THE WILLIE NELSON MYSTIQUE

"Consummate country songwriter . . . redneck/hippie mediator, culture hero, man most likely to succeed, hometown boy made good . . . he is the ideal father figure for a generation which needs to dance with its daddys but doesn't know how."

Patrick Carr,
Country Music Magazine

"Willie just gets inside your head and then plays on your memories as if he were softly chording a guitar."

Nat Hentoff,
noted jazz critic

"I swear to God, being around Willie is like being around Buddha. He gives off these positive attitudes. Next thing you know, you're acting like him."

Kris Kristofferson,
in a recent interview

"Willie Nelson legitimized country music for young people . . . his highly acclaimed STARDUST album introduced a whole new generation to the music of the 1930s and the 1940s . . . Willie Nelson beat the system, shattered a lot of myths and changed a lot of people's views about country music and American heroes."

Michael Bane,
from the book

An Unauthorized Biography of
WILLIE NELSON

by Michael Bane

A DELL/JAMES A. BRYANS BOOK

Published by
Dell Publishing Co., Inc.
1 Dag Hammarskjold Plaza
New York, New York 10017

Dell TM 681510, Dell Publishing Co., Inc.

ISBN: 0-440-09290-6

Printed in the United States of America

First printing—July 1984

ACKNOWLEDGMENTS

To *Country Music* Magazine, both for their unreserved help and their permission to use a wealth of material from their back issues, books and files.

To researcher-extraordinaire Rich Kienzle, who was instrumental in helping pull material together, find obscure background, steer me away from dead ends and twisting alleys, and, in general, provide his unqualified help and support, regardless of the hour of the night.

To Bob Allen, for his thoughtful works on Willie and Waylon and his unprecedentedly generous offer of unpublished interviews with Willie and friends.

To Mary Ellen Moore, who probably listened to enough Willie Nelson albums to cause brain damage.

Thanks.

CONTENTS

DEDICATION

For Russ Barnard, Patrick Carr and Rochelle Friedman, the all-new Hole In The Wall Gang.

God open my eyes
 so I may see
And feel Your presence
 close to me...
Give me strength
 for my stumbling feet
As I battle the crowd
 on life's busy street,
And widen the vision
 of my unseeing eyes
So in passing faces
 I'll recognize
Not just a stranger,
 unloved and unknown,
But a friend with a heart
 that is much like my own...
Give me perception
 to make me aware
That scattered profusely
 on life's thoroughfare
Are the best gifts of God
 that we daily pass by
As we look at the world
 with an unseeing eye.

Helen Steiner Rice

Guideposts

CARMEL • NEW YORK 10512

God, teach me
to be patient—
Teach me to
go slow—
Teach me how to
"wait on You"
When my way I
do not know...
Teach me sweet
forbearance
When things do
not go right
So I remain
unruffled
When others
grow uptight...
Teach me how
to quiet
My racing,
rising heart
So I may hear
the answer
You are trying
to impart...
Teach me to let go,
dear God,
And pray undisturbed
until
My heart is filled
with inner peace
And I learn to
know your will!

Helen Steiner Rice

PROLOGUE:
THE ROAD

It's the contradictions that jump out, the differences between the calm Colorado aerie and the gritty reality of backstage at a Willie Nelson bash. The contradictions stand out even more strongly the closer you get to Willie Nelson. He is the calm at the eye of a storm of his own making, Ground Zero of a multi-million-dollar organization that moves like a smooth juggernaut across America in the year of our Lord, 1984.

Yet Willie is quiet and gracious, a man comfortable with silences and unwilling to be drawn into the maelstrom that surrounds him. Like the Plains Indians, whom he has long admired, Willie has been pushed farther and farther by encroaching civilization. The newest "reservation" is forty miles outside Denver, a compound of four houses and a tepee on 122 acres nestled in the mountains. Cold Colorado mornings sometimes find Willie Nelson, owner of all he surveys, wrapped in a scratchy woolen blanket, sitting at the door of the tepee, looking out across the mountains, as if, in the distance, he can see the shiny haze off the asphalt.

When he's home—which isn't that often—morning begins with Willie pulling on an old t-shirt, shorts, and his battered Nike running shoes for at least five miles before breakfast. He's thin and wiry, and more than one person has pointed out that every day Willie Nelson more and more resembles the tough old leather he sometimes sings about.

He runs alone or with wife Connie, who usually runs three miles to Willie's five. When his manager, Mark Rothbaum, is staying at the ranch, he joins Willie for the morning run, although by Willie's own admission his manager can run him into the ground, making it tough to discuss business.

After the run comes the exercise machines. Willie has learned a secret truth having to do with both age *and* mileage—both can kill you, but when your mileage starts approaching that of Willie Nelson, some serious preventative measures are called for. He doesn't drink as much as legend has it; his smoking habits are widely documented but apparently harmless. Over the last couple of years Willie has lost thirty pounds. His legs could belong to a high-school track star, which is a far cry from the kid who once took up pole vaulting because "you didn't have to train as much."

Most of the time in Colorado is rest time, a

chance to spiritually gird his loins for the next trip out on the road. It is an odd family life, made all the odder because it seems so *normal*. At thirty-nine years old, Connie Nelson doesn't look at all like what one might expect the wife of Willie Nelson to look. She is blonde, statuesque and poised; when she stands next to Willie, he looks more than ever like an explosion in a Woolco.

She is a consummate hostess, treating intrusive writers with the same courtesy she extends to friends and guests. She cleans the house and does much of the cooking herself; answers the phone when Willie's home to buffer him from the world and make sure that his house is really a *home*. One of the things that sets Willie Nelson's houses away from those of many—maybe even most—other country singers is the sense that Willie and Connie *live* there, which is a neat trick, since Willie is usually just passing through. Part of the attraction of the Colorado house is Paula, now thirteen years old, and Amy, ten. It's not unusual for Willie to bundle the family up and take them on the road—Amy and Paula traditionally join their father on-stage for his closing numbers.

For Amy and Paula, a life on the road is the only one they've ever known, and Colorado represents a major sanctuary from the glaring light of celebrityhood. The Austin spread was hardly on the main drag, but as Willie's fame spread, the farm came to be something of a Mecca for country music fans from around the world. He was sure they meant no harm, Willie said, but for his family it made living any sort of "normal" life out of the question. Colorado, with its indigenous rich and famous, was a little more inured to celebrities and more suitable for Willie's family. Amy and Paula both attend a public school, and although the road looms large, the Colorado house offers a way out.

The road hangs over Willie Nelson's life like a fat harvest moon, waning and waxing, but rarely disappearing. After jogging, exercise and breakfast, Willie and Connie's day is usually low-key, doing the things that most married couples might think of as commonplace. A day in front of the television set watching old movies, an afternoon of dominoes with in-laws, a nap and a swim, are all luxuries to Willie Nelson. One of the great ironies of the country music business is that once you are a success, you no longer have the time to do the things you wanted to be a success to do. Willie once claimed that he would never allow himself to be fenced in like Elvis Presley, watching his world shrink around him and his family until there was no world left. Yet stardom of the magnitude Willie has achieved leaves very little choice. A trip into town guarantees a crowd, and Willie is too much the gentleman of the old school to send the crowd packing. Instead, his world shrinks a little more.

The road is, truly, a problem without resolution. Connie knows that the road has ahold of

Willie Nelson and that it's never going to let him go.

"I trust Willie completely," she says. "But sometimes I feel that he doesn't need me. He's got the road and he's got his life. It's real easy to feel pushed aside."

For all its pleasures, there is no doubt that Colorado is a way station between the 200 to 250 nights a year that Willie Nelson is on the road. Getting him to rest, Connie says, is a constant problem. Willie fears that people will believe "success has changed ole Willie," and bends over backwards to prove it ain't so.

But Willie's never going to rest for long, though, not as long as there's one honkytonk left unplayed. "I get restless," he says, "staying in one place."

After a few days in Colorado, days of resting and happiness, Willie grows edgy, staring off into the hazy distances. There are suddenly phone calls that have to be made, deals that have to be done. Connie and the kids recognize all the signs, and maybe they sigh a little bit each time the inevitable comes.

What follows are goodbyes worn as smooth as stones in a fast-moving stream, followed by a quick trip to the airport in Denver. *Air Willie*, a million-dollars-worth of Learjet, is warmed up and waiting, ready to take Willie Nelson to the next show. The jet, he says, is worth every penny, since it brings him and his family closer together. It is a freedom purchased with hard cash, a lot of nights honkytonking.

Willie's real home is the back of a Silver Eagle tour bus, and his life—the night life—begins just about when most people are feeling their first yawns of the day.

Although Willie might roll into town in a Learjet, his heart stays in the buses, the self-contained miniature world of the traveling musician. A tour bus is better compared to a private railroad car from days gone by than anything else. In fact, Willie's traveling entourage is more like a private train without track. The usual trip calls for three Silver Eagle buses—including a 40-foot "chuck wagon" mobile kitchen and 16-seat portable restaurant that once served as the dressing room for Porter Wagoner and Dolly Parton—and two semis carrying light and sound equipment for the show. The buses are equipped with color television sets, video recorders and a healthy selection of tapes, a microwave oven, beds, bathroom and kitchen and, fittingly, an excellent sound system. The road may be long, but nowadays it's not unpleasant.

For Willie, the back of a tour bus is the most stable home he'd known, a place as secure and as isolated as the high country in Colorado. And with necessity—as country shows have gotten bigger and bigger (and Willie's is the biggest), it's gotten harder and harder to protect the artist from the sheer overzealousness of the fans. It's especially hard with Willie, who's willing to talk to anybody at anytime about anything.

It's easy to romanticize being on the road,

because being on the road is hopelessly romantic. The towns and cities roll by with regular monotony; the lives of the people in those towns become insubstantial, unreal. The cramped inside of the bus becomes a sealed ship, pausing to touch any town for only a few hours.

When the buses arrive, the man of the moment is T. Snake, Willie's de facto road manager. A road manager makes everything work, from seeing to it that the lights are hung properly, that the sound sounds right, that Willie shows up on time, and that every one of a million and one other details are taken care of.

There are almost as many stories about Snake as there are about Willie. It's told that he was once a Marine, that he once worked for IBM, that he once had another name. Of course, all of that was B.W. —Before Willie. Unless you've actually seen it from up close, it's hard to imagine how many details go into making a show look spontaneous and unrehearsed. Everything from high voltage to free passes has to work a certain way, in a certain *groove*, or people go away muttering unkind things. The music is part of it, but there's also a *feeling*, a sense of Karma, that has to be exactly right.

One of Snake's biggest jobs—and it's undoubtedly the hardest—is keeping as many of the hordes of fans as possible away from Willie. Snake routinely wears a t-shirt that reads, "I Don't Know Where Willie Is." He's the man with the backstage passes, and everybody is looking for Willie. Some people really need to find him—at one Willie concert a rock singer who had a song riding *Billboard's* Top-Ten begged to get a backstage pass and couldn't. His name wasn't on "the list," a guest list of people to be allowed backstage. Sometimes the list isn't there at all. Or, in a really big concert (like most of Willie's), there are *several* lists, describing just what access that person has. An "All Areas" pass, for example, might not allow the person access to all areas. That might take a "Restricted Area" pass.

Think of a concert as a military operation. If everything works smoothly, the people in the front of the stage are fairly unaware of what is going on behind the stage. The best concerts don't look "staged" at all. Willie's shows seem more like Willie just happened to wander by and thought he'd play a little.

Much of Willie's day before a show is hurry up and wait, lots of time for cards or dominoes on the bus, or working out a new song with his guitar, or just trying to come to grips with the paperwork of running what amounts to a business empire. Before a show, Willie waits at a hotel, visiting with friends or just resting. Unless his band members can figure a way around it, he still tends to answer his own phone and chat with whoever's calling.

The show, though, is the thing, and the shows tend to last at least three hours, whether it's a sold-out Superdome or a nearly empty honkytonk (although there are far too few of those anymore).

The idea for a show is as old as the medicine shows and older. Give 'em a little, an opening act. Let the Family Band play a few numbers while the crowd yells for "Willie! Willie! WILLIE!!" Willie sometimes arrives just a few minutes before going on stage, surrounded by members of the entourage who serve double duty as the star's bodyguards. He's just as likely, though, to amble in early, see who's around. Depending on where the show is, there are a lot of people around; Kris Kristofferson and Leon Russell are regular drop-in visitors, both backstage and on-stage.

"I made a living playing the road," Willie says. "I think I still make a living playing the road."

Maybe it was easier in the old days, when Willie and Johnny Bush would pull into town with one guitar between them and just start picking. The audience was probably too drunk to notice a couple of missing chords—or even band members! It's hard to be intimate with 100,000 people, a fact that has sent more than one career down the drain. Willie's answer is both simple and eloquent—keep it simple, and always remember that the audience comes first.

Sounds simple, doesn't it? Yet for a performer of Willie's magnitude, it's almost impossible. He's been singing some of the same songs over and over again for maybe forty of his fifty years, yet in his hands they seem as fresh as the first time he picked the chords out on his old Stella guitar.

The secret of Willie Nelson may lie in the flint-edged religion of his youth. The very root of that religion is that man is but a vessel, an instrument of an even greater Singer; that, sometimes, the singer is not nearly as important as the Song.

The show ends with "Amazing Grace" and "Will The Circle Be Unbroken?" a nightly acknowledgment and thank-you to a hard-dirt Texas religion that never goes away. Amy and Paula and Connie join Willie onstage, and the applause, applause that was so long in coming, seems to go on forever. With a little luck, Snake has him out of the building after the last encore.

Snake hasn't had any luck in almost ten years.

1

Two Sides to Every Story

The singer sits in the back of the battered tour bus, dressed in jeans and a t-shirt with a worn red bandana tied around his head. His sneakers are worn and dusty, and the battered old Martin guitar looks on the verge of falling apart. But the singer is smiling, grinning even, and the young journalist is uncomfortable.

Willie Nelson takes a long draw on a fat, hand-rolled, non-tobacco cigarette and leans forward in the chair that takes up most of the cramped rear of the bus.

It is 1975. The big news in country music is that Australian singer, Olivia Newton-John. Rock and roll swings to the Southern beat of the Allman Brothers and the Marshall Tucker Band. Willie Nelson knows all that and accepts it benignly. He knows something that the young journalist is just beginning to feel. Willie Nelson knows the times they are a-changing, changing the way he has always known they would.

In Nashville, he has just recorded an album that is going to change country music forever. Country music, that silly cry-in-your-beer music that was good for a laugh in the movie *Five Easy Pieces*, will grow to rival rock and roll. People who still wear American flags sewn on the back of their jeans will buy cowboy boots and Stetson hats. Willie Nelson draws deeply on the weed and leans back.

The young journalist is puzzled. The man in the back of the bus is so sure, so certain. *Red-Headed Stranger* is a good album, to be sure; maybe even a great album. It certainly caught the young journalist off-guard. Raised in Memphis, a hotbed of rhythm and blues, the young journalist had always considered country music to be, well, *un-hip*, affectation rather than affection. Something you listened to for only as long as it took to hit another button on the car radio.

But *Red-Headed Stranger* is something else again, Willie Nelson's thin, raggedy voice accompanied mainly by his own guitar and sister Bobbie on piano, a morality tale set in the mythical Old West. It is a hypnotic and moving album, and the young journalist has come to ask Willie Nelson for the whys and hows.

But Willie Nelson is having no part of it. He is funny and charming, and he wants to talk about his plans for the future. He is, he says emphatically, going to do all the things he's wanted to do, all the songs he's dreamed of singing.

"I think I'm going to record an album of

Lefty Frizzell songs," he says, his eyes twinkling.
"You do know who Lefty Frizzell is, don't you?"

The young journalist nods dumbly. In the
thick smoke in the back of the bus, he is having
severe reality slippage.

"Then I think I'm going to do a gospel album,"
he continues. "I grew up listening to gospel,
and I love it."

One by one Willie Nelson ticks off his agenda,
his goals, his loves.

"All those great old songs from the 1930s
and 1940s," he says. "There's a whole generation of people who have never heard 'Stardust.'
You've heard 'Stardust,' haven't you?"

The young journalist nods.

"Duets," he says emphatically. "You know, I
just want to sing songs with my friends. Ray
Price, Roger Miller, Waylon Jennings—I think
I'm going to do a record with each one of
them."

The young journalist is aware that he's thrown
a switch, but he is still slightly puzzled. Who
does this Willie Nelson think he is, anyway?
From the way he is talking, you'd think he
changed the world or something. The young
journalist asks a question about being on the
road, about being away from home all the time,
year after year. Willie Nelson just smiles benignly.

"There is nothing," he says, smiling, "I would
rather do than play music. Nothing."

Country music is, as more than one critic has
said, the white man's blues. Before the coming

of Willie Nelson and the music *Country Music* Magazine dubbed "outlaw," country music was rooted deeply in the rural South. Ironically, it was music that shared both black and white roots. As Frye Gaillard wrote in *Watermelon Wine: The Spirit of Country Music,* "Even in the years of peak segregation, the separation was never as complete as the mythology insisted it was."

Country music was the music of the Appalachian Mountains, the high, lonesome sound, filtered through the black honkytonks that dotted the South like fleas on a blue-tick hound. Consider the landscape. Music was *everywhere,* from barn dances to field chants to the budding technology of radio. "A musician would be open to sounds from every direction," wrote Englishman Tony Russell in *Blacks, Whites and Blues,* "from family and friends, from field and railroad yard, lumber camp and mine; from street singers and traveling show musicians; from phonograph records and radio; from dances and suppers and camp meetings and carnivals; from fellow prisoners in jails, from workmen everywhere. A white youngster could learn a song or a tune not only from the bosom of his family but from their black employees—mammy, Uncle Remus or anyone . . ."

So it was with Willie Nelson, who grew up in the flatlands of Texas listening to black fieldhands and white country singers on the radio; who absorbed in equal parts the heart of the blues and the soul of Hoagy Carmichael.

Of all the stars in country music, Willie Nelson is second only to Hank Williams in his influence and talent. Not only has Willie Nelson written some of the classic songs of country—"Hello Walls," "Crazy," "Night Life (Ain't No Good Life)"—and been a party to some of the most stunning successes in popular music, but it was Willie Nelson who first realized that a whole generation of kids raised on the Beatles and the Rolling Stones were really hankering for some down-home country music.

In these post-Urban Cowboy days with country music blaring out of jukeboxes right alongside rock and pop, that might not sound like much of a revolution. But in the early years of the 1970s, Willie's discovery was something akin to finding a pot of gold at the end of an unlikely rainbow. Those were polarized times—rednecks hated hippies; hippies hated rednecks. Country music was boring junk for old people, and rock and roll was nothing but noise for stupid kids with burned-out ears.

But Willie Nelson saw through all that, right into the heart of what the music really meant. Then he risked his reputation—which was substantial—and a lot of public ridicule on what he believed he saw. And, ultimately, he was proven totally right. Willie broke down the dam, and in the flood that followed, country music grew up.

Ironically, when Willie and his cohorts had legitimized country music for young people, Willie Nelson kept right on a musical path he'd charted years before. His highly acclaimed *Stardust* album introduced a whole new generation to the music of the 1930s and 1940s. He sang honkytonk music with Waylon Jennings and internationalized pop with worldwide recording star Julio Iglesias. His album tribute to Lefty Frizzell sparked renewed interest in that classic country performer. His gospel album put traditional gospel at the top of the country charts and, not coincidentally, introduced the young country audience to the old music of camp meetings and the sanctified church. On the "Austin City Limits" television show, Willie devoted a whole show to the music of guitar jazz master Django Reinhardt.

Yet through it all, Willie Nelson has hardly seemed like a person to foment revolution.

"That's exactly why everything changed," says Tompall Glaser, another Nashville legend instrumental in the stunning success of country music. "It changed because it *was* Willie ... When Willie left Nashville, he didn't leave in anger or in a rage or anything. He left with *love,* and everybody knew that if it was so bad that Willie Nelson had to leave, something was *wrong!*"

Stardom is a mercurial thing, and probably no subject has so dominated the public attention as the way a person can or—too many times—cannot come to grips with that stardom. Fellow outlaw Waylon Jennings found his life rocked and buffeted by his tremendous success, eventually driving him into seclusion. Yet Willie

Nelson has remained amazingly unaffected by the waves of adulation that surround him. Like the country singers he idolized while growing up in the Depression years in Texas, Willie Nelson has a personal relationship with his fans. He works the road as much as any newcomer, his customized buses (and now the customized Learjet) crisscrossing the country like the honky-tonk hero he portrayed in the movie *Honeysuckle Rose*. His shows still exceed three hours in length, and his fans still holler for more.

It is, more than anything else, a question of *myth*. Willie Nelson doesn't subscribe to the Myth of Willie Nelson. The rest of the world can wear t-shirts that read, "Matthew, Mark, Luke and Willie," and everyone else in the music business can admire him for being a "canny businessman" or damn him for being a heartless, calculating bastard.

Willie doesn't care one way or the other.

What he does, how he perceives himself, is as a man who makes music.

"See, there's a whole generation of people who have never heard songs like 'Blue Skies' and 'Stardust,' " Willie told me not long after the release of the *Stardust* album, "just like they'd never heard country music. We're bringing them those songs."

Sort of, I suggest, like a musical evangelist?

"I guess you could say that," Willie says, grinning. "Yeah. A musical evangelist."

* * *

Willie Nelson leans back and smiles his perpetual smile, caught up for a moment in his cherished vision of the future. The young journalist doesn't have an inkling at the time, but Willie's smoke-filled dreams are conservative. Ahead lies success beyond the wildest dreams of any country singer, a career in the movies, an invitation to the White House, a kind of public adulation seldom granted to anyone, much less an aging country music singer.

Willie Nelson smiles, then shakes his head briefly, the dreams of tomorrow slowly dissolving in the smoke.

"Gotta go now," he says, rising. "Time to go play some music."

2

My Heros Have Always
Been Cowboys

The Texas Rangers have a saying that goes
something like this: A Little Man Will Whip a
Big Man Every Time If He's in the Right and
Keeps a'Comin'. Indeed, there are as many
sayings as legends in Texas, and Texas has
enough legends to fill the flat dry plains that fill
so much of the state.

In Abbott, Texas, the summer wind can scour
the parched prairie like a sandblaster, eating away
at the white clapboard houses and giving the
square brick buildings the sad, worn faces of aging
war veterans. Time moves slowly in Abbott, the
steady progression of winter to spring to summer
to autumn, in time with the planting, the culti-
vating, the harvesting of the crops. It was said
that a boy with a good, strong right arm could
toss a rock from one end of Abbott to another.

But the little town on the prairie held all the
promise in the world for Ira and Myrle Nelson
in the grim, dark days of 1929, when success

was defined as survival and the hot winds that blew across Abbott seemed to moan with the cries of the Great Depression. Certainly the farm town of Abbott held more promise than the poverty-stricken Ozarks of Arkansas, where the rocky, unyielding soil of the family's 40-acre homestead near Pindall, Arkansas, refused to yield even a bare living.

Ira Nelson was sixteen years old when he married Myrle, only fifteen, and took her and his momma and daddy to Abbott. Ira had a knack with machines, a godsend for farmers struggling to make ends meet, and if there was nothing else, there was always the cotton, and never enough blacks to pick it all. A man with a strong back, Ira Nelson reasoned, could feed a family in Abbott. And there would be money, a little money, coming from Daddy Nelson, William Alfred Nelson, Ira's father, and a blacksmith.

And every penny would be needed. Myrle was quickly pregnant with her first child, a little girl they named Bobbie Lee. A couple of years later, on April 30, 1933, a second child, a red-headed boy she and Ira named Willie Hugh, was born.

Life was gruelingly hard in Depression Texas. Ira continued to get work as a mechanic, but he was constantly traveling from small town to small town, leaving Myrle alone in Abbott. The dust and the isolation and the grinding nightmare of the Depression took their toll on Myrle. If the Great Depression could be said to have a good side at all, it was that the preconceived

notions on which America had functioned for
generations were being broken down. Myrle
dreamed of the road, of places other than Abbott,
Texas, of a world without dust and poverty and
cotton, cotton, cotton. She lasted until Willie
was two and Bobbie was five, then she told
Mama and Daddy Nelson that she was going to
look for a job outside of town. In a few days
they'd realized she'd left for good.

Years later, with Willie Nelson a star, she
would explain that she'd left for the kids' own
good, so they could be raised in the church and
grow up safely in Abbott. She came back to
Abbott one more time, sick and afraid of dying,
and then stayed only long enough to be cured.
Wherever her path was taking her, Myrle Nelson knew that it didn't run through Abbott,
Texas. After the divorce was granted, she married a man named Ken Harvey and moved to
Oregon. Ira Nelson, too, remarried, and after a
brief try at being one big happy family in Abbott,
he loaded up his new wife Lorraine and their
two sons, Charles and Doyle, and moved on
down the road to Ft. Worth. Willie and Bobbie
stayed with Mama and Daddy Nelson.

While the situation could have been tragic,
instead it turned into an almost ideal situation
for the two children. Mama and Daddy Nelson
were old-school Christians, steeped in the teachings of love and the necessity of doing good in
this world. Instead of an added burden, Willie
Hugh and Bobbie Lee were gifts from God,
blank palimpsests on which images of goodness

could be inscribed. There is a photo in the Nelson family album showing Mama—Nancy Elizabeth Smothers—and Daddy—William Alfred Nelson—just before their move to Abbott. The photo is reminiscent of the Farm Service photos that would soon be commissioned to chronicle America in the Depression. The picture shows a sturdy farm couple, he in coveralls turned up at the ankle, she in a plain dress covered with a white apron. Her hand is on his shoulder, and the overriding impression is one of quiet strength.

Life in Abbott, Texas, wasn't all that different from life in Pindall, Arkansas. Life revolved around the cotton, and there was little call for a farmer who broke horses as a sideline. Daddy Nelson worked hard as a blacksmith, and, as much as possible, the family raised their own food.

The Nelson household, however, revolved around two sometimes complementary poles, religion and music. Ira had been a musician, a guitar player, and both Mama and Daddy Nelson had wanted to be music teachers. Of course, the only way open to them was through a mail-order correspondence course, and the two Nelsons threw themselves into learning music with the same combination of gusto and love with which they approached the rest of their lives. Although the little house in Abbott had no electricity, the Nelsons stayed up late, studying music by the light of a kerosene lamp. Early on, the Nelsons had traded an old pump organ for a piano, and Nancy Nelson soon began transferring her new musical knowledge to Bobbie.

"My first piano book," Bobbie Nelson remembered, "was a Methodist hymnal. The first
song I played was 'Jesus, Lover of My Soul.'
My grandmother showed me how to read . . . It
made sense to me right away."

Young Willie Nelson, too, was taken with
the musical landscape. On weekend nights he
listened to the sounds of the Grand Ole Opry
from Nashville, Tennessee, blanketing most of
the South with the high, lonesome sound of the
hills. He went to all-day gospel sings with Mama
and Daddy Nelson, and listened to the black
field chants in the cotton fields. He heard the
soul-wrenching sounds of black gospel music,
the sanctified forerunner of rhythm and blues.

On Saturday afternoons, when there was
money, Willie Nelson went to the movies to see
the cowboy serials. The cowboys who rode the
musical range became his heroes—Gene Autry,
Roy Rogers, Ken Maynard, Tex Ritter, Ray
Whitley and the others. Men who shot straight,
respected their women, treasured their horses
and were likely to break into song at a moment's
notice. The plots might have been as flimsy as
the artificial backdrops used in some of the
lower-budget movies, but the feeling—the legends of the American West, of the cowboy—
shaped more than one young life. In the singing
cowboys, Willie Nelson saw everything that
wasn't readily visible from dusty Abbott, Texas.
A life of glamour, free from the aching poverty;
a life filled with horses and sixguns and, most
of all, music.

According to country music historian Douglas B. Green, the music of the singing cowboys helped legitimize country music, turning it from a quaint Appalachian anomaly into an accepted part of the American scene (along the way, forever linking "western" to "country"). Every kid in the Depression dreamed of growing up to be a cowboy, and in the dust-swept streets of Abbott, Texas, such a dream seemed as real as the coming winter. A kid from Abbott really *could* grow up to be a singing cowboy, at least, that's what a young kid named Willie Nelson fervently believed.

Willie Nelson played his first "gig" when he was "about five." He'd been taught by Mama and Daddy Nelson to recite short poems, and Mama Nelson decided to take Willie to an all-day gospel-sing and picnic to "perform."

"My grandmother dressed me in this little sailor suit, all white, and took me to one of those picnics. You know, singing and eating and praying and praying some more," he remembered. But the day was long, and the fidgeting Willie began to pick his nose.

"So I got up there to recite the poem she'd taught me," he continued. "My nose started to bleed. There I was, doing the poem and holding one side of my nose with my hand."

He recited:

"What are you looking at me for?
I ain't got nothing to say.
If you don't like the looks of me
You can look some other way . . ."

"I think everybody was glad when I sat down," Willie said. "I know I was."

Both Mama and Daddy Nelson encouraged Willie's and Bobbie's music, hoping, in fact, they would some day play together at the big gospel sings or maybe even, hoping against hope, make a gospel record.

"When I was six years old," Willie said, "my grandparents bought me a Stella guitar, and my granddad taught me a couple of chords and gave me a chord book."

Willie had no sooner begun the guitar under his grandfather's tutelage when fate dealt the little family another nearly crushing blow. When Willie was six, Daddy Nelson died, leaving the family to once again sink or swim in treacherous waters.

The first major change was that everybody in the Nelson family now had to work for the family to get by. Mama Nelson took an $18-a-week job in the local school lunchroom, and Willie began working after school picking cotton for $1.50 a day. It was hot, back-breaking work. The black fieldworkers sang the blues with their resonant voices—one would call, the others respond, a style of music that traced its roots back to Africa.

"Picking cotton is a real bad job," Willie said. "As hard as you make it. If, like me, you picked awhile and sat on your sack awhile, it's not as hard as it was for some. I first heard the blues picking cotton in a field full of black people. One would sing a line at this end of the field, another one at that end. I realized they knew more about music, soul, *feeling* than I did. Plus they could pick more cotton."

As he bent to pick the cotton, he unconsciously moved his body to the rhythms of the blues, dreaming, wishing, hoping, *praying* that he could be someplace else.

"I didn't like picking cotton one bit," he said. "I used to stand in the fields and watch the cars go by and think, 'I want to go with *them.'"

Ironically, although his guitar work was stalled—"My grandmother couldn't play a guitar; she played the piano. I learned to read music just enough so that after I was grown up, I knew what key I was playing in." —Willie had begun writing songs.

"Mainly, I'd write 'em down and leave 'em laying around, see if somebody'd pick 'em up and comment on 'em. I was a little shy," Willie recalled. "I kept them hid a lot."

Perhaps an even greater irony, the type of songs he'd begun writing were cheating songs, although even he himself was puzzled about where a seven-year-old kid in Abbott, Texas, would pick up enough to start writing soul-searching songs about love betrayed. "Maybe I got 'em from the soap operas on the radio," he said much later. "But I always seemed to be able to write the sad side of everything. It was always easy for me."

Since he was writing cheatin' songs at seven, it was only fitting that Willie Nelson should go on the road when he was ten. The turning point in Willie's young life was hearing Ernest Tubb, the first of the great honkytonk singers. Ernest Tubb was a Texas boy, too, from Crisp, in Ellis County, and grew up idolizing the music of Jimmie Rodgers. When he moved to San Antonio several years after Rodgers' untimely death, Tubb was surprised to find that Rodgers' widow still lived there, and that her telephone number was listed. He called her up, hoping to get a picture of his idol. He ended up getting a career. With the backing of Jimmie Rodgers' widow, Tubb was able to crack the tough Nashville music establishment.

What Ernest Tubb brought to country music was a rip-roaring honkytonk style and vocals that can only be described as "unique." His strange phrasing was at first criticized, then imitated. "I want to sing in such a manner," Tubb said later, "that the boy out there working in the fields can say, 'Hey, I can do that!' " Tubb also brought to Nashville two other honkytonk mainstays—the electric guitar and the pedal steel guitar. The electric guitar was made necessary by the noise level in honkytonks, generally thought to be loud enough to cause brain damage in the uninitiated. People simply couldn't hear an acoustic instrument, so Tubb wired a guitar up to an amplifier and let 'er rip. The steel, a variation of the Hawaiian guitar, would soon come to be identified with country music around the world.

Tubb wasn't the first artist to bring an electric guitar on the stage of the Grand Ole Opry (Sam McGee, Pee Wee King and Paul Howard are all contenders, and the title probably be-

longs to Pee Wee King). But Tubb made the
hard amplified music the basis of his sound.
Working with just an electric guitar, the steel
and a bass, Ernest Tubb got out there and
wailed. Young Willie could not help but be
moved, and moved in a honkytonk direction.

True to Tubb's later declaration, Willie Nelson heard Ernest Tubb on the Grand Ole Opry
and thought, "Hey, I can do that!" By the age
of nine he was chafing to hit the road, but
Mama Nelson was holding him back. While she
had wholeheartedly encouraged a career in music,
she was less than enthused about him going out
on the road. Bobbie was already working the
revival tent circuit, playing the piano, so Mama
Nelson finally relented.

Willie joined John Raycjeck's Bohemian Polka
Band.

"With no amplification, and all those tubas
and trombones and drums, there was no way
anyone could hear me," he recalled, "so I could
make my mistakes without being noticed."

He also began working with a band headed
by Bud Fletcher, Bobbie's young, handsome
husband—like her mama before her, Bobbie had
married at fifteen. Willie's dreams of being a
country music star seemed closer to fulfillment
than ever.

In truth, they were farther away than he ever
would have believed.

3

Bob Wills Is
Still The King

Musical wave after wave rolled over the Texas flatlands, and young Willie Nelson absorbed every one of them.

"There's a sense of *sprawl* to Texas that gives a person a sense of freedom," he says. "Growing up in Texas, radio was the only thing we had. I had a radio in my ear all the time, spinning the dial constantly—so I heard pop, jazz, country, blues. I was accustomed to all types of music. Good music doesn't need to be broken up into pieces and labeled."

Ernest Tubb had changed Willie's ambition from being a cowboy singer to being a honky-tonk hero. He listened to the music of black fieldhands and Mexican migrant workers, gospel singers and black revivalists. He listened to the blues and country and their bastard offspring, the honkytonk bar music that would one day in the not-so-far future become rock and roll. He listened to crooners like young Frank Sinatra.

But there was a new music rolling across the flatlands of Texas, a music that would have a major effect on Willie Nelson and on American music. Like the music beginning to swim around in Willie Nelson's head, it was a melange of the many sounds of the Lone Star State. As Willie Nelson entered his teens, swing bands were popping up all over Texas. The music drew heavily on big-band swing, but it was, at its roots, happy music to dance to. An evening's songs might include a few big-band numbers, some up-tempo rags, a little squaredance fiddle music, a Cajun dance tune and, in between the dance numbers, the big hits of the day, maybe "Rosetta" or even "Stardust."

The music was called Western Swing, and of all the groups that played it, none was greater than Bob Wills and His Texas Playboys.

Western Swing was as deeply rooted in the Texas prairies as the fiddle music and dour gospel songs were in the mountains of Tennessee and Arkansas. Western Swing was first and foremost a *social* music, the music of Saturday night get-togethers after a week of deadening toil in the dusty land.

"In the Southeast, social needs were filled by closeness of kin and by the physical presence of the warm (though often far from rich) mountains and foothills—a presence that somehow seems to affirm continually strong religious beliefs," wrote historian Douglas B. Green. "The Southwest, on the other hand, offered millions of acres of flat, sunbaked prairie, and with them hot, hard work, aching loneliness, and the intense need to break loose from the grinding, dusty toil to be with neighbors, dance with neighbors, even raise a little hell with neighbors . . ."

Western Swing grew out of the specific needs of the people of the Western flatlands, the need to escape the tyranny of the land. All over Texas, bands like the one headed by Bobbie Nelson's husband, Bud Fletcher, were springing up, and every Bud Fletcher saw himself as the very next incarnation of the great Bob Wills.

Before the coming of Hank Williams, Willie Nelson said, "Bob Wills was *it*!"

Wills himself grew up in the hardscrabble land around Turkey, Texas, giving up the hard life on the farm to work in a blackface medicine show. He was originally a fiddler of the old school, the kind found scattered throughout the mountains of the Southeast.

In the 1930s, though, Wills fell in with a group of musicians around Ft. Worth called the Light Crust Doughboys, so named by their leader Wilbert Lee O'Daniel because it was the name of the brand of flour he represented. O'Daniel originally heard Wills on the radio playing in a band called Aladdin's Laddies, and figured that since the Grand Ole Opry sold a lot of Martha White's Self-Rising Flour, a band in Texas ought to do at least as well selling Light Crust Flour.

Not only did O'Daniel eventually become governor of Texas and a U.S. Senator partly because of the popularity of the Doughboys, but the Western Swing music of the group quickly became a local, then a regional, then a national phenomenon. Ironically, the only place Western Swing was not particularly popular was in the Southeast, where a different kind of music, closer to rhythm and blues, was bubbling up.

In September 1933, Wills, his brother Johnnie Lee and singer Tommy Duncan split from the Doughboys to form their own group, Bob Wills and his Playboys. The next year the group, with the addition of Leon McAuliffe on pedal steel guitar, moved to Tulsa, Oklahoma, to play on radio station KVOO. They also became Bob Wills and His *Texas* Playboys. The Playboys featured jazzy solos, big-band arrangements and a swinging beat, a musical stew of the styles that rolled across Texas like the wind.

"If you cut up what they call Western Swing," Willie Nelson said, "you'll find there's some jazz and some blues and maybe that's it ... There were very few, if any, full-time country music radio stations in those days, so you listened to a station that had country music maybe an hour a day, and the rest of the time it would be playing popular music—'Stardust,' 'Harbor Lights,' 'Coming In On A Wing And A Prayer' —the popular music of the war years. I was raised up on all kinds of music. Country was the one that was more easy for me to play, and I enjoyed playing it more."

"The one thing Wills did for Willie's music was to make it a bit more eclectic," according to Rich Kienzle, musicologist and expert on the music of the Playboys. "Willie listened to jazz early on—he listened to a station in New Orleans— but Wills' eclecticism has stayed with

Willie throughout his career. Willie didn't really record any swing until much later. But he listened to Wills and he heard not only a mixture of styles, but a mixture that was commercially successful."

"Everyone I knew when I was a kid was a Bob Wills fan. I didn't know anybody who didn't like Bob Wills' music," Willie said. "With his fans, there was a communication. You really had to be there to see how he communicated, and the magnetism, how those people *love* him. And *he* loves *them,* too."

The Playboys continued to grow not only in their successes, but in the band's size as well. By 1943 the band reached a peak of twenty-two members, including four fiddles and a full brass section. The magic of Bob Wills was the blending of traditional jazz with the rural instrumentation of the South, the fiddles and steel guitar. Bob Wills wasn't afraid to add any instrument or style, make any change, no matter how radical. This was so shocking to the more conservative musicians of the era that the local musicians' union in Tulsa initially refused to let the Playboys join on the grounds that what they were playing was not "music," so they obviously weren't musicians.

The wildly swinging jazz, coupled with such dreamy ballads as "San Antonio Rose" and "Faded Love," helped shape a generation of musicians, Willie Nelson among them. Along with playing in Bud Fletcher's band, Willie and his brother-in-law booked other acts into local bars. When Willie was thirteen, he booked Bob

Wills into Whitney, Texas, in an outdoor dance pavilion. Wills was past his golden years—Tommy Duncan was no longer with the band, and Western Swing was on the decline. That's not, however, what Willie remembered.

"By then, Bob Wills was already a legend," Willie has said. "There's no other way to describe what a Bob Wills show or dance was like unless you were there. That man had the magnetism, or whatever a man has which has every eye in the house glued on him all night long. He had good bands and he had mediocre bands, but it didn't seem to make any difference. The people who were there listening weren't really hearing the music that was being played on the bandstand: They were hearing the records, and they already knew them. They knew what Bob Wills was going to sound like before they got there, so it didn't really matter whether he was having a good night or a bad night. The people were such Bob Wills addicts and fans that every night was a good night. It was just indescribable."

About 1200 people turned out for Bob Wills in Whitney, Texas—"A lot of beer drinkers who liked to dance," Willie said—and they all had a great time. At the end of the show, Willie Nelson got up on stage and joined Bob Wills in a song, a Bob Wills song. It was the high point of Willie Nelson's young life.

Unconsciously, young Willie Nelson absorbed more than the music of Bob Wills and His

Texas Playboys. If Ernest Tubb had turned him away from riding the range toward the honkytonks, Bob Wills laid down rules of, for lack of a better word, *style* that Willie Nelson still follows today.

In addition to retaining Wills' sense of adventure and eclecticism in music, Willie began seeing himself as a *bandleader,* just like Bob Wills.

"He was a bandleader," Willie said. "He *directed* the band, and he was respected probably more than any other bandleader."

The musicians watched Wills like a hawk, because, true to his jazz styles, he could point his fiddle's bow at any band member, and he'd better be able to take over and *fly*—"You'd better be ready to know where it was at and jump in and do *something.*"

Moreover, Bob Wills had a special relationship with his band members, a relationship that Willie would someday imitate.

"Even though he had arrangements, which came on in certain places in a song, Bob allowed his musicians to *play,*" Willie explains. "He'd give them individual breaks and let them do their stuff, play their licks. Other bands weren't doing that at the time. That was Bob Wills' technique. He'd make individual stars out of everyone on the bandstand, or at least he tried to . . ."

Years later, Willie would remember Bob Wills in his relationship with his own Family Band, making sure that each person on stage was an individual star. But, like Wills, he would demand that the band members watch him like a hawk, ready to take over in an instant.

The love that Willie Nelson felt arcing between Bob Wills and his audience was manifested in the fact that Wills obviously loved being on stage. He'd start playing around eight in the evening and play straight through until midnight, never taking an intermission. Ironically, Willie would find that exactly the opposite was the case with touring country musicians, who usually did a quick two shows a night, packed up and went home. One of the first things mentioned in reviews of Willie Nelson and the Family Band was that they "seemed to play all night."

Finally, Willie learned a hearty respect for arrangements.

"It used to be that when you learned a Bob Wills song, you also learned the exact arrangement, because the arrangement was so good," he said. "They were head arrangements of jazz riffs which the musicians would put together and add three- and four-part harmonies. Now that was *real* unusual to hear in a Western band."

Each incarnation of the Texas Playboys followed the same arrangements—the same arrangements, in fact, that were used on the records. When people went to a Bob Wills concert, they heard the Texas Playboys play the songs they were familiar with in the same way they'd heard them on the radio. This is something else that stuck with Willie through the years.

Although it was not all that uncommon in the years after World War Two, the coming of rock and roll changed the dynamics of the music business, and in some ways changed it for the worse. Suddenly touring musicians didn't want to play the songs the audience heard on the radio. Arrangements were juggled around and new songs and styles became the order of the day. The traditional bond between the audience and the performer was changed, sometimes broken. People went to concerts to listen, not to dance. The audience became observers rather than participants, critics rather than fans.

Willie Nelson, though, would go back to the old-time ways, the way Bob Wills did it.

When Willie Nelson stepped onstage in Whitney, Texas, though, in the ebullient days after World War Two, all that was yet to come. Instead, he was a thirteen-year-old red-headed kid, maybe a little too smart, maybe a little too old for his age. A kid who snaked his idol into letting him sing along, which wasn't likely to hurt Willie's local reputation any, bet on that.

There are people who, to this very day, will swear to you on a stack of Bibles that Willie Nelson knew, even when he stepped on that stage with Bob Wills, what was coming down the line; that he saw the future stretched in front of him like a string of musical notes, the highs and lows, the sharps and flats, an endless procession of one-night stands leading to multi-million-dollar success. Of course, Willie always scoffed at people like that.

4

Crazy

One of the most difficult things to get a grip on in Willie Nelson's life is that so many things happened so *quickly*, as though the first years of his life were all viewed from the wrong end of the telescope. While most kids were learning their alphabets, Willie Nelson was learning chords. While most kids of that period dreamed of cowboys, Willie Nelson dreamed of cowboy singers. While most kids were at home dreaming of sandlot baseball, Willie Nelson was at Frank Clements' barbershop in Abbott, serenading the customers for fifty cents a day. Seven-year-old Willie writing cheating songs; thirteen-year-old Willie onstage with Bob Wills—before his sixteenth birthday, it almost seemed as though Willie Nelson had lived a lifetime.

There was, however, another side to growing up Willie, a "normal" side that both he and Bobbie managed to maintain despite his youthful honkytonk nights.

Like a million other kids, Willie Nelson was taken with sports (an obsession he retains today). In high school, he played baseball, softball, volleyball, football, even basketball. He competed in track, was a fierce, if slightly undersized, halfback for the Abbott High School Panthers, was, for a while, a member of the Boy Scouts and the Future Farmers of America, worked on the school paper and the annual and even finished with pretty good grades for a kid who was staying up to all hours pickin' in honkytonks.

Bud Fletcher's band, sometimes even featuring Ira Nelson, was working steadily in the honkytonks of nearby Waco, considered by the God-fearing people of Abbott to be only a small step above Sodom. In fact, Myrle Nelson would appear periodically in town, making no bones that she disapproved of how Willie's and Bobbie's lives were going. She had left town, after all, to make sure the two got a good religious raising.

But all the honkytonking was having a surprisingly slight effect on Willie. The main problem, in fact, seemed to be that he was getting less and less sleep. Those missed hours of sleep, ironically, would shape much of his later life, because the lack of sleep might have been the overriding factor that launched Willie irrevocably on the road to music. In high school, he had temporarily put aside his burning ambition to be a honkytonk singer and bandleader for the lure of professional sports. When he finally graduated, the game plan had become professional baseball. There were tryouts for a baseball scholarship at a nearby junior college, and Willie imagined himself a shoo-in.

Maybe he would have been, too, if he hadn't been up all night honkytonking. Inside curves look different through bloodshot eyes, and there simply aren't words to describe the vicious *cra . . . a . . . a . . . cking* noise of a bat colliding with a ball in the bright sunlight. No baseball scholarship. No college career. In the cold light of the day, it must have seemed like no future, either. It was 1951. Willie Nelson joined the Air Force.

The stint in the military lasted less than a year, a year that Willie dismisses with as few words as possible. Thanks to a bad back, maybe the unwitting legacy of picking all that cotton, he was soon back on the road again, working in Bud Fletcher's band and still trying to figure out what he was going to do with his life. Not, mind you, that he had anything at all against a life in music—that was certainly the most appealing prospect. It was just that a life in music seemed to offer almost no hope of making any money, much less enough money to live on.

And Willie now needed money to live on not just for himself, but for his new wife, sixteen-year-old Martha Matthews, a carhop at the Lone Oak Drive-in in Waco and a full-blooded Cherokee Indian. Marrying Martha began a phase in Willie's life that would provide enough fodder for a million country songs. Willie's relationship with women has been, at best, tumultuous. Being on the road is hardly conducive to good marital relationships, nor is having a knack for picking, as one interviewer delicately put it, "demonstrative" women. Marriage, Willie now claims, is not as important to men as to women.

"Maybe the man shrinks away from it a little bit, because to him it signifies the end of freedom and to her it's security," Willie said. "I'm not saying I got married every time I did to make the girl happy, but maybe I did—I don't know. I've been married three times now, and I still don't know whether it's better to be married or not to be married. They both have their drawbacks."

About the time he married Martha, Willie Nelson began a hopscotch succession of day jobs to support his music. He sold vacuum cleaners, encyclopedias, even Bibles door-to-door. He gave up selling encyclopedias door-to-door when he realized that he was selling encyclopedias on the time payment plan to people too poor to even own furniture. Willie's car was so beat up that the biggest challenge was finding a hill in flatland Texas to park the car on, to give the decrepit vehicle a running start. Selling Bibles disgusted him so much that Willie decided to go to college to learn about agriculture, getting as far as trying Baylor ("I majored in dominoes," he says, grinning a Willie Nelson grin). For a while—a very short while—he considered becoming a professional football player.

Willie figured, though, that he ought to at least make a stab at bringing his night life and day life together, and the ideal job to Willie seemed to be that of disk jockey. He quickly decided to get a job at a radio station, not at all deterred by the fact that he had no experience and, outside of singing on radio shows, only the vaguest understanding of how a radio station worked.

He'd already made the jump from Abbott to San Antonio, a honkytonking, wide-open border town, and he'd even linked up with a new band, The Mission City Playboys, headed up by another ne'er-do-well named Johnny Bush.

Willie applied at a small radio station about half-an-hour from San Antonio in a wide place in the road called Pleasanton. He might not have known anything about radio, but Willie Nelson knew plenty about talking fast. While knocking around the radio stations around Abbott, Willie noticed that the equipment had the distinctive RCA logo on it, as did most of the radio equipment of that time. When the Pleasanton station owner asked whether Willie had done that kind of work before, Willie answered, sure, but he was used to working with RCA equipment. He started out with a ten-minute news and commercial show, making what at the time seemed like the lordly sum of forty dollars a week.

He opened the station up at the nearly unbelievable hour of 5:30 a.m., usually with one of the mind-numbing homilies described by Lana Nelson Fowler, Willie's oldest daughter, in her *Family Album*: "Your old cotton pickin', snuff

dippin', tobaccer chewin', stump jumpin', gravy
soppin', coffee-pot dodgin', dumplin' eatin', frog
giggin' hillbilly from Hill County . . ." Which
was probably enough to wake up the dead,
although not necessarily Willie Nelson, at the
crack of dawn.

Every night was a honkytonk night, and the
stretch of road between San Antonio where he
played and Pleasanton, where he lived with
Martha, was probably the longest, hardest stretch
of highway in the world. He sat in with all sorts
of bands, from hardcore honkytonkers to letter-
perfect Bob Wills imitators. It was the first great
period of musical experimentation for Willie.

"It was easy for me to learn a song," he says.
"I learned all kinds of songs—country, blues,
jazz and pop standards. I learned everything I
could. Every time a song would come out, I'd
learn it. If it had an unusual melody, or an
unusual chord in it, well, I'd try to learn to sing
the melody and play the chord."

It was crazy times, and times that get a little
larger with each retelling. Willie and Johnny
Bush, soaking up the whiskey and dead, stone-
cold broke, trying to hustle up enough cash to
make the next gig; not having enough gas to
make that long trip from San Antonio to
Pleasanton, causing the good farming citizens
of Pleasanton to wake up to dead silence rather
than the old Stump Jumper himself. There is the
perhaps slightly stretched story of Willie and
Johnny, too broke to make it to a gig, trying
their luck at hopping a freight train. After all, it

sounded so easy on all those Jimmie Rodgers records. The two men threw their bags and their guitars into an open boxcar, and then the train sped up, leaving the breathless singers to watch their possessions disappearing down the rails.

Meantime, Martha had begun to take offense at Willie's crazy hours and drinking habits—"I am not," Willie has said, again and again, "a successful drunk." Nor was Martha a successful house-mouse. What had begun as limited sniping showed all the potential of breaking into full-scale war. Willie's response was typical —he went on the road. He moved around, usually with Martha in tow, taking odd jobs here and there to keep them going. At one point they were so broke that he was forced to fill the gas tank of his car by siphoning off gas intended for school buses and government vehicles. Think of it as building an experience bank, which would later prove invaluable to him as a songwriter. At the time, it seemed more like purgatory.

After a quick lap of the country, he found himself and Martha back in Texas, this time Fort Worth. He got a job at KCKN, resumed playing the honkytonks and bought a used car, $25 down, from a "shady" local character named Paul English, whose brother played drums occasionally with Willie. Probably of all the things he did in Fort Worth, that used car provided the biggest pay-off in the long run.

English was born near Vernon, Texas, and

raised in the church. When he turned sixteen, though, he was drawn to the 'tonks that infested Ft. Worth. He was, he claimed, a skinny kid. He was also a Golden Gloves champion, and in no time at all the head of his own street gang, called the Peroxide Gang, because, Paul remembers, "We all peroxided our hair." He got in fairly serious trouble with the law, got out and got into illegal gambling.

He stuck to his specialties, gambling, hustling, numbers, cardrooms—getting by while his friends were getting dead. He was thrown out of one suburb of Ft. Worth after another. Through it all, he retained the attitude of, as one Austin club owner described him, "a cavalier, a gentleman."

Then Willie Nelson walked into his life to buy a used car. The old saw is that opposites attract, and it certainly held true in this case. Mild-mannered Willie became fast friends with Paul the Hustler. Willie taught Paul to play the drums, and the two played pool together in honkytonks where Willie Nelson alone would have been hung up and dried. Although Paul was knocking down big bucks in his "sidelines," he played with Willie for $15 a night. When times were really tough, English popped for some of Willie's bills.

They played the honkytonks along the Jacksboro Highway (usually referred to as the "Jaxbeer" Highway). "My friend used to say that the 'tonks that lined the Jaxbeer Highway were the easiest places in Fort Worth for a white man to get killed by his own kind," recalls Dave Hickey, no stranger to those very 'tonks. They had names like Blood Bucket and The County Dump, and sometimes the management graciously strung chicken wire in front of the stage to keep the performers from getting whacked with a thrown beer bottle. One joint was so tough that the band was hired just to cover the noise of a dice game. "One evening my cousin took a night off," Paul says, "and the guy who took his place was killed. He was stabbed over a hundred times."

While surviving the honkytonks, Willie took a fatal blow to his religious affiliations. He was teaching Sunday School at the Metropolitan Baptist Church in Fort Worth when one of the church members discovered Willie was a musician in the 'tonks. There is sacred music, and there is secular music, and in the South, never the twain shall meet. Never ever. Play for the church, the pastor told Willie, or play the Godless honkytonks. A man can't do both. Willie Nelson, a strongly religious man, thought differently, but, given the choice, he took the honkytonks.

5

Night Life
(Ain't No Good Life)

One of the things that has set Willie Nelson apart from a slew of other excellent country music performers is his impressive abilities as a songwriter.

"A great song has to have its own personality—as well as a good lyric and a good melody," Willie says. "And it has to be simple. If it gets to be too complicated, you have to listen to it too many times to appreciate it. And that makes it too hard for John Doe on the street to pick it up. The first time he hears it, it's got to hit him between the eyes."

Probably the hardest single action in the whole music business is writing a simple song. Human emotions are very complex, and the more complicated the situation is, the more complex the emotions. The gift of a songwriter is to take a whole string of complex, interwoven emotions and make them seem both simple and immedi-

57

ately recognizable—"There," the listener says, "I felt that way."

Probably the greatest country songwriter of them all was Hank Williams, a haunted, tormented genius who set a tone for country music that remains strong today.

"As you read through the lyrics of a Hank Williams song," wrote Frye Gaillard in *Watermelon Wine: The Spirit of Country Music,* "the words are so simple, so obvious—the kind of vocabulary you would expect from a small-town Alabama boy who grew up during the Depression with an utter lack of interest in formal, or even informal, schooling. But if the songs themselves are uncomplicated, the emotions they captured are not, and that's what gives them the kind of gut-stabbing realism that country music fans have always remembered."

Substitute Willie Nelson for Hank Williams, and change Alabama to Texas, and the sentence would still be pretty accurate. Like Hank Williams, Willie Nelson's songs are surprisingly simple, pegged to an event surrounded by an emotional hurricane. Take an early song like "Night Life (Ain't No Good Life)." For the singer of the song, the night life isn't a good life, but it's the life the singer has chosen. The song conveys a sense of seduction—the night life is seductive—but there's a hint of the old Christian guilt lurking around as well, and a sense of loss. The night life is the last stop, the only choice left.

Or take a song like the enormous hit, "On

The Road Again," from the movie *Honeysuckle Rose*.

"We (Willie and producer Jerry Schatzberg) were flying in this private airplane from somewhere to somewhere else, and we were talking about the script and the movie and the music we would need," Willie told disk jockey Lee Arnold. "I guess I was probably showing off a little bit, but they wanted a song that would be like a theme song for *Honeysuckle Rose*. I asked what they would like the song to say. And either Jerry or Sidney (Lumet, the director) said, 'Well, we'd like it to say something about being back on the road again.' So I said, 'Give me a pencil.' "

In approximately five minutes, on a piece of scrap paper, Willie, much to the amazement of the movie executives, wrote out all the lyrics to "On The Road Again." When they asked about the melody, Willie shrugged. Don't worry about that, he said. That'll come later.

"I had in my mind the melody I wanted," he recalled, "but I didn't put the melody to it until several months later, when we were getting ready to start rehearsals on it. But, you know, it wasn't really hard to put a melody to it, since I knew I wanted an uptempo thing that sounded like a bus going down the highway."

Even a simple song like "On The Road Again" is filled with emotional overtones, this time *happy* emotions, the joys of playing music, of being with the extended family of the band and the hold the road has on Willie Nelson.

"I never write more than ten or twelve songs a year," Willie says. "But I've done it since I was ten or eleven years old, so it adds up. I go for months without writing anything, then maybe I'll write two songs in one day. Songs are like labor pains. You just have to wait for them to come. Sometimes the tune comes first, but usually it's the idea. It starts out in my mind, and I think about it while I'm driving, and I put the melody around the lyrics. Only later do I get to working on it with a guitar. Almost everything I write is autobiographical . . ."

The pool halls in Fort Worth began to wear pretty thin, and in 1956 Willie decided to move to Vancouver, Washington, where Myrle had remarried and was living. He quickly got a job as a disk jockey on KVAN and even more quickly became one of the top disk jockeys in the area. With all those fans tuning in every afternoon, Willie figured it was time to start a recording career, so he financed his first recording, "No Place For Me," a country cry-in-your-beer weeper he'd written, backed with the upbeat "Lumberjack." He sold 2000 copies at a dollar a copy. For the first time in his life, Willie Nelson was a star.

For the first time also, his songwriting was beginning to show some financial return. Although he'd had songs published before, it wasn't until he teamed up with another songwriter named Jack Rhodes to write "Too Young to

Settle Down" that he himself began to settle
down in the role of songwriter.

"If I had a choice," he says, "I'd play four
hours a night, seven days a week. The playing is
the fun, the writing is the work. To write songs,
I usually need a reason. Like not having any
money."

Despite his successes on the radio in the
Northwest, Texas pulled at Willie like a magnet.
He lasted two years in Vancouver, then bun-
dled up Martha, who was sick of the whole
thing, and headed back to Fort Worth and the
honkytonks. This time, however, he didn't stay
long. Willie quickly moved to Houston, a big
city with a bit more opportunity for an aspiring
performer. As usual, his first stop was at the
local radio stations, where he nailed down a job
at KCRT as a disk jockey. He also got a pretty
good playing gig six nights a week at a joint
called the Esquire Club.

He also got a job teaching guitar at a music
school owned by country musician Paul Buskirk,
which was something of a laugh since Willie
didn't read music. Buskirk agreed to tutor Willie so Willie could tutor his students.

The most important thing to happen in
Houston, though, was the maturing of Willie's
talent as a songwriter. The situation was very
similar to Vancouver, and Willie quickly became locally well-known. But instead of weepy
ballads, his songwriting jelled into tight, autobiographical verses. One of his earliest songs
was "Family Bible," a song dedicated to Mama

Nelson and inspired by the family Bible she kept.

It was in Houston, as well, that Willie wrote "Night Life." He and Martha, now with three kids, lived in Pasadena, about thirty miles from Houston. It was a drive Willie knew well enough to drive with his eyes closed, and it was stupefyingly boring. As he drove along, he wrote songs. One particular snatch of lyric in particular kept nagging at him, a few words about the night life. What was worse, he would write most of the song in his head on the way to work at the Esquire Club, and after a night of hard honkytonking, the song would be almost gone. Each trip, he'd do a little more work on it, until, finally, it was finished.

While Willie Nelson was long on songwriting talent, he was, as author Bob Allen has put it, a bit short on business acumen. Dollars seemed to slip through Willie Nelson's hands faster than songs sprang up in his fertile brain. He was always broke, always hustling for a few dollars more. The one thing Willie had that he could sell was his songs.

Selling songs isn't the same thing as getting a song *published,* either. Publishing a song means royalties for the writer each time the song is published. When a song is sold outright, though, the writer loses all financial interest in the song. In fact, in many cases the writer doesn't even have to be acknowledged.

Much to the distress of his family, Willie sold "Family Bible" for $50 to a person he'd met while teaching music. The song went on to become a country music classic. And in perhaps one of the saddest deals in popular music, Willie Nelson sold the rights to "Night Life" for $150. As he later told an interviewer, some people rob convenience stores when times get hard; some people sell their songs.

Incredibly, he couldn't even find one person with enough money to buy the song. First he offered the song to the bandleader of the Esquire Club for $10. The bandleader, appalled that Willie would let such a song go, offered instead to loan Willie some money. But the money slipped away, and Willie went looking for another buyer. Willie finally sold two-thirds interest in the song to Paul Buskirk and his business partner, Walter Breeland. The song was originally recorded by Paul Buskirk and His Little Men, featuring Hugh Nelson. Willie "Hugh" Nelson played the bluesy guitar in the chorus of the song that has gone on to become its trademark.

"Night Life" went on to become one of the most recorded songs in country music history. Beginning with Ray Price's classic 1963 recording, "Night Life" has been recorded by more than seventy artists and has sold over 30 million copies.

The 1960s were not shaping up auspiciously. Willie Nelson was broke, getting broker and had all the prospects of being a broke, tired, drunk, unhappy honkytonk singer for the rest of his life. It was time, he thought, to test what he would later call the Law of Karma, "What goes around, comes around."

If Willie Hugh Nelson wanted to be a famous singer and songwriter, then he had to *be* a country music singer and songwriter. What was required was a simple act of faith, something not unfamiliar to a man raised in the hardscrabble church.

Accordingly, he bought a 1946 Buick, already on its last legs, and told Martha and the three kids that he was moving to Nashville to be a country singer and songwriter. He'd send for the family when he was settled.

When he was a star.

6

Down At The Corner Beer Joint

When Willie Nelson got to Nashville, the car promptly died, leaving Willie to move into a $25-a-week trailer park, Dunn's, on the wrong side of Nashville's tracks. It was worth, Willie later recalled, closer to $3 a week. The sign on the trailer park read, "Trailers For Sale Or Rent," and another Nashville songwriter, Roger Miller, would see in that sign a summation of life on the road.

In a couple of weeks, Martha and the three kids arrived by bus from Waco, where they had been staying with Martha's parents, and Willie Nelson began making good on the Law of Karma. No disk jockey this time, no peddling Bibles, vacuum cleaners, encyclopedias—no day job at all. Instead, Willie would concentrate on making contacts, the true secret of making a dent in the music business, and Martha would get some kind of job to support the family. To

Willie, it sounded like a great deal. To Martha, it sounded like slavery.

So Willie began the process of "making contacts". To the uninitiated, "making contacts" was only marginally different than being a no-count worthless bum. One of the biggest necessities for making contacts is a bar, where the person wishing to make contacts spends endless days and nights, playing music and drinking until dawn. This is repeated until said contacts are made.

The bar in this case was Tootsie's Orchid Lounge, a dingy, down-and-out bar right behind the Ryman Auditorium, home of the Grand Ole Opry. If there had been no such place as Tootsie's, some country songwriter would have had to invent it. Its facade was painted a garish purple—the color of an orchid—and the inside of the joint was darker than a dungeon. Even on its good days, it seemed about to collapse. The decor consisted of ratty chairs, ratty tables, all of which bore the carvings of a million country music fans— "Billy From Tulsa," "I Love Hank Williams." The walls were plastered with the photos of thousands of Nashville's best-known, least-known and unknown, as if watching your photograph grow yellow on the wall of Tootsie's was stardom of a sort.

Presiding over it all was the tiny figure of Tootsie Bess, born in Hohenwald, Tennessee, and once married to the singer-comedian-ticket seller for Big Jeff Bess and the Radio Playboys. When the two broke up, some time in the late

1950s, Tootsie opened her bar. Right off, the street people around South Broadway in Nashville figured Tootsie's was the place to be. For a start, it was convenient to the Opry. Big stars could zip out the back door and be at Tootsie's swilling down a Budweiser quicker than an emcee could say "Thankee, thankee, thankee."

Willie did, however, have some immediate problems, the biggest of which was his almost uncanny knack for being slightly out of sync with the rest of the world. Since everyone in Nashville was starting to get into rhinestone suits and powder-blue performing outfits, Willie favored turtle-neck sweaters and jeans. Later he would wear a bandana and a shoulder-length ponytail to the White House.

More important than the way he looked was the indisputable fact that Willie Nelson sang funny. He *phrased,* sang country music songs the way he'd heard Frank Sinatra.

"His voice is grainy but it cuts clean," wrote noted jazz critic Nat Hentoff. "In no way does it try to overpower or surprise the listener with virtuoso effects. Willie just gets inside your head and then plays on your memories as if he were softly chording a guitar."

Country music has always been a medium of distinctive voices—Ernest Tubb and Jimmie Rodgers come quickly to mind—but it is not a medium that has always been happy with those voices. At various times, Nashville has wished that all those strange voices would just *disappear.* The fact that Willie's monotone baritone was evocative and perfectly suited to Willie's moving songs didn't cut a bit of ice with the Nashville powers-that-be.

Country music was on its way to becoming big-time stuff. The way it had chosen to become big time, though, was by moving closer to the mainstream, trying to come to grips with the legacy of Hank Williams and the honkytonk—issues that would, ultimately, shape the career of not only Willie Nelson but the whole of Nashville and country music in the 1970s.

Ole Hank has become so much a part of the Nashville cultural unconscious and the country music landscape that his myth is recycled constantly, at a seemingly ever-increasing rate. Hank's most profound impact on country music was not found among the countless imitators who dominated country through much of the 1950s, but among the young pickers who saw a genius go down in flames while his friends and admirers stood on the sidelines, studiously ignoring the smoke. One veteran Nashville observer who knew Hank commented, most eloquently, "Those people on the Opry didn't give a shit. He had no friends until he died." The example that Hank Williams left for the young pickers was, for the first time in country music, a page from the Gospel According To Hollywood—live fast, die young and leave a beautiful corpse.

The saddest thing, perhaps, was that for Hank there really didn't seem to be any other end. When Hank Williams arrived in Nashville in

1946, just seven years before his death, he had been roaring hard since he was twelve years old and had won his first talent contest in Montgomery, Alabama, singing his own "W.P.A. Blues." By the time he was fifteen, he was hitting the brutal north Alabama honkytonk circuit with a band he called the Drifting Cowboys. Driven by a bitter childhood—he had been raised by his mother after his father left for a veterans' hospital—he was a virtual alcoholic well before his twentieth birthday. Then there were the pills to ease the pain of a chronically bad back; the pills, of course, soon became an end in themselves.

Yet what he had when he came to Nashville in 1946 was the same kind of drive that would be reflected in Willie Nelson a little more than a decade later. Hank Williams brought with him the natural, stunning ability to drive a simple song straight into the gut, to bypass the head and score an immediate, direct hit on the heart. He was best, perhaps, at evoking a sense of despair, of the sheer pain of the small failures of everyday life.

Country music in the late 1940s, wrote Greil Marcus in his book on popular music, *Mystery Train,* "so perfectly expressed the acceptance and fatalism of its audience of poor and striving whites, blending in with their way of life and endlessly reinforcing it, that the music brought all it had to say to the surface, told no secrets and had no use for novelty. It was conservative in an almost tragic sense, because it carried no hope of change, only respite . . . Country music lacked the confidence to break things open because it was not even sure it could find the space to breathe. Hank Williams was eloquent, but his eloquence could not set him free from the life he sang about; he died proving that, overdosing in the back of a car, on his way to one more show."

On New Year's Day, 1953, Hank Williams died in the back of his Cadillac, on his way to a show in Canton, Ohio. He'd already been thrown off the Opry for his drinking, relegated to the less-prestigious Louisiana Hayride, where his career had really begun. Ironically, he was selling more records than ever. He was, in fact, the biggest star country music had ever produced.

But before he'd had a chance to really reach his full potential as a singer and a songwriter, Hank Williams was gone, leaving behind a catalog of songs that would grow staggeringly valuable and a myth that would partially shape the life of every aspiring kid with a guitar. In four years—from his first appearance on the Opry in 1949 to his death in 1953—he had given country music its first national audience, an audience that Nashville has only recently been able to find again, and only with the help of Texan Willie Nelson. Hank Williams was a star, not just a country music star, and country music singers have been acutely aware of that distinction ever since.

But the legacy of Hank remains a two-edged sword. For all the good that he and his music did, he gave country music a *tragic* figure to revere and to emulate. He provided a prototype of the hard-living, hard-drinking, got-no-future-but-I'm-sure-as-hell-on-my-way hillbilly singer, and that image held true until the *second* success of Willie Nelson in the mid-1970s.

Ole Hank launched an era of miserable hillbillies. There was a nagging feeling in Nashville—and you can still feel it today, if you know where to look—that so what if Hank *died* doing it, it's still the only way to go. When Willie Nelson arrived in Nashville in 1961, the spirit of Ole Hank hung over the place like a pall, which, in fact, it was.

The other thing that Hank Williams did, which would mean everything in the world to Willie Nelson, was give songwriters a good name. Before him, country songwriters tended to be fairly anonymous contributors to an artist's success— the emphasis was on the singer, the *bandleader à la* Bob Wills. But the success of Hank Williams' material, especially in the hands of pop crooners, helped bring the country songwriter out of the closet. Pretty soon the Nashville bus station was drawing a new breed of starry-eyed newcomer. Although these newcomers might pack a battered guitar of their own, they came primarily to write songs. People like Harlan Howard ("Busted," "I Fall To Pieces"), Marijohn Wilkin ("Long Black Veil"), John D. Loudermilk ("Tobacco Road"), Mel Tillis ("Detroit City") and Roger Miller ("In The Summertime," and, of course, "King of the Road") began to drift into town, and suddenly Music City began to seem like a real music city.

By the mid-1950s, the recording industry in Nashville was gearing up for its headlong rush into the next two decades. Besides the actual industry portion of Music Row, at one time a deteriorating middle-class neighborhood near the Vanderbilt University campus which included studios, record company offices and the miscellaneous flotsam and jetsam of the industry, Nashville's biggest asset was its talent. The first and most obvious skin of the Nashville onion was made up of the pickers—the musicians who played on almost every record coming out of Nashville. Nashville pickers were so good that they would very quickly develop a "sound," a particular style that would mark a record as a Music City product. That style, that Nashville feeling, would draw such mainstream artists as Bob Dylan to the city to record. The second obvious layer was the producers, the engineers, the technical people in charge of the actual studio sessions.

But the most important third layer—the songwriters—was just beginning to form when Willie Nelson arrived in Nashville. The songwriting community was unique. It resembled in some ways the awakening of the Beat Generation in New York City—artists banding together to pursue their craft—but unlike the Beat counterpart to the north, this community was strictly a commercial venture. You were accepted because you wrote hit songs, and you kept your place by writing more hit songs. The people who held on were, quite literally, the cream of the crop.

The first to arrive was Mel Tillis, who recalls arriving in Nashville around 1956. He came to Nashville out of the service and broke, looking for some kind of work, and quickly wrote such hits as "Detroit City," a masterpiece of the dispossessed Southerner trying to make it in the industrial cities of the North.

"When I got to Nashville, there was no one else," he remembers. "Then Harlan Howard showed up, Hank Cochran, Roger Miller and Willie . . .

"We all hung around together," Tillis says. "I mean, we all knew each other, and we'd gather down at the Orchid Lounge and have a guitar pullin', you know, a jam session. Sing each other our songs. It was really close knit."

There were other things going on in the songwriters' community that would have a long-term effect on the life of Willie Nelson. When the guys would get together down at Tootsie's or Linebaugh's restaurant across the street, they wouldn't necessarily sing their latest hit single. Instead, they'd sing songs that had a major effect on them, songs they liked, tunes they enjoyed. And as a rule, a songwriter's taste is not necessarily going to reflect what's popular at the moment, or even what will ever be popular. The folks down at Tootsie's had heard a lot of songs, and what they were listening for

was that little something extra, that special touch
that gave a song its shot at immortality.

Pretty soon some of the more canny people
along Music Row were hanging around Tootsie's
themselves, listening to what the songwriters
sang to themselves and looking for tomorrow's
Next Big Thing. The result was the formation
of a kind of Nashville underground, a constantly boiling musical stew to satisfy the city's
ever-growing hungers.

The regular guitar pullin's at Tootsie's or
Linebaugh's were fertile ground for new and
radically different ideas and styles, like, say a
singer who *phrased* like Frank Sinatra instead
of Hank Snow. In the smoky atmosphere of the
Lower Broadway clubs, commercial potential
was not the name of the game. What mattered
was originality and uniqueness, and it was inevitable that at least some of that originality and
uniqueness would find its way into Nashville
music.

But not necessarily immediately.

"I was trying to sell a new style of singer,"
Willie remembers. "They didn't have a category
to put me in."

Music City was having its problems, and many
of those problems stemmed from a reaction to
none other than Hank Williams. An important
thing to keep in mind here is that Nashville had
always shunned Texas as a source of musical
inspiration. Although Bob Wills was the King
of Texas, Nashville had little use for swing
music in the 1940s. And the upbeat, amplified

music of Ernest Tubb of Texas took a back seat
to the honkytonk visions of Hank Williams of
Alabama. The biggest thing rocking Nashville
in the mid-1950s, though, came not from Texas
or Alabama, but from Tennessee. Memphis, to
be exact, where a man named Sam Phillips had
been conducting a search for the Next Big Thing
on his own. The Next Big Thing he was looking
for was a white man who could sing black;
what he found was Elvis Presley. The cataclys-
mic birth of rock and roll gave a huge boost to
the recording industry in Nashville while almost destroying country music. After the eloquent fatalism of Hank Williams, country music
had sort of painted itself into a depressing corner.
In 1955, the country charts were dominated by
such country weepers as Kitty Wells' "Making
Believe" and Porter Wagoner's "Satisfied Mind."
The next year there were four Elvis songs in
the country top ten, including "Heartbreak
Hotel," penned by Nashville songwriting star
Mae Borden Axton, "I Want You, I Need You,
I Love You," "Don't Be Cruel" and "I Forgot
To Remember To Forget." Also on the charts
that year were Johnny Cash ("I Walk The Line"),
Carl Perkins ("Blue Suede Shoes") and Marty
Robbins ("Singing The Blues"). In fact, the only
country acts on the charts were Kitty Wells
("Searching") and two honkytonk classics, Webb
Pierce and Red Sovine doing "Why Baby Why"
and Ray Price doing one of the greats, "Crazy
Arms." A sudden breath of fresh air had blown
into the dusty halls of country music. The

music was wild, violent, overtly sexual and rebellious; music for a generation more akin in spirit to Marlon Brando in *The Wild One* than to A.P. Carter. The new music had none of the doomed quality that seemed to permeate the best music of honkytonk kings like Hank Williams. It was music for *young* people.

In the beginning, as the charts make clear, rock and roll as practiced by the Memphis rockabillies like Elvis, Johnny Cash and Carl Perkins, was heavily country-oriented. Elvis, taking a page from the book of Hank Williams, first played the Louisiana Hayride, where he was introduced as "The Hillbilly Cat." In one of the great stories of country music, Elvis even auditioned for the Opry, where that venerable institution's talent director suggested Elvis Presley should go back to driving a truck.

The fact that the early rock and rollers saw themselves as country musicians scared the living cleft notes out of Nashville. It was obvious from the beginning that country music could not compete with the new music—the death of Hank Williams had hit country music harder than anyone would admit, and many of the old Williams' fans were looking for an escape from the Williams' despair. In country music, the energy to fight the brash newcomers simply wasn't there, especially since the battle looked so hopeless. The charts told the story, so little by little, country music began to change.

At first, the change was slow—the charts of the late 1950s reflect a thrashing around, looking for an identity in the wave of rock. Rather than go one-on-one with rock, country shifted more and more toward pop, the smooth mellow sound of crooners like Jim Reeves and Eddy Arnold, essentially washing its hands of its honkytonk past. Since the kids were plainly entranced with something different, then country music would go after their parents.

That decision left a lot of people out in the cold. While the Tootsie's crowd began cranking out songs for crooners and flourished as never before, the country-oriented rockabillies like Waylon Jennings and "Cowboy" Jack Clement were suddenly frozen out. If you liked the beat, sang in a funny way, wanted to really honkytonk, then Nashville wasn't for you. You had to fit in with the crooners, and after that movement had peaked, you had to be a part of the Nashville Sound.

When Willie Nelson arrived in Nashville, country music had already gone suburban. For Willie, that meant tremendous promise for his songwriting career, because somebody had to keep those crooners stoked up. But it meant just the opposite for his singing career. Nashville's decision to veer away from young people and concentrate on their affluent, suburban parents set the stage for the phenomenal success of Willie Nelson and country music in the mid-1970s. The music would come full circle, and Willie Nelson would be the point on which it would pivot. His allies would be his buddies from Tootsie's; the songwriting underground would

be seen as something of a revolutionary underground. For the first time since young Willie
Nelson had leaned his head against Mama
Nelson's old Philco radio, searching for WSM
and the Grand Ole Opry, country music would
rival rock and roll in the marketplace.

All because Willie Nelson insisted on staying
the same.

7

Phases & Stages, Circles, Cycles & Scenes

Willie continued to make contacts at Tootsie's, and Martha just got madder and madder. She'd been the one to take a day job, bartender at the Hitching Post, a down-and-out bar across the street from Tootsie's on South Broadway. Unlike Willie, Martha had a knack for organization, and she was soon running the Hitching Post and working some in the bar next door, the Wagon Wheel. After a night's hard work at the bar, it didn't help to have Willie come staggering in during the wee hours of the morning, all contacted out.

The battles between Willie and Martha escalated into open warfare, and the warfare has grown in the retelling over the years into something akin to a myth-like battle between good and evil. In probably his most oft-quoted quote, Willie once remarked that Martha was a full-blooded Cherokee Indian, "And we replayed

79

Custer's Last Stand every night." Sounds suspiciously like a country song.

In one legendary battle, Martha sewed a drunken Willie into a bedsheet, although the more probable version of the story has Martha tying a passed-out Willie into the bed with their daughter's jump rope and beating him with a broom. Then she took off with the kids and Willie's clothes. She didn't come back for four days, leaving Willie to sit in the ratty trailer in his underwear, without a phone and afraid to drop in on his neighbors largely in the buff. Another time she threw a fork at him so hard it stuck in his chest. Once she chased him through a nearby graveyard with a butcher knife.

Willie's personal life veered closer and closer to disaster.

As if to compensate, all his "contacting" down at Tootsie's suddenly began to pay off, and pay off big.

At first, the situation looked grim. As soon as Willie had arrived in Nashville, he ran into fellow Texan Billy "The Travelin' Texan" Walker, a solid star on the Grand Ole Opry. Introductions aside, Walker asked to hear some of Willie's songs and was so impressed he took Willie to Starday Records, suggesting to Starday that they sign Willie right up as a singer and a songwriter. The folks at Starday took a listen to Willie's off-beat phrasing and painfully personal lyrics and said no dice.

One of the mainstays at Tootsie's, though, was Hank Cochran, a one-time oil field worker who had given up roughnecking for entertaining in small clubs in California. He linked up with another Cochran, an Oklahoman named Eddie, and the two began playing clubs as The Cochran Brothers. Originally, they were a country duet, but one night in Dallas the two saw Elvis Presley perform. Rock and roll, they decided, was the way to go. They performed together for two years, then decided to split. Eddie stayed with rock, eventually recording the rock classic "Summertime Blues" and starring in such movies as *The Girl Can't Help It* and *Bop Girl* before dying in a car crash in England in early 1960.

Hank Cochran, on the other hand, had decided to get back to country music. First he went to work on a television show in Stockton, California, called "The California Hayride." He already had a contract with a California-based song-publishing company, Pamper Music, and in 1959 he decided to make the big move, to Nashville. Once in Nashville, Cochran teamed up with a Tootsie's regular, Harlan Howard, to write "I Fall To Pieces" for Patsy Cline, a top song in 1961. That year Cochran also began his own recording career with "Sally Was A Good Ole Girl."

Cochran's star was clearly on the rise when Willie Nelson made his way to Tootsie's, and the songwriter was clearly impressed with what he heard Willie picking. In fact, impressed is not nearly a strong enough word. He convinced his bosses at Pamper Music, which was partially owned by Ray Price, to hire Willie as a staff songwriter for $50 a week, the same salary Cochran was making.

Willie had already had a bittersweet taste of success. "Family Bible," the song his family had not wanted him to sell, had become a major hit for Claude Gray in 1960, the year before Willie went to Nashville. Unfortunately, when Willie sold "Family Bible" for fifty bucks, he sold all rights. His name didn't even appear on the record.

As soon as he signed with Pamper, however, Willie appeared to make the breakthrough he had always sought. Hank Cochran was as good a knockaround buddy as there was, and the two of them had a knack for writing songs together. They wrote such songs as "Undo The Right" and "You'll Always Have Someone," then Willie would hustle up studio time and record the songs as demos, hoping to stir up interest in his singing. The spare, clean arrangements and Willie's simple vocals didn't stir up anything in Nashville at the time, but, ironically, the demo recordings sound fresh and contemporary when played today.

Willie also went into a frenzy of writing songs. The ideas just seemed to flow from his pen; as fast as he could get one done, another would come to him. One of the first was "Funny How Time Slips Away," one of the only songs he claims to have written specifically for someone else to sing. He wrote it for Billy Walker, perhaps in thanks for Walker's ongoing support.

Walker's recording quickly became a hit, then a standard, and is now considered a classic. The same week Willie wrote "Funny How Time Slips Away," he also wrote "Crazy," which he thought would be just great for a girl singer like Patsy Cline.

Patsy Cline didn't think so at all. In fact, she hated the song, which was mostly a recitation. After much pushing and persuading by her producer, Owen Bradley, a dubious Cline agreed to record the song. It went to Number Two on the country charts, and Number Nine on the pop charts.

About the same time, Willie wrote what was to become his breakthrough hit, "Hello Walls." He and Hank Cochran worked in a garage on Pamper's property. "There was a door, a window and a guitar," Willie recalled, "and that was about it. We were out there this one particular day, and I started talking to the walls."

He called Hank Cochran over to help him write the song, but Hank had a phone call and had to leave. By the time Hank got back, Willie had written all the lyrics to "Hello Walls" on a piece of cardboard. He claimed, later, to have written a string of "house songs," among them "Hello Roof," "Hello Car."

With "Hello Walls" in hand, Willie headed on down to Tootsie's and began picking. Among the visitors for that particular session was Faron Young, one of the most consistently successful artists in Nashville throughout the 1950s. A promotion man for a record company had heard Willie play "Hello Walls" and went straight to Faron, who was coaxed into Tootsie's to hear the song. Faron didn't get to be a star by not knowing a hit song when he heard it. In fact, Faron had a reputation for listening to young songwriters and helping them out when they were in a bind, a generosity that had paid for itself time and time again.

Faron Young snapped up "Hello Walls" and cut a classic crooner version, where the walls answered back in a high little voice, "Hello, hello." That version soared to the top of the charts, even crossing over onto the pop charts. When "Crazy" was released (it was recorded before "Hello Walls") and began its climb up the charts, Willie Nelson was a struggling song-writer no more. In Nashville, then as now, there is no one quite so valued as a writer who can cross over, write a song that goes onto the pop charts as well as the country charts. There's no mystery about it, either—it's a simple matter of dollars and cents. A successful pop song in the 1960s sold two, three or even ten times as many records as a big hit country record. A country music artist would be riding high with sales of 100,000 records; a comparable pop song might sell a million. "Hello Walls" went on to sell more than two million copies. Ray Price recorded "Night Life;" Billy Walker did "Funny How Time Slips Away." Big-name non-country acts like Perry Como, Little Anthony and the Imperials, Lawrence Welk, even Eydie

Gorme, began recording songs by the little red-headed songwriter from Nashville.

By the end of 1961, after one year in Music City, Willie Nelson was a rich man, a respected songwriter, the new king of Tootsie's Orchid Lounge. But he wasn't a *star*.

Author Jan Reid in his book, *The Improbable Rise Of Redneck Rock,* correctly pointed out that if a songwriter had had the tremendous success of Willie Nelson in the new Nashville of the 1970s, "He would have been an immediate recorded superstar even if he sang with no teeth and a cleft palate. But Nelson arrived a decade early."

Nashville was willing to concede that old Willie Nelson was a songwriting devil, but they'd be damned if they'd put somebody who sang that funny on a record. About the time "Crazy" was climbing the charts, Willie heard that Donny Young, also knows as Johnny Paycheck, was quitting as the bass player and front man for Ray Price's Cherokee Cowboys.

"I heard that Ray Price needed a man to play bass and front his band," Willie says. "I didn't know how to play bass, but I told Ray I did, got the job, went out and got a bass and learned real quick. If he ever knew I didn't know how to play, he was kind enough not to mention it."

In many ways, Ray Price was the perfect man to enter Willie Nelson's life at that point. Born in East Texas, Ray Price grew up around Dallas and originally intended to become a veterinary surgeon. He began playing clubs and college campuses, though, and finally landed a job on the Big D Jamboree. In the early 1950s, Ray Price fell in with Hank Williams. Williams took the young singer under his wing and filled him in on the finer points of honkytonking. It was an interesting match—Price, like Willie Nelson, was steeped in the Texas tradition. Like Willie Nelson, he'd shared the multiple influences of growing up in Texas: Bob Wills and Western Swing, black and Latin music, the Opry over the radio. Under the tutelage of Hank Williams, Southwest met—some say for the first time— Southeast. In Ray Price, the high, lonesome sound of the Appalachian Mountains met the dance rhythms of the flat plains of Texas. As Price became more sure of himself as a performer, all those influences found their way into his music. His band, the Cherokee Cowboys, were in fact formed from the remnants of Hank Williams' Drifting Cowboys, unemployed when Williams' life crashed against the rocks.

Like Bob Wills, Ray Price was an artist not constrained by labels or trends. He could shift effortlessly from honkytonk *à la* Hank Williams to crooning *à la* Jim Reeves and do either with equal talent and verve. For a year, Willie toured with the Cherokee Cowboys, a band that included one of Willie's oldest friends, Johnny Bush, fiddler Wade Ray and pedal steel master Jimmy Day.

Willie was making $25 a night playing for Ray Price. When the royalty checks started rolling in, his annual salary quickly rose into six figures. For a country boy who once siphoned gas out of government vehicles, that kind of money meant that every day was payday, and every night was Saturday night. While Ray Price, one of the biggest stars in the history of country music, was riding on the bus with the band, Willie Nelson, bass player extraordinaire, was flying to the dates and staying in penthouses.

"(I was) throwing my money away with both hands," a rueful Willie says today. "I thought that was the way everybody did it."

It was on the road as a bass player that Willie finally did in his crumbling marriage to Martha. The more time he spent on the road, the lousier things got at home, of course, making it a *lot* more attractive to stay on the road, even at $25 a night. While on one of the swings through Los Angeles with Ray Price, Willie met a red-haired country singer named Shirley Collie, wife of respected country disk jockey Biff Collie. She already had a recording contract with Liberty Records in California, and Willie had approached her to pitch one of his songs.

"It was instant love," Shirley later told *Time* Magazine. "I saw things in him that give me goose bumps now."

At the same time Willie was boiling over with Shirley, Hank Cochran had once again stepped into Willie's life and given things a lift. At Cochran's recommendation, Liberty Records had signed Willie as a singer. Willie's first Liberty release featured a Willie Nelson-Shirley Collie duet on "Willingly," a song written by Hank

Cochran. That song cracked the Top Ten in March of 1962, and an enthused Liberty released "Touch Me" with Willie solo. That song went to Number Seven later that year. Liberty released a Willie Nelson album, . . . *And Then I Wrote*, which debuted to a world of praise. The album liner notes, from disk jockey Charlie Williams, were bright with promise. "It is rare that a truly great songwriter," he wrote, "is also an exciting vocalist . . . Johnny Mercer, Hoagy Carmichael and a handful of others. Now, with pride, Liberty Records presents the latest member of that select group. His name is Willie Nelson."

The year 1963 dawned clear and full of promise. After all the years, all the disappointments, Willie Nelson was in love—although not with his wife—and on the charts with his own songs.

He would be a star.

8

Pretend I Never Happened

The headlines in the country music fan magazines read, "Mr. Progress Weds," and the pictures were of a very short-haired Willie Nelson and an attractive Shirley Collie, now Shirley Nelson. The two were appearing at the Golden Nugget in Las Vegas, according to the reports, when they decided to tie the knot. Steel guitarist Jimmy Day was best man; Johnny Bush was "flower girl." The date for the wedding in the fan article was January 12, 1963, which is probably wrong, since Willie wasn't divorced from Martha until that October, according to Nashville court records.

In any case, the marriage with Martha hadn't survived the road. Later Willie would reflect on the fact that he'd met and married each of his wives when he was on the road, and it would be the road that destroyed two out of the three marriages. Absence, he will say with a typical Willie Nelson turn of phrase, does not necessarily make the heart grow fonder. Sometimes it makes the heart grow distant and cold.

"When I met each of my wives," he remembers, "I was on the road—goin' up and down the highway to play music. And that's what I'm still doin.' It's not that my wife and kids are second best or anything. It's just the nature of what I do."

Shirley encouraged Willie to start a band of his own, and Willie got the best band he could find—Ray Price's. Johnny Bush, Wade Ray and Jimmy Day joined Willie on the road, and Willie later reflected that buying the band "a station wagon and a credit card" was probably not such a good idea after all. After about half a tour, Bush and Willie hitchhiked back to Texas from California. He and Shirley moved from Nashville to Fort Worth, then to Los Angeles, then back to Nashville.

The middle years of Willie Nelson's career seem to flash by like pages ripped from a cinematic calendar. At the beginning of 1963, Willie Nelson seemed a sure bet, the Next Big Thing. His songwriting was legend; his single and duet with Shirley were high on the charts; his album was getting rave reviews. Based on that response, Liberty decided to release a second album, *Here's Willie Nelson,* and suddenly Willie Nelson wasn't hot anymore. People were still recording his songs, but his own songs— and his duets with Shirley—were suddenly going nowhere.

There are a couple of schools of thought on

the strange and fragmented career of Willie Nelson at that time. Part of the revisionist school, headed by Chet Atkins, head of RCA Records during the 1960s, was that everybody loved the way Willie sang and that Nashville was always on the lookout for a unique voice. This particular version is hardly borne out by the cold reality of Music City, where a genuinely unique talent will cause nine out of ten producers to break into hives. The history of country music is filled with unique talents surfacing in spite of every roadblock the record business could throw in their way.

The other traditional version is that Willie was so far ahead of his time that he was discriminated against, the vision being a cabal of insiders plotting the failure of Willie Hugh Nelson among others.

There's an element of truth to both versions, but the real explanation has much to do with sheer bad timing, a function more of luck than anything else. The early 1960s were some of the best years for country music artists since the great heyday of Hank Williams. Country music had good reason to be proud—it had weathered the rock-and-roll crisis and come out stronger than ever. Country artists were coming on strong. Bobby Bare sold a million copies of Mel Tillis' "Detroit City;" Johnny Cash was coming on strong with "Ring of Fire;" Skeeter Davis had "The End Of The World," and Ray Charles had come to Nashville and sung the gospel of country music. "Wolverton Mountain" and "Six

Days On The Road" were selling like hotcakes. Elvis Presley and Roy Orbison were treading a road that was still pretty close to Nashville. Nashville felt *good*.

Late in 1963 a British group named the Beatles entered the American charts with "I Want To Hold Your Hand." Within thirty days the world of popular music was shattered and reformed. The British Invasion was off and running, and Nashville found itself with another even bigger storm to weather. Ironically, the only people to stand in the face of the British Invasion were novelty acts, including Willie's old friend Roger Miller, who left Nashville for California, arrived broke, wired Willie for money and became rich beyond his wildest imagination with "Dang Me" and "King of the Road."

Country music retreated to the only safe ground it knew, the suburban audience it had been courting since the death of Hank Williams. More than even the first violent bursts of rockabilly, the British Invasion turned the "generation gap" into the Grand Canyon. Mom and Dad, who at long last had been convinced that Elvis Presley could *sing* and Roy Orbison wasn't necessarily the devil in disguise because he wore shades all the time, were finally presented with something they couldn't grasp—English boys with impossibly long hair singing adenoidal American rhythm and blues to their screaming children. Better to stick with country music, conservative country music, *crooning* country music. In the face of the British Invasion, coun-

try music retreated to the bastion of the Nashville Sound: slick, heavily laid-on production
behind smooth, usually male singers. Jim Reeves,
Eddy Arnold, a smoother Ray Price and Sonny
James rose quickly to the top of the charts.
The off-beat artists, the old honkytonkers, the
"distinctive" vocalists found themselves out in
the cold.

The rise of the Nashville Sound was rooted in
two factors—the increasing number of excellent
musicians who made Nashville their home and
the ascendancy of Chet Atkins at RCA Records.
The Nashville pickers worked together behind
almost every act. They worked from "head"
arrangements rather than formal charts or written music; sometimes it seemed they knew each
other better than the fingers on a guitar player's
hand. They evolved a very distinct sound, a
style capable of enhancing the music of anyone
who came to Nashville to record. The sound
itself was almost a reaction to the music on pop
radio—a sedate, mildly jazzy melange of guitar
melody and slip-note piano *à la* Floyd Cramer
of "Last Date" fame.

The rise of Chet Atkins cemented the wall of
Nashville Sound. A superb guitar player from
Luttrell, Tennessee, Chet Atkins played with
the Carter Family and was something of a revolutionary himself when he moved to Nashville.
After working on the RCA Elvis Presley sessions in the mid-1950s—sessions that guaran-
teed Nashville's place as a recording center—

Atkins took over as head of the powerful RCA Studios.

Although sensitive to new and upcoming talents, including Willie Nelson, whom he respected tremendously, Chet Atkins was moving toward a style of music that had little to do with Willie's honkytonk ways. The music Atkins favored was an easy-going, tensionless rhythm, exactly the opposite of the jerky steel guitar and fiddle and rhythms of old country music.

Chet Atkins' style became just what the country music industry was sure it needed, a sound to appeal to the people who liked neither the electrifying tension of rock and roll nor the similarly funky sounds of classic Hank Williams/Jimmie Rodgers-style country. In itself, Atkins' influence was good—any music either advances or it dies. But in the supercharged atmosphere of Nashville, with the barbarians just outside the gates, the Nashville Sound was embraced as the *only* way to make a successful record.

Producers like Billy Sherrill, a master of rhythm and blues, expanded the concept of the Nashville Sound by pushing it even closer to mainstream easy-listening pop, adding huge banks of orchestral-style strings to "sweeten" his recordings. He bounced his singers on this bed of violins, softening every note with echoing and double-tracking recording techniques until every singer sounded like a chorus of country angels.

On the surface, there would seem to be no reason for such tight controls to operate. The reason is in the economics of the business. If country records sold proportionately less than their pop counterparts, then the records had to be made proportionately cheaper to guarantee a profit. The albums were cut in two or three days with the same Nashville Sound musicians, and the dominant feature of the recording studio was the clock. With these factors controlling sessions, there was little room for new (read, "time-consuming") and different (read, "expensive") styles. A well-oiled machine was not only prudent but mandatory, and one of the first things anyone learns about an assembly line is that all the pieces have to be interchangeable or it just doesn't work.

The real irony of the whole episode is that Nashville built its own trap and fell into it. Like Detroit cars in the 1950s, the Nashville Sound kept getting bigger and bigger, more of this, more of that, until it was more expensive than any other type of recording. In fact, it wasn't until none other than Willie Nelson started cutting songs with only sister Bobbie on piano and his own guitar that Nashville realized the corner it had painted itself into. Of course, it was also Willie who proved that a country album could sell just like a rock album, but that was later, in his third incarnation.

"You know, I always thought I could sing pretty good," Willie has said. "And I guess it kinda bothered me that nobody else thought so . . . I was into a lot of negative thinking back then. I did a lot of bad things, got into fights with people, got divorced, all that stuff. My head was just pointed the wrong way, you know."

Liberty Records stopped cutting country music, leaving Willie without a recording contract. Although Chet Atkins at RCA made Willie an offer, he instead went to Monument Records, a label owned by Fred Foster, who'd also had a hit with one of Willie's songs. After an overly long period, Monument released a single record, which went nowhere. In the same period of time, Roy Orbison, Monument's mainstay artist, recorded Willie's Christmas lament, "Pretty Paper," which remains a season standard.

In disgust, Willie Nelson decided to quit the music business.

He and Shirley retreated to his Ridgetop, Tennessee, farm so he could become a gentleman farmer and raise hogs. The secret to hog-raising seemed to elude Willie, though. "Hogs is an art," Shirley said, "but we didn't know that. We just left those feeders full and the hogs ate until they ruptured or died."

Crack businessman Willie Nelson finally figured out a way to buy hogs at twenty-seven cents a pound and sell them for nineteen.

"Songwriting was better than that," he says.

Songwriting was, of course, what was financing the Ridgetop farm. Oddly enough, the farm eventually did grow into a going concern. But Willie Nelson was hardly cut out to be a hog farmer. Probably the most interesting thing to come out of the farm was Willie's estrangement with Ray Price. Ray Price could forgive a lot, could forgive, even, Willie stealing his band. But a man's got to draw the limit somewhere.

The line came over some of Ray Price's prized fighting roosters. Cockfighting was (and is) not a sport unknown to Nashville, and Price's roosters had a reputation as winners. He lived near Willie and asked one day if he could bring one of his roosters on Willie's farm for exercise.

"I said sure," Willie remembers, "but I've got some hens out there, he won't bother those hens, will he?"

Ray Price assured Willie that the fighting cock would be a pussycat. There were eight hens, and they were Shirley's pets. Two days later, Willie got up and discovered one of the hens dead. One thing Shirley shared with Martha was temper, and Willie hastily called Price and told him to remove the rooster.

No problem, hoss, Ray said. Be right over.

"About three weeks later he still hadn't come over to get the rooster," Willie says, "and I got up one morning and there was another hen dead."

Shirley went through the ceiling, got the shotgun and headed out to do permanent damage to Ray Price's fighting cock. Willie, fearing barnyard carnage, took the shotgun himself and killed the rooster and gave it to the housekeeper, who cooked the stringy fighting bird into a dinner.

Ray Price was furious. You just killed a thousand-dollar chicken, he told Willie, who replied that no fighting rooster was worth one good laying hen.

"Of course I was bullshitting," Willie says. "I knew it was worth a lot of money."

Not only was it worth a lot of money, Ray Price continued, but it was going to cost Willie a lot more than one thousand dollars, because Ray Price would never again record a Willie Nelson song.

For years, he didn't, either.

9

What Can You Do To Me Now?

The bucolic farm life wasn't what it was cracked up to be. After a few disasters, such as losing $5000 on a single load of hogs, the farm settled into a fairly profitable routine, and routine was the one thing Willie Nelson could not abide.

"I tried to be like other people," Willie told a reporter. "I tried to come home and watch TV. That just wasn't me."

More than anything else, Willie Nelson could not pull himself away from the road. For a traveling musician, the road represents all that is good and most of what's bad about playing country music. The life is incredibly hard—it's not unusual for an act to play 300 nights a year, trying to hustle up that spark of recognition in an audience. Country musicians pioneered the use of tour buses, big Silver Eagles that came to resemble small ocean liners on cruises that never seemed to end.

In the small world of a tour bus, problems seemed a bit more manageable. The problems, the lives and hopes and fears of the people outside the bus in each little community it plowed through, took on an air of unreality. The rhythms of the road and the rhythms of the music blended together into a steady beat. The road never really lets a performer go. No matter what happens, on the road there's always a sense that tomorrow is another day, another stage, another city, another shot at life. Failures and triumphs end at the city limits, and you're only as good as your last show.

Willie, Shirley remembers, needed his own little kingdom. He needed the road.

With the pig business percolating along, Willie Nelson decided to go back on the road. One of the first things he did was a symbolic act. On November 24, 1964, he joined the Grand Ole Opry.

He also told Chet Atkins that he was ready to record for RCA Records, recording an album called *Country Willie: His Own Songs*. Chet Atkins was at the helm, and the result was a good album, but not necessarily a Willie Nelson album. He also began touring with his old friend, Western Swing fiddler and vocalist Wade Ray, working as a duo and picking up a local band. Like the touring musicians of another era, Willie Nelson and Wade Ray played what the people wanted to hear. If the crowd wanted Bob Wills, they did Bob Wills; if the crowd wanted the Beatles, they did the Beatles. "We weren't interested in trends or the Nashville Sound," Ray told musicologist Rich Kienzle. "We did what we felt our fans wanted to hear from us."

The touring with Ray reinforced Willie's eclecticism, reminding him that despite what the recording industry chose to believe, music fans were more interested in *music* than *music categories.*

"When I got into the record end of the business," Willie says, "I found out they had music sliced up into a bunch of different categories. That was very confusing to me—I had to start slicing up what I knew. 'Well, you can't play this one because it's not country,' or 'You can't play that one because it's not commercial.' There's still a lot of people who live under the illusion that music is sliced up, but it's not. A 'G' is a 'G'. A quarter note is a quarter note. Whoever's doing it makes it different, I think."

Aside from Beatles' songs and Willie Nelson favorites, the duo found themselves being asked again and again for the standards Willie had grown to love—"Georgia On My Mind," "Stardust," even a few gospel songs.

"The people I was singing to in beer joints and clubs didn't know about labels like pop and country," he says caustically. "All they liked was songs and music."

The recording, however, was not going nearly as well. Despite assurances to the contrary, recording with RCA wasn't working the way Willie's master plan called for it to work. The problems were vague and ill-defined, as much

Willie's fault as RCA's. Willie had trouble explaining the music he heard in his head, the
music he played on the road. Musical categories
meant nothing to Willie; they meant everything
in the world to Nashville. The operative word
in Nashville had become "commercial," a word
that stuck in the craw of the by-now legendary
songwriting crew down at Tootsie's.

"There was a big argument over the word
'commercial,' " Willie says. "And it became a
word that was, I don't know, *hated* by the
writers. We hated to hear the word 'commercial,'
'cause there was some guy who didn't know
anything at all about songwriting and, we felt,
didn't know a fucking thing about the music
business, standing up there telling us what was
'commercial!' They were trying to tell us what
the people wanted to hear when we had just
come from the people. We knew what the people liked where we came from, and maybe we
didn't know what people *everywhere* liked. But
when all of us got together, coming from
everywhere, we realized people were liking pretty
much the same thing—good songs—and they
were having trouble finding them. 'Cause good
songs were being stopped—if they weren't
'commercial,' they never got out."

After a couple of years recording for RCA
and touring with Wade Ray, Willie decided—
against a lot of people's better judgment—that
he wanted a band. Bands were luxuries, mainly
because they were expensive to carry on the
road. The sound was much, much better, the

options for eclectic Willie Nelson that much greater, but a band was still a major production and a major commitment to the road.

One of the first things he did was call his old friend, Paul English, to ask if English knew whatever became of Skeeter Davis' drummer, who was well-regarded.

English was working as a drummer at a dive in Houston, making $150 a week for drumming and $1,000 a week in his "sidelines." When he got Willie's call, his only answer was, "I'm a better drummer than him." English promptly signed on for what would become a permanent gig with Willie Nelson.

"When I got with Willie," English remembers, "that became my total life."

Willie also signed up Dan "Bee" Spears, a crack bass player, added Johnny Bush as yet another drummer (at various times) and opening vocalist, and persuaded Wade Ray to come along. He called his band "The Record Men," after the flip side of one of his early singles and maybe just a little bit of wry commentary on Nashville's flat refusal to let a performer record with his band instead of the regular pickers.

Willie also signed up Charley Pride, country music's first—and back then *only*—black singer, to join him on a swing through some of the deepest areas of the Deep South at a time when racial tensions were at their very worst. The signing of Pride undoubtedly appealed to Willie's sheer sense of perversity, but the main factor was that, in Willie's own words, Charley Pride could "sing his ass off."

"When we got to Dallas," Willie recalls, "I made out the program to where I'd follow him. Pride walked out and said, 'I guess you're wondering what a man with a permanent tan like myself is doing singing country music, but I like it and hope you enjoy hearing it as much as I enjoy singing it.' He Uncle Tommed them into a standing ovation. They were yelling for Charley Pride all through my set. The next night I said, bullshit, I'm not following him, so I went on before and Hank Williams, Jr., went on after. They couldn't boo Hank Williams."

When the show got to Shreveport, the racial situation was extremely iffy, so Willie did the one thing that would guarantee his place in some cosmic country music hall of fame: He went on stage and kissed Charley Pride.

"Kissed him right on the mouth," Willie says. "Of course, we had to move on fast to something else, but by the time they got over the shock, he was already playing and he had them hooked."

Oddly enough, many music critics have focused on Willie's use of the word "nigger" as some telling point on Willie Nelson's psyche, totally overlooking the fact that he has consistently gone to the wall for talent, regardless of the color of the performer.

Although he was recording in Nashville, most of his concerts were in Texas. The reason was that there were simply no places to play around

Nashville. Nashville was a recording center; a performing musician could starve to death. While there were still plenty of places to play in the North and on the West Coast, there were usually not enough places clustered together to really pay off. It took a long time to drive from Nashville to New Jersey or Oregon, and sometimes the money from the dates wasn't even enough to cover the costs. To make money, a touring musician was faced with one of two choices. He could go south, to Memphis and the deadly Southern bar circuit, or southwest, to Texas and the dancehalls and honkytonks in Texas and Oklahoma. The bars in Alabama and Georgia leaned toward rockabilly, rhythm-and-blues or Hank-done-it-this-way country music. Willie and band would head west every weekend to play the dancehalls and 'tonks in Texas Friday and Saturday night, then haul ass back to Nashville to record. And the recording sessions were getting worse and worse.

"I was an artist on RCA, but it seemed like there was no money being spent promotionwise on Willie Nelson," Willie says. "It seemed like I was only cutting my albums there as dub sessions ... It was just lack of communication between me and Nashville and New York. I felt like I was working for a giant computer in New York, and everytime something came up, we would have to check with New York and everything had to be cleared through New York, so I could see ... well, one day the computer is going to say Willie Who?"

He grew increasingly bitter. RCA, he reasoned, was the biggest and most powerful record company in Nashville and ought to be able to do anything they wanted with an artist, including make that artist a star. Willie Nelson was not becoming a star.

"They (the producers) figured if they added strings and other voices, there was a chance of crossover sales," Willie says. "I didn't feel at the time I was qualified to tell them how it should sound. I felt they were supposed to know more than me, but I found out later they really didn't."

There were always the obvious pleasures of the road, the drinking and the drugs and the running around, and it quickly became obvious that those pleasures were quickly destroying his marriage to Shirley. Both of them drank and drugged and ran around, then fought, then reconciled. In one memorable incident, Shirley, who was a student of the martial arts, tossed a drunken Willie head-first through the door of their house. Willie still has the scars. Just as it had with him and Martha, the road was methodically destroying the relationship between Willie and Shirley.

There were also rumblings of big events in Nashville as the 1960s drew to a close. Country music *was* beginning to change, tiny cracks appearing in the walls of the Nashville Sound. One of the first cracks came from Bobby Bare, who'd soared to the top of the charts with "Detroit City." Bare was getting disgusted with the whole of Music City.

"There was a while when people would put out records and it didn't matter whether it was good or bad or a piece of shit—it would go to Number One," Bare says. "At that point, I went over the Top Hundred records, and I think I counted three or four legitimate hits. Anyway, at that point I was sick of what was going on. That's about when I decided that I didn't give a shit if I *did* go down the tubes and lose it all, 'cause I didn't care what was going on anyway."

What Bobby Bare did was demand complete creative control of his career—what songs he recorded, what musicians played on the records, the photographs used on the album covers, everything. What surprised everyone was that he got it. The record company caved in, and a ripple of secret thrill passed through the denizens of Tootsie's. Maybe, just maybe, it *was* possible to fight city hall and win. A lot of people, including Waylon Jennings, Tompall Glaser and even Willie Nelson, stood on the sidelines and watched.

One more revolutionary ingredient was needed, and that ingredient was Kris Kristofferson.

Kristofferson's story has achieved a mythic quality—how he grew from a skinny guy with skinny ties, a Rhodes scholar and Vietnam helicopter pilot to become a shaggy hippie and famous songwriter; how he turned country music around on its nose by singing about sex and drugs and all the things a person could see on the six o'clock news any night of the week; how he rode out of Nashville one day to become a matinee idol, and how the little darlin's lined the streets and wept.

In truth, Kris Kristofferson had a liberating effect on country music songwriting. Before "Help Me Make It Through The Night," one would be hard pressed to figure out what a honkytonk angel did when you got her out of the honkytonk.

The second major effect of Kristofferson and crew was a question of *style*, a critical question for Willie Hugh Nelson. Kris dressed weird, and his band dressed weird, and they all acted weird, and in no time at all they were the biggest act in country music. They drank and they did other taboo things, and they sang about drinking and taking drugs like it was *fun*. They sang about men and women the way men and women really were, and nobody booed them off the stage or threw brickbats or even beer bottles. Kris Kristofferson and his merry men were loved, and that gave a lot of people pause. Either Kristofferson was a mirage, or all that conventional wisdom floating around Nashville was wrong. Moreover, Kris Kristofferson sang country music to *kids*, rock-and-roll refugees, and they loved it. If they would love a mangy freak, maybe they would love a mangy cowboy as well. Maybe it was time for some hillbilly liberation.

Maybe Willie Nelson didn't need to wear natty suits and string ties. He tried it. Every weekend Willie would play in Texas, Big G's in Round Rock, Panther Hall in Fort Worth, the Broken Spoke in Austin, selling out huge houses.

"There were a few other people who knew there was a bigger audience for country music," Willie says. "I knew it because I'd been out there in Texas all those years."

On each trip, Willie's hair got a little longer; suits gave way to jeans and t-shirts. As with Kristofferson, nobody threw bricks.

"I always knew it didn't make any difference," Willie said. "I just had to do it to get the fucking attention. I knew it would draw some attention, definitely get some fire from certain areas and I couldn't get arrested up until then."

Willie Nelson, playing his offbeat brand of music, was a star in Texas, a chump in Nashville. He was still hailed as a songwriting genius, sometimes even mentioned as the Next Big Thing. He became increasingly bitter, working for "that computer in New York," working for men whom Willie perceived neither cared for nor knew country music.

"Some people do not know and will not learn," he says. "And will *never* learn. And yet they're in a position to hurt a lot of people who are trying to make their way as whatever, a singer or a songwriter. And there's people there, at the top, who have lost contact—if they ever had contact—with people and don't know what's going on. I mean, they sit behind a desk for so long and answer the telephone, and pretty soon they become telephone salesmen."

The marriage to Shirley joined the marriage

with Martha as a victim of the road, and there wasn't anything left to do but drink. "A lot of bad luck was going down," he remembers. The 1960s were almost over. A decade that had dawned so well for Willie Nelson was ending up in the toilet. He and Hank Cochran drank and commiserated, drank and commiserated, then, just before Christmas, 1969, retired to the basement of Willie's house to write a song to sum the whole lousy mess up.

The song was titled, "What Can You Do To Me Now?"

A few days later, his Ridgetop house burned down.

"It's the only time I've seen Willie rattled," says friend Waylon Jennings. "Willie walked past me and said, 'Can't talk now, man. My house is burning down.' "

Willie raced to the scene, pushed past the firemen and ran into the burning house, returning with a guitar case. The guitar case was filled with prime Colombian marijuana.

Holding his dope, he watched as hundreds of unpublished songs—the only copies—fueled the bright fires.

The next day, Willie Nelson, family, friends and band, moved back to Texas.

10

Comin' Back To Texas

Willie Nelson left Music City for the tiny town of Bandera, Texas, where a friend of Willie's owned a crumbling dude ranch.

"It's *still* a great place to go to get away from the world," Willie says. "We moved onto a golf course— the Lost Valley Country Club. It wasn't much of a country club. It really wasn't that much of a golf course, but we didn't care . . . I'll never forget the times we had there."

In addition to a new home, Willie Nelson had a new woman in his life, beautiful platinum-blonde Connie Koepke, a glass-factory worker whom, typically, Willie met on the road.

Once he'd settled into the five guest houses around the golf course, the first thing he did was reassemble his band, buy a ratty old bus, and begin touring Texas.

"I knew that a man could make a living doing nothing but playing Texas," he says. "I'd already been doing it for years."

His life alternated between the quiet afternoons in Bandera, where Willie and the band were just home folks like everybody else, and wild nights on the road. All the stops were pulled out—if Willie wanted to play "Stardust," then The Record Men would damn well play "Stardust." If the crowd wanted to hear "Whiskey River," pal Johnny Bush's contribution to the growing Willie Nelson legend, then The Record Men would play "Whiskey River" until the crowd was drowning in it.

What he was doing was honing an already canny sense of what the audience wants, indeed, what the audience *demands*. In Texas, Willie and his audience were so close that they really didn't need any overt communication. The audience didn't have to tell Willie what he could get away with—he knew instinctively. He knew he could open with "Whiskey River" and close with "Amazing Grace," because his audience shared the same kind of pulls between Saturday night and Sunday morning. He could flirt with rock and roll, then sing Hank Williams and the audience loved it.

Willie was, in fact, one of the first artists to realize just how much the audience for popular music had changed. The more he played Texas, the more he looked out through the stage lights and saw that something had fundamentally changed. It was a change that would affect all of popular music.

"Well, I felt I could no longer make any progress in Nashville," Willie says. "I felt like I had gone as far as I could go with my record label there. I felt I had gone as far as I could go with the town. I was already established as a songwriter, and I didn't feel that I was ever going to be able to sell any records as an artist in the environment I was in. I'd been going down to Texas and living there off and on for years, so I knew what was going on."

What was going on was the kids. Willie Nelson looked out in the audience and saw *hippies*. It was wonderful. After Willie played some of the joints in Austin, he'd go over to a new club, the Armadillo World Headquarters. One night Willie asked if he could get up and pick. The proverbial die was cast.

"I got up and picked at the Armadillo one time, and there was this brand new audience!" Willie says with awe. "I discovered that there were young people who liked what I had been singing all my life to people my age or older. There was a whole new audience there, and I felt like Texas was where I could come and, if worse came to worse, I could still make a living singing around Texas and singing for the people I've been singing for all my life, except I'm singing for their children. Sing the same songs I've always sung, and sing them the same way I've always sung them."

Much of the time in Bandera was spent in simple contemplation, the quiet working and reworking of songs. Willie had always had a strong mystical bent, and the quiet time at Bandera gave him a chance to explore more fully the writings of Kahlil Gibran and Edgar Cayce. Despite it all, Nashville still had a solid hold on Willie in the form of the remainder of the RCA contract, two more albums. The first of the two was *Willie Nelson And Family,* which sounds more like a grab-bag than a coherent album. The second album, however, was the creative breakthrough Willie had always sought, an album that integrated the sense of old and new, remaining faithful to both. The album was called *Yesterday's Wine* and was a concept album, an album that as a unit told a story—common in rock, unheard of in country.

"I started restructuring everything and taking a good look at what I had been doing on stage and what I had been doing in the studio and what I had been doing in business," Willie says. "I started looking at everything and trying to start all over again."

The idea of starting over again had been gnawing at Willie, and, as usual, his first thoughts were of the stage.

"I wanted to do something on stage that was a little different," he remembers, "and the concept idea was what I had in mind to do on stage."

His idea was to tie his songs together into a storyline, an overall structure that would, he hoped, make the finished product greater than the sum of its parts. The songs didn't have to be new songs specifically written for the concept—as was most often the case with rock. In fact, it didn't matter whether Willie wrote the songs or not. Any number of songs, by any number of artists, could be adapted to the concept.

"I really didn't know whether it was going to be that great an album idea or not," he says. "But I felt it would be good in concert—the concept-type program rather than just standing up there and singing one song after the other."

In the calm atmosphere of Bandera, Willie began reworking his stage shows. He only worked where he wanted to work. Legend has it that he even helped open a few car lots for friends. The stage was a laboratory for experimentation, and Willie watched the audience closely, gauging both its response and his own reactions. Willie Nelson was bitter and frustrated, and he knew from hard-won experience that no performer could risk translating those feelings into his stage shows. He dug deep into his own mind, analyzing his successes and failures.

Two streams of thought were coming together. The concept idea of performing was filling a very strong Willie Nelson need—the need to tell a story. Even the greatest songwriter at some point recognizes the limitations of a three-minute song, and the storyteller longs for room to stretch out and grow. The second stream of thought in Bandera was that Willie Nelson was going to take a stand for the kind of music he believed in—"A statement," he says. "This is where I am. Period."

It was something that easy-going Willie Nelson had never done—something, in fact, that a professional songwriter couldn't *afford* to do.

No songwriter gets rich by writing only one kind of song, aimed at one particular artist or style. Times and styles change, and the audience is forever fickle.

"There have been a lot of times," Willie says, "when I first went to town, I would have done whatever they said to do. Where do you sign? Over here. Okay. Here, sign some more. I signed everything they had. I thought that was a sign of success—how many contracts you signed. I found out different."

One Friday afternoon Willie got a call in Bandera. RCA wanted the last album, and could Willie Nelson please be in Nashville the next Monday to record? Willie—still the easy-going red-headed guy from Texas—agreed. He flew to Nashville, took some little white pills to stay awake, and cranked out seven songs for the album—a metaphysical tale of an imperfect man trying to sort some meaning out of the personal chaos around him—overnight. To those songs he added some of his own favorites—the much abused "Family Bible" and an incredible song about the road, a capsulized autobiography titled "Me And Paul." He capped the album with "Yesterday's Wine," one of his finest songs ever.

It was beautiful—"a spiritual album, in a sense," Willie says. RCA released it and it sank like a stone.

Not commercial, was the general consensus.

"If it had more than three chords in it," Willie recalls bitterly, "it was non-commercial."

More single releases on RCA went nowhere,

although, Paul English notes incredulously, Willie and band were packing them in by the thousands in Texas. RCA requested that Willie renew his contract early, although the company didn't seem all that interested in having Willie Nelson as an artist on its label. If anything, Willie was disgusted by the whole wheeling and dealing, but he retained a core, a certainty, that he was right.

"Even though I was frustrated and bitter," he says, "I never got really discouraged to the point where I would throw it all away. I felt like if I stayed with it, something had to happen. I knew that what I was doing wasn't that bad. I knew the songs were okay and I could sing fairly well—as good as some people I had heard on the radio. I didn't see why I shouldn't at least be played on the radio more than I was."

Willie had also made a crucial connection with a show-business lawyer from New York named Neil Reshen, who agreed to leap into the contract morass and teach Nashville a thing or two about the way contracts should be written. Or, as the case may be, unwritten. RCA didn't really want Willie Nelson, and Willie Nelson didn't really want RCA. The label cut Willie loose, provided he return a small amount of overpayment.

Without a label, Willie Nelson went back to Texas.

Things weren't really hopeless. If RCA didn't want to record Willie Nelson, there were at least a few other labels that did. With Reshen at the business helm of Willie's career, he was already a step ahead of most Nashville acts. Business as usual in Nashville consisted of sort of a "good ole boy" network of record company executives, artists' managers, producers, public relations people and journalists. Once an artist was plugged into the network, everything tended to go smoothly—as long as the artist (or any of the other links in the chain) didn't make waves.

And, in truth, the system worked pretty well right up until the early 1970s, when Willie Nelson and friends hammered it apart with a vengeance. The basic problem with the system was that it was predicated on being *small*. Country music was a family, with shared roots, shared dreams and aspirations. The fact that some of the "family" members did amazingly better than other "family" members was looked on more as an act of God than bad business practices. The failure of a record company to really promote or push a record—something critical to a record's success—could be dismissed with a shrug and a comment like, "It's not commercial enough."

Sometimes a record will take off on its own, something that Willie would soon learn, but even that requires that the radio stations, perhaps the most important link in the whole chain, have the records to play.

Nashville had responded to the wave after wave of pop music growth in a typically country-and-Western way: They had drawn up the wagons in a circle and got down to serious us-versus-them.

Willie came to Nashville with the idea of fitting in and no other knowledge of what critic Joe Nick Patoski called "the music bid'ness." All Willie wanted to be was a star.

"I was sure it wouldn't take long," he says ruefully. "I knew all I had to do was just make the record and they would put it out and everyone would go buy it and we would all live happily ever after."

When Willie moved to Texas and hired a New York hotshot to represent him, he declared in the most eloquent way possible that the old ways were no longer good enough. Although it took Nashville a couple of years to figure it out, the failure of *Yesterday's Wine* and the changes in Willie Nelson marked the end of an era in country music, the destruction of the Nashville good-ole-boy system.

These days it has become fashionable to downplay what Willie did—it is impossible to find anyone in Music City today who wasn't one thousand percent behind Willie Nelson in those grim days in the early 1970s. It's hard to remember back to those days when cars had bumper stickers that read "America: Love It Or Leave It," and the quickest way to start a riot was for a longhair to walk into a truckstop. Those were polarized times, and there's a tendency, once those times have passed, to look back on them with a bit of embarrassment. Hair was never *that* important, was it? Was there ever a time when *hippies* didn't listen to country music; when *Rolling Stone* Magazine didn't review Merle Haggard right along with Mick Jagger?

Willie Nelson went back to Texas, and the musical world pivoted on that point.

11

Ol' Waylon

With Willie Nelson in Texas, there was still another piece of the puzzle needed before country music could sweep the nation like a steel-guitared tidal wave.

The final piece of the puzzle was a haggard-looking guitar player named Waylon Jennings, a fellow Texan and near legend in Nashville, where he was struggling to overcome the same problems besetting Willie Nelson.

For many listeners today, Willie and Waylon are a sort of matched set, WillienWaylon. One song was once released by *Waylie and Willon*. Without a doubt in the world, the two men are the most popular act country music has ever spawned. Such songs as "Good-Hearted Woman" and "Luckenbach, Texas" put country music over the top, completed the changes that Willie foresaw and Waylon struggled to bring about. Willie and Waylon, together with Tompall Glaser and singer-songwriters like David Allan Coe,

121

Billy Joe Shaver, Lee Clayton and others, were the Outlaws, the folks who carried the message of country music to the kids.

The irony has always been, as Frye Gaillard pointed out in *Watermelon Wine*, that none of the so-called "Outlaws" were particularly radical, not nearly as radical as even Hank Williams or Ernest Tubb in their day. If anything, Willie and Waylon issued a clear call for tradition, for not losing the music's roots in a morass of strings and production.

"Why heck," Waylon said for years, "I just wanted to play my music . . ."

Waylon Arnold Jennings was born in Littlefield, Texas, on June 15, 1937. Littlefield is part of the "other" Texas, closer to the New Mexico badlands than Abbott. The one thing Littlefield shared with Abbott was cotton, and Waylon Jennings picked his share of it.

His father was a truck driver who also played guitar in a country band. Like Willie, Waylon was given a guitar just about as soon as he could hold one, and he was imitating his idols Ernest Tubb and Hank Williams by the time he was ten. Within a couple of years young Waylon had his own radio show, a fifteen-minute spot on KVOW. He quit school at fourteen—"Seemed like a good idea at the time," he said—and set about to make his way working in his father's newly acquired feed store and working the honkytonks.

Waylon played amateur shows and theaters across West Texas. On one of his trips, he ran into another West Texan trying to make his break into country music. Buddy Holly, from nearby Lubbock, was impressed with Waylon Jennings' picking and singing, and the two became friends. They were both committed to country music until they heard Elvis Presley.

"We were still playing country—hell, there wasn't anything else, really," Waylon told Peter Guralnick in *Lost Highways*. "I saw Elvis Presley in 1955, I guess it was, in Lubbock. Well, it changed things in a way. I think it changed Buddy, too—at least it had a bearing. Actually, it changed almost everything, really . . . It was like an explosion . . ."

While Buddy Holly went on to become part of that explosion, Waylon Jennings stayed in Lubbock to become a disk jockey.

"I was still playing," he says. "I was still aiming to be a singer. I was just using radio as a kind of stepping stone."

Buddy Holly came back to Lubbock in 1958 to find his old friend Waylon still singing and spinning records. Buddy liked what he heard and hired Waylon as his bass player. The catch, of course, was that Waylon couldn't play bass. Buddy Holly went out and bought him a bass, which Waylon learned to play in a couple of weeks.

"I was his protégé, more or less," Waylon says. "He cut the first record on me, you know, for Brunswick in 1958. Got King Curtis to play on it, just called him to come down. He was really hot then, too. We did an old country thing, 'Jole Blon.' We did it up-beat, with the saxophone on the lead part. We didn't even know the words."

"We never had a cross word," Waylon recollects. "He was easygoing, easy to get along with, and he sure was a monkey in a lot of ways, a real cut-up. We sure did have a lot of fun. He was one of the best people I knew in my life. Really."

Things were really cooking for Holly, and the future for him and his band, the Crickets, couldn't have looked better. Holly's rockabilly music, a bit milder and less threatening than the stuff from Sun Records in Memphis, had taken America by storm, and after a brief hiatus, Holly was cooking again. Things were falling into place for both Buddy Holly and Waylon Jennings. All that came to an end, though, early in 1959, when Holly decided to charter a small plane to fly to a gig in Fargo, North Dakota. The plane crashed, and Holly, J.P. Richardson—the Big Bopper of "Chantilly Lace" fame—and Richie Valens were killed.

"We'd been on the road for days, man," Waylon says. "Our clothes were all dirty and we were all dirty and tired and everything. Even the bus had frozen up one time."

Because things were so hectic, Holly decided to charter the plane for himself, Waylon and band member Tommy Allsop.

"The three of us were going to fly from Mason City—we were playing in Clear Lake, a little place out of Mason City, Iowa—to Fargo,"

Waylon remembers. "We were going to play in Moorhead, Minnesota, and the airport was between Moorhead and Fargo.

"So we were backstage when the Big Bopper asked me if he could take my place on the plane because he had the flu," he continues. "I told him it was all right, and he made it all right with Buddy. Then Richie Valens asked Tommy if he could take his place. A lot of people say it was Buddy who took my place, but that ain't the way it was. You know, it was real funny. That night after the crash, we played some auditorium in Moorhead, and after we played, they tried to dock us for the money that Buddy and the Big Bopper and Richie Valens would have gotten—after begging us to play. We just wanted to go home, you know."

After that show, Waylon Jennings did go home—"I just kind of quit"—back to Lubbock, where he took a $75-dollar-a-week job as a disk jockey. It took two years before Waylon Jennings was ready to face the performing side of the music business again. Finally, though, he took off to Arizona to start his own band. What he carried with him was the beat, that driving, soul-twisting rhythm that had turned rock and roll into gold. He represented the flip-side of the Texas music coin, rockabilly and rhythm and blues instead of Western Swing and pop favorites. When he got that band together, country or not, that beat was still there, still pounding, and they loved it in Arizona.

Waylon landed a recording contract with the

help of Don Bowman, a country comedian who was also born in Lubbock. Bowman had a hit with the novelty song, "Chet Atkins, Make Me A Star," which he reprised years later as, "Willie Nelson, Make Me A Star." The contract was with A&M Records, and Waylon's producer was Herb Alpert of the Tijuana Brass. "I kept trying to hang on to country," Waylon says, "but I think they kept hearing Al Martino."

At the urgings of Bowman and Bobby Bare, RCA head Chet Atkins listened to Waylon Jennings and was impressed. Around 1965 Atkins suggested that Waylon leave Phoenix and move to Nashville. Atkins also arranged for Waylon to get sprung from A&M and sign with RCA Records.

Before he gave up Phoenix, where he was making a good living and was something of a local celebrity, he sought the advice of a man he'd come to respect through his songwriting. When Willie Nelson swung through Phoenix, Waylon asked whether he should take Chet Atkins' offer and move to Music City or stay in Phoenix and play the clubs.

Stay in Phoenix, Willie advised emphatically. Nashville is no place for such a good singer.

It is advice Willie still stands by today.

Ignoring Willie's advice, Waylon moved to Nashville.

The early days in Nashville were both the best and worst of times. Waylon set up house-keeping with another Nashville firebrand, Johnny

Cash, and it was quickly a case of Western crazy meets Southern crazy.

"Yep, there's a lot of stories," Waylon says. "We did some fishing together, you know. I dunno. I ain't *never* caught a fish. I've been fishing with Bobby Bare, Harlan Howard, Johnny Cash, a lot of people, but I never caught a fish."

The two tore around Nashville, drinking and raising general hell. They were loaded all the time, kicking down doors, wrecking cars and, when the heat was really on, retreating to the lake to sit and stare for hours at a fishing line. Unlike Willie Nelson, though, Waylon and Cash were solid commercial successes, which, in many ways, made it worse. While the powers-that-be could neatly ignore Willie Nelson, it was harder to ignore a half-stoned cowboy dressed in dirty denims and about twenty pounds of silver and turquoise jewelry. Country stars looked like Porter Waggoner, for heaven's sake, with powder-blue performing suits and garish rhinestones. They might drink themselves into a stupor in private, but in public they were expected to be the perfect gentlemen and ladies. To his credit, Chet Atkins did his best recording Waylon Jennings, catching Waylon's flair for eccentricity —good music, Waylon Jennings insisted, was good music. He didn't give a goddammed whether it was called country, rock or soul. Waylon insisted on looking beyond Tootsie's for good songs. One early collection featured songs by such diverse figures as Mick Jagger and George Jones, all done with the same classic Jennings interpretation. He insisted on—and, amazingly, got—the right to use his road band in the recording studio. While that might not seem such a major change now, in Nashville it was tantamount to suggesting that the Grand Ole Opry be turned into a bordello. A singer might work the road with a certain band, trying out new things in front of audiences and constantly experimenting. But when the same artist went into the studio, he was faced with a solid wall of Nashville studio pickers, the best in the world, to be sure, but in the case of Waylon Jennings and Willie Nelson, too good, too slick, too polished. All that experimenting on the road was lost. All the feedback from the audience tossed away. Waylon insisted, and RCA agreed.

"I couldn't conform," he says. "I wasn't understood, and some of it was maybe my fault—drugs, that stuff. They thought I was out to destroy, when all I wanted to do was survive. And country is ... very suspicious. Country people are very suspicious and they're slow to change. And they're afraid change means destruction. But it doesn't. I wouldn't do anything to destroy anything. But there's a lot of wrong that's been done to us, and there's a lot of wrong still going on. And I'm not a big defender or anything, but I'll tell you what: If they put it in front of me, I'll be right or else."

For a while Waylon turned to the same cure as Willie—the road. He toured 300 crazy nights a year, criss-crossing the country like a dervish

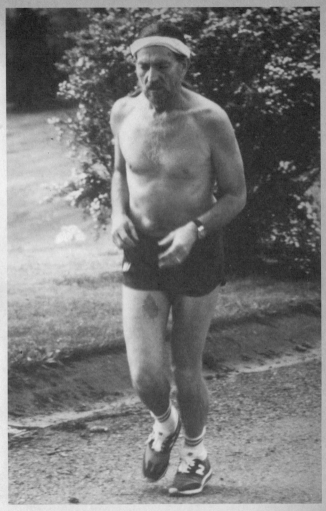
ON THE ROAD AGAIN with a vengeance: Five miles of running every morning under the new Willie Nelson program for health and long life. *(photo by John Lee)*

TWO WHO CAME UP THE HARD WAY: Willie, the Depression kid from the Texas flatlands, and Merle Haggard, whose Okie family made the long, poverty trip to California. *(photo courtesy CBS)*

WILLIE AND WIFE MEET THE MAN WITH THE HORN: Connie Nelson and Willie with the great jazzman Miles Davis, who named a song "Willie Nelson." *(photo courtesy CBS)*

ROCK MEETS COUNTRY: Leon Russell, who made his name with Joe Cocker on tour with MAD DOGS AND ENGLISHMEN, got together with Willie to make the topselling album of oldies, ONE FOR THE ROAD. *(photo by John Lee)*

THE HEART OF WILLIE'S FAMILY BAND: Mickey Raphael, harmonica virtuoso; Paul English, drummer and Willie's old honkytonk buddy; sister Bobbie, who plays a tasty piano with gospel roots. Missing is Bee Spears, sterling bass guitarist. *(photo by J. Clark Thomas)*

THE GREAT WILLIE NELSON FOURTH OF JULY PICNIC: This one (in 1976) was the third in what has become an annual event, and drew 250,000 people, mostly young. Willie used it to showcase underrated talents such as George Jones (ex- of Tammy Wynette) shown onstage, and with picnic-giver Nelson in inset photo. *(photos by J. Clark Thomas)*

WILLIE LOVES KIDS...he has five of his own, and here he harmonizes with a group that includes close pal Kris Kristofferson's. *(photo courtesy Michael Putland/Retna)*

Right, SUPERSTAR TIME: an impromptu get-together at a New York nightclub, including Rita Coolidge (ex-Mrs. Kris), Kristofferson, Candice Bergen, Willie and a clean-shaven Burt Reynolds. *(photo courtesy CBS)*

THE TWO BOSS OUTLAWS
TOGETHER AGAIN: Willie
Nelson and Waylon Jennings,
who together shook up the Nashville music Establishment, have

teamed up once more, after a period of estrangement, to produce a hit album and single, TAKE IT TO THE LIMIT. *(photo courtesy CBS)*

LEGENDARY HERO: Willie Nelson in his first starring movie role, as Barbarosa, an aging gunfighter headed for his last showdown. Willie, who got into films through Robert Redford (ELECTRIC HORSEMAN), is said to have "the greatest movie face since Bogart." *(photo courtesy CBS)*

Below, HONEYSUCKLE ROSE was Willie's top movie hit thus far. Here, as a rambling and roguish country musician, he appears with Dyan Cannon and friend and old-time fiddler, Johnny Gimble. *(photo courtesy CBS)*

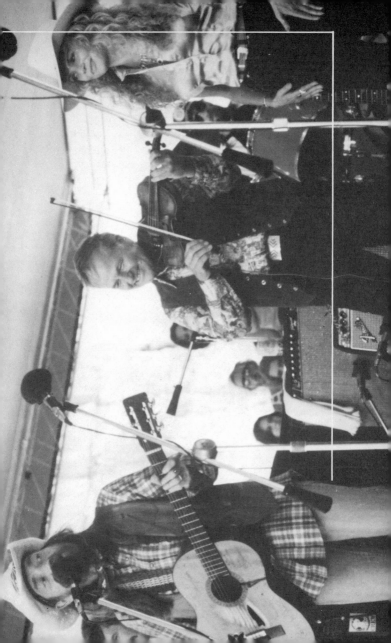

RUMORS OF OFFSTAGE ROMANCE with youthful HONEYSUCKLE ROSE co-star Amy Irving (who steals him from Dyan Cannon in the movie) concerned Willie for its possible effect on his solid marriage with third wife, Connie, who was the inspirer of his smash RED-HEADED STRANGER album *(photo courtesy CBS)*

Right, WILLIE THEN: Young Mr. Nelson, circa 1963, on his first trip out of Texas to Nashville, for his first recording date in Opryland. *(photo courtesy of the Country Music Foundation Library and Media Center, Nashville, Tennessee)*

WILLIE NOW: He looks sagely to the future: more albums, more playing time on the road, and a new movie (SONGWRITER) with Kris Kristofferson, who says "being around Willie is like being around Buddha." *(photo courtesy CBS)*

in an all-black bus Waylon claimed was haunted by the spirit of Hank Williams. Waylon painted Hank's name on the bathroom door of the bus with a little gold star under it, and, according to legend, always kept an empty bunk on the bus for Ole Hank.

Like Willie, Waylon found that the road was not easy on relationships. He quickly went through three marriages, commenting bitterly at one point that his alimony payments resembled the national debt.

Unlike Willie, though, Waylon kept having hit records. Songs like "The Only Daddy That'll Walk The Line," "The Taker," "Cedartown Georgia," "Rainy Day Woman," and "Mississippi Woman" kept Waylon, if not on the top of the charts, at least *on* the charts. Waylon's version of the already overwrought "MacArthur Park" won a batch of awards, and by 1970 even *Rolling Stone* Magazine, the ultimate arbiter of pop taste of the period, had portentously declared Waylon Jennings a pop artist.

Interestingly enough, one of the biggest songs in the history of country music was written during that period. Willie dropped by Waylon's house for a game of poker, and right in the middle of the game Waylon mentioned that there was a song he'd started writing but had gotten stalled on. Waylon read Willie the first verse and chorus of "Good-Hearted Woman" and told Willie that if the master songwriter would give him a hand, Willie could have half the song. He also mentioned that Willie should hurry, since Waylon wanted to record it the next day.

Willie stayed the night, and woke up the next morning to write the rest of the song. They finished it right after breakfast, and Waylon called a studio session to record it.

The decade ended with Waylon, like Willie, feeling trapped by the Nashville Sound. Despite his successes, the pressure was on Waylon to conform, and the more pressure put on him, the more certain he was that he was having no part of what was being dished out.

He was sick and in hock up to his neck and his third marriage was on the rocks. The music wasn't fun and the drugs didn't help.

What he needed was a shot of Willie Nelson.

12

Shotgun Willie

Willie Nelson went back to Texas. The original plan had been to move to Houston, but Willie took offense at the sprawling city and opted for Austin, where Bobbie had been living.

He had also done something else to send a small shockwave through Nashville. With the RCA connection cut loose, Willie went shopping for a new record label. There were several labels in Nashville willing to sign Willie up, if for no other reason than to get an inside track on his songwriting, but Paul English was spooked. Although Willie was into Paul for more than $5000 in back wages, Paul remained Willie's most faithful friend. Paul sensed correctly that events might be coming to a boil soon in Nashville, and that Willie's budding reputation as an outsider might lead the Nashville record companies to freeze him out entirely. Stranger things had happened in Music City.

Take Neil Reshen's advice, English pleaded.
Go to New York.

In New York, there was $25,000 waiting for
Willie to sign with the legendary Atlantic Records,
which had never signed a country artist before.
Atlantic's vice-president, Jerry Wexler, wanted
to expand the label into country music.

Atlantic started out in the late 1940s as a jazz
label, quickly expanding into rhythm and blues.
The record label quickly came to dominate the
rock market in the years after rockabilly and
before the Beatles with groups like the Coasters
and the Drifters. In the 1960s Atlantic surged
back into the limelight with the rise of soul
music. As one of the heads of Atlantic, Wexler
had an uncanny ear, the ability to sense the
drifts in popular music before they were appar-
ent to everyone and his aged mother. Wexler
had long been fascinated with Southern music
and had engineered Atlantic's biggest successes,
including Wilson Pickett and Aretha Franklin.

In the early 1970s, Wexler's sensitive anten-
nae began hearing a sound in Nashville that
Wexler felt could be the Next Big Thing. Wexler
himself was familiar with the work—both the
singing and the songwriting—of one Willie
Nelson, but he'd never seen him perform until
late 1971.

"I went to a party in Nashville after some
banquet or other," Wexler remembers. "All these
big country stars were there, passing the guitar
around, of course, all of them playing a couple
of songs. Then Willie got up, ice cold and

unknown, and took over. In that setting, it was the most remarkable thing I'd ever seen."

Afterwards, Wexler stayed to introduce himself to Willie.

"I've been looking forward to meeting you for a long time," the record executive said.

"Hey," Willie replied, smiling, "have I been looking for you for a long time."

Wexler correctly perceived that all Willie Nelson needed was a studio and a little time, which Atlantic Records was quick to provide in New York City. Wexler also told Willie that he could have any musicians he wanted on the album.

Willie asked for his band: Bobbie "Bee" Spears, Paul English and Jimmy Day. He also opened the studio up to anybody who might want to drop in. That particular list grew to tremendous proportions and included Waylon Jennings, Jessi Colter, Larry Gatlin, Johnny Gimble (Bob Wills' fiddle player), Texas rocker Doug Sahm and a slew of other people.

The session was launched in the best rock-and-roll tradition—throw a bunch of musician-type people in a room, close the door and come back in a week or so and pick up the tapes. Willie Nelson hit the Atlantic studios like a madman, "like a dog released from its kennel for the first time in weeks," wrote Jan Reid in *The Improbable Rise Of Redneck Rock*, "spinning off in all directions because of the pent-up energy."

Just to get a feel for things, Willie knocked off a whole gospel album in just two days. The album was released as *The Troublemaker* in 1976. It refined the style Willie had used in *Yesterday's Wine,* simple, nothing flashy. Larry Gatlin, Sammi Smith, Dee Moeller and Doug Sahm sang back-up; Gatlin also joined the band for the simple instrumentals.

With the gospel album in the can, Willie started into a second album. The sessions were going very well, but Willie still needed a song to peg the album on; not necessarily a concept, but a song to define the feeling of freedom that was blooming in the New York studios. Sitting in the bathroom of the Holiday Inn, he picked up a wrapper for a sanitary napkin, and after staring at the wrapper—which read, "Another Individual Service Provided By Holiday Inn" and "Preferred By Particular Women"—for an appropriate amount of time, he grabbed a pencil and wrote the lyrics to "Shotgun Willie."

Yesterday's Wine represented an artistic statement, but *Shotgun Willie* was the breakthrough album Willie had been looking for. It captured some of the feel of those Texas dancehalls, some of the sense of the many kinds of music Willie Nelson represented. In fact, with *Shotgun Willie,* Willie Nelson laid down the template for the rest of his life.

With beer in hand, he and the band cut Johnny Bush's "Whiskey River," the song Willie still uses to open most of his shows. They did Willie's own "The Devil Shivers In His Sleeping Bag," another ode to Paul English and the road, "Sad Songs And Waltzes" and "Local Memory." Nor could Willie neglect the music of his idol; from Bob Wills' heyday he recorded "Stay All Night" and "Bubbles In My Beer."

Willie also recorded two songs by a man who was, at that time, a major rock-and-roll star. Willie recorded "Look Like The Devil" and "A Song For You" by Leon Russell, the high-rolling Tulsa sideman who had captivated rock with his electrifying performance in the movie *Mad Dogs And Englishmen*. Russell had played on Willie's second Liberty album, but it wasn't until Willie heard a copy of the *Mad Dogs And Englishmen* soundtrack his daughter had that he really became interested in meeting the long-haired Russell.

Willie went to a Leon Russell concert in Houston, then arranged to meet him. As soon as they met, Leon Russell, idol to a million young fans, announced to Willie that his favorite song was "Family Bible."

The result? Two Leon Russell songs on *Shotgun Willie*.

Even before cutting *Shotgun Willie*, Willie had had a brief vision of the future.

That particular vision came in a cow pasture just outside Austin. The event was the First Annual Dripping Springs Reunion, a country music extravaganza cooked up by some promotion men in Dallas. The idea was to put together what amounted to a country music rock festival, *à la* Woodstock. The twist would be that there would be acts not only for traditional country folks—acts like Loretta Lynn, Tex Ritter,

Roy Acuff, Charlie Rich—but acts for younger fans, for *kids*. Kris Kristofferson, Waylon Jennings, Tom T. Hall and Billy Joe Shaver were already attracting something other than the old crowd, so why not put them all together in a cow pasture and see what happened?

What happened was a disaster, a classic case of non-planning in which 60,000 people got wet, got cold, got drunk, got stoned and got rowdy. The promoters lost a fortune; the crowd had a wonderful time.

"It was the first time anyone had seen all types of people together listening to country music," Willie says. "It was actually the first time the hippie and the redneck had gotten together."

The day after the 1972 festival, the Austin newspaper ran a picture of Willie, Leon Russell and University of Texas football coach Darrell Royal. It was, Willie says, "the best thing to come out of Dripping Springs . . . In my mind, it brought it all together."

Shotgun Willie, all thirty-three cuts, was finished in one week, a record of sorts for Atlantic Records. Willie Nelson went back to Austin ready to kick ass.

He'd played all around that part of Texas, just about in every nook and cranny. About the only place he'd never played was the Armadillo Club in Austin.

"I never played the Armadillo because it was considered a place for rock and roll," he says. "Strictly rock and roll."

Willie and Paul went to the Armadillo and listened. In truth, the Armadillo was a hard-core hippie bar, catering to the college crowd from the University of Texas and concentrating on bands with hot licks and funny names—Man Mountain and the Green Slime Boys comes to mind. The walls were covered with psychedelic posters and flower-child paraphernalia.

Willie and Paul asked if they could sit in one night.

The owners of the Armadillo thought the idea was crazy, but not without merit. The idea was that if they could combine their college regulars, who wouldn't set foot in a shit-kicking bar on a bet, with some of those regulars who patronized the bars Willie and The Record Men played, they might be able to finally make some money.

Willie played, and the crowd of long-haired freaks went wild. The local newspaper even reported the event, stating that it "boggled the mind."

"I didn't know there was a country audience over there," Willie says. "They might not have known there was a country audience over there either. It just kind of happened that when they were exposed to it, they liked it."

It was the ultimate vindication of Willie's basic belief that good music was good music.

"A whole new audience had grown up," he adds. "A new, more progressive audience—progressive thinking, liberalized thinking. Liber-alized to the point where they don't believe everything they're told. If someone sends out a record to them, just because it's a name artist on a name label, that doesn't mean it's a good song."

What Willie saw was an embryonic audience, and he assumed the dual role of performer and teacher, sort of a musical evangelist, he would say much later.

"The audience progressed along with the rest of us," he says. "We entered into a new field—there were young people out there who didn't know Ernest Tubb from anybody. They didn't know anything at all about country music. They heard maybe their dads and their mothers playing it when they were out of the room or something, but it was all new to them."

And Willie Nelson, unlike many other singers thrust into a similar situation, recognized that he had an obligation to that audience.

"Anybody they saw had a good chance of selling them . . ." he says. "The audience is eager to listen to anybody who has anything to say."

Willie Nelson began playing the Armadillo regularly, and true to the predictions of the Armadillo's owners, some of Willie's older audience began making their way past the debris of the counterculture to hear Willie Nelson sing. Although the number was vastly smaller, a few brave "hippies" made their way to the shit-kicker country clubs like Big G.'s or the Broken Spoke, although, in truth, that was somewhat the more daring trip. Hippies seldom broke beer bottles over people's heads.

Shotgun Willie outsold anything he had ever done in Nashville, and he quickly began work on a second Atlantic album titled *Phases And Stages*, a concept album. In between, he worked the road. After his stunning success at the Armadillo World Headquarters, he found himself in demand on the college circuit, billed as a "folk-country" act like the Nitty Gritty Dirt Band. By 1972 Willie Nelson and The Record Men had logged 160,000 miles, the next year playing every state in the union.

The next thing he did was send for reinforcements.

"Willie called me and said, 'Hey, hoss, I think I've found something,'" Waylon Jennings remembers.

Willie invited Waylon down to play the Armadillo World Headquarters, not bothering to tell Waylon a thing about the audience. Waylon, caught up in the Nashville wars, had no idea what was about to happen.

"So I got down there and walked in and saw all those long-haired kids," Waylon says. "I thought, 'What's that crazy sonovabitch done to me now?' I said, 'Goddam, Willie!' and he said, 'Just trust me. If they don't go for it, you're going down with me.'"

Of course, Waylon never had to worry one bit. The Armadillo crowd, every pound of excess hair, went totally crazy over Waylon, just as Willie figured they would. Good music, Willie said.

"I couldn't believe it," Waylon continues, still incredulous after all these years.

"I think we found something," Willie said. "I think we found people who understand us and who believe in what we're doing; who like us and take us as people and can relate to our music."

"I think he was right," Waylon says.

13

Hello Walls

The gate is six feet high, three feet thick, topped with electrified barbed wire and made of stone. The signs say "Positively No Hunting; No Trespassing," "No Admittance," "Keep Out." After waiting for an hour, staring into the blind eye of a television monitor, the young journalist begins screaming at the television camera.

"You invited me," he screams at the camera. "Goddamn it, Willie, open the gate."

The metal gates swing open, and the young journalist drives down the long driveway for his first meeting with Willie Nelson in nearly three years. The old bus has given way to new buses; Willie Nelson has gone from being a little-known man with a strangely certain dream to something of a national hero. So much of a hero, in fact, that his farm in Austin, Texas, is surrounded by a brick wall, yet the fans still make the long trek to stand in front of the wall, hoping for a glimpse of the bearded, long-haired cowboy singer.

Willie Nelson greets the young journalist at the door with a handshake and a cold Coors beer from Connie, the third Mrs. Nelson. "You looked," Willie says, "pretty funny out there, yelling at the television camera."

The young journalist opines that he felt pretty funny out there in front of the television camera.

He's been so busy, Willie says, that there hasn't even been time for songwriting. Willie Nelson laughs, and the young journalist settles into the overstuffed furniture. The room is comfortable and quiet, only the slight noise of the air conditioning breaking the silence and keeping the stifling Texas heat at bay. There is a large picture window, and outside are the green rolling hills that surround Austin. A river flows through a patch of cottonwood trees, and the young journalist thinks that for an old cowboy, this must be the pot of gold at the end of a rainbow, the end of the road.

Last time we talked, the young journalist says, you said the one thing Willie Nelson never wanted to become was a star like Elvis Presley, unable to stick his nose out the door.

Willie nods seriously. That's true, he says.

Congratulations, the young journalist says with what passes for cleverness, you can't stick your nose out the door. Do you feel, Willie Nelson, that you're living in a bunker?

"A fishbowl, actually," he says, "And no, I don't like it at all. I don't really know how much good the gate does; maybe it does my mind some good. There's nobody really bothering me now . . ."

The unspoken implication that there was somebody bothering him *before* hangs in the air. Does, the young journalist suggests, all this success change the way Willie Nelson relates to his audience?

"No," he says. "I fight against it. I realize these people who came out here are people who would go to the trouble of bothering me. They would probably never pay ten or five dollars to hear me sing. So it's a different group of people—usually someone who wants something from me. I'm just like everyone else."

This, the young journalist thinks, is the central irony of the country music business, something the best singers and songwriters understand instinctively. The people who sing and write those pretty country songs are really no different from the people who listen to them, except that the first group is caught up in the maelstrom of hype, hangers-on and just plain nonsense that swirls around the music business.

For a long time, the young journalist says, country music was considered an embarrassment, sort of like a country cousin who didn't wear shoes and drooled at the table. What happened?

Willie pauses at the question. It is the central point in the gospel according to Willie Nelson, the basis of the great leap of faith.

"Well," he says slowly, "there's something going on, not only in Texas, but all over the United States. There's a desire for country music; people want to dance and holler and do some shitkicking and raise some hell. The kids want to do this, and I see no reason to keep it from them."

Why kids? the young journalist asks. It is a personal question. Like so many others, he has gone from the hard rock of the 1960s to the country music of Willie Nelson and others in the 1970s. It is, the young journalist thinks, a question that covers a lot more than music.

"I think it's a new way to express themselves," Willie says. "Something they've been told is hayseed all their lives, and they're finding out that maybe it's not so hayseed. That maybe there's something really there. It's a nice, easy, simple music. It's our American heritage, so to speak. They can say: This is country music; this is ours. And the kids have decided that they like it."

That's not good enough, the young journalist challenges. Rock and roll, to one extent or the other, helped shape a whole generation of kids, helped change the direction of America in many ways. Now those very same kids are buying Willie Nelson and Waylon Jennings records, wearing cowboy hats and launching the boot industry into the stratosphere.

What happened, Willie Nelson says, is that those kids grew up. When life grabbed ahold of you and shook you, when loves collapsed and dreams lay like a fine coating of dust over your life, somehow it didn't seem appropriate to crank up Mick Jagger on the radio.

Crying in your beer, Willie Nelson says, is only funny until you've cried in your beer once. Then it's not so funny at all.

The afternoon passes pleasantly, part interview, part friendly get-together. The cottonwoods cast long shadows in the late afternoon light, and the young journalist gets up to leave.

Come back again, Willie says, when there's time to use the swimming hole or a chance to go fishing. It would be nice, he says wistfully, to go fishing again. The young journalist shakes hands with the calm man; Connie waves goodbye.

Soon Willie Nelson will have to move out of the Austin ranch, to some place even more secluded.

The road, however, will go on.

14

Call it "Outlaw"

Kris Kristofferson was impressed. Things were finally beginning to move in Nashville, and now his buddy from Tootsie's, Lee Clayton, had written a song that somehow seemed to sum it all up.

Sounds like, Kris offered, you've just written a hit song for Ole Waylon. Clayton rallied—why shouldn't it be a hit for Waylon? It was written about him. Maybe with Willie in the back of his mind, too. And Lee Clayton had latched onto a great hook—ladies do, after all, love outlaws.

And it was a hit for Waylon in 1972. He liked the song so much he named a whole album after it. The whole thing might have ended there if a tiny radio station in North Carolina hadn't started bugging Hazel Smith about what to call the "new" music they were playing. People wanted to hear that new music by Willie Nelson and Waylon Jennings. They were calling in and asking for the beat, and now they needed a Name.

Hazel Smith occupied a strange position in Nashville—she served as both a public relations arm and gossip conduit for Waylon, Tompall Glaser, Willie when he was in town, and all of what amounted to the Nashville Underground. Information passed through Hazel like muddy water along the Mississippi; the best of it ending up in her gossip column in *Country Music* Magazine, the rest being routed to farther destinations.

It was one day in early 1973, she remembers, when a disk jockey from WCSE in Ashboro, North Carolina, a little town in the central part of the state, called for a chit-chat. He had a Sunday afternoon show, and all he was going to play was music by Willie, Waylon, Tompall and Kris. But he needed a good hook, something to call the show to make it special. And since he'd heard of Hazel—who hadn't?—and since Hazel called North Carolina home, well, maybe she had some suggestions.

What did the folks at Hillbilly Central, local slang for Tompall Glaser's recording studio, call the music they were making?

To Hazel's mind, this was crucial. Being a songwriter herself, she knew what a good hook could mean. The difference, for instance, between airplay and no airplay. And Hillbilly Central needed the airplay. Record sales and airplay are sort of a chicken-and-egg proposition. A record with no exposure usually doesn't sell—

the very point Willie had been arguing for the better part of a decade. If the record companies weren't going to support the songs, then it became absolutely critical to have the disk jockeys themselves behind them.

The solution hit her like the proverbial bolt from the blue. Call it "outlaw" music, Hazel Smith said. Call it Outlaw.

"I discussed it with Lee Clayton later," she says, "and I think the term was in the back of my mind from his song. But later I looked it up in the dictionary and found it meant, literally, someone who lives outside the law. And I knew people like Willie and Waylon and Tompall . . . were not going along with the Music Row establishment, the Nashville Sound. So I figured they could be living outside the law."

The music was so popular that WCSE became an "outlaw" station, and the college kids— the same breed of kids who in Texas were flocking to the Armadillo, loved it. And since they loved it, Hazel loved it. She even got Willie to autograph a bunch of eight-by-ten glossies for the station to give away as prizes; then she started badgering record companies to send *outlaw* records to radio programmers. The station's ratings soared, then other stations followed suit, most notably KOKE in Austin, Willie's new home town. A columnist in the *Baltimore Sun* mentioned *outlaw* music in his column. Finally Dave Hickey, writing in *Country Music*, had a story headlined "In Defense Of

The Telecaster Cowboy Outlaws" that pulled the pin out of the floodgates.

"Now, as you know, I'm just an old foot-tapper, bottle-thrower and freelance layabout," Hickey, sounding like Willie Nelson's early radio shows, wrote. "And I don't know much about these guys except by watching and listening. But just by watching and listening I can tell you they're the only folks in Nashville who will walk into a room where there's a guitar and a *Wall Street Journal* and pick up the guitar . . ."

You couldn't have gotten more of an effect with a hand grenade rolled into the Country Music Hall of Fame. For the first time, it was obvious to anyone who cared to look: Something big was going on in country music; Nashville was boiling.

Later that year Willie Nelson came to Nashville to pal around with Waylon and get inducted into the Nashville Songwriters Association Hall of Fame. At the banquet, Willie started singing his hits . . . and more hits . . . and more hits. Up until that moment, a lot of people at the banquet hadn't put it together yet, hadn't really connected the long-haired Texas guy with one of the most awesome song catalogs in the history of Music City. The crowd sat there in awe, until a voice from the back of the room shouted, "Hell, Willie! What *didn't* you write?"

Neil Reshen set up a Waylon and Willie concert the week of the Disk Jockey Convention, a week-long party where all the disk jockeys in the world come to Nashville to see and meet acts, to listen to new music and, in general, get together and *boogie*. They planned on having a couple of thousand people, but more than 6,000 people crammed into the small room, a mob scene unlike anything Nashville had experienced. At the nationally televised Country Music Awards Show the same week, smiling Roy Clark won Entertainer of the Year; most of the other awards went to Charlie Rich for "Behind Closed Doors," the top song of the year and a huge pop crossover. The Nashville Sound was a bulwark, as strong as the dollar. Of course, the dollar wasn't what it used to be, either.

Later, both Willie and Waylon would explain again and again how they hated the term "outlaw," how it was all bunk and how they'd prefer never to hear it again. To hear them talk, it's probably a miracle Hazel Smith wasn't strangled in her sleep. All things considered, however, "outlaw" wasn't such a bad term. It played on the cowboy mythology that ran through the works of both Willie and Waylon; it captured their looks at a time when appearance was of tremendous importance. Outlaw also separated the music of Waylon and Willie and the boys from "cowboy" music, the music of the Singing Cowboys Willie had listened to growing up in Abbott. For a while "progressive" country music, *à la* the progressive rock of the period, looked like it might overtake outlaws. Problem was that "progressive" just sounded too much like hippie music, and that was never the point. The changes in country music weren't coming from

that direction—the direction everybody expected
the change to come from. Rock was perceived
as strong; country as weak. But the outlaws
weren't rock-and-roll bandits, riding into Nashville in the middle of the night and riding out
the next morning with the goodies. Just a few
years earlier, Willie and Waylon *were* the
Establishment. They'd paid their dues, then discovered that it didn't mean a thing.

"Outlaw" had enough cowboy machismo to
excuse all the denim, leather and turquoise
trappings; all the cowboy boots and Stetson
hats; all the Lone Star State wahoo-ism and
general insanity that grew up around it. In fact,
the whole concept of "outlaw" came at a breaking point for popular culture. Rock music had
just about mellowed itself to death. A lot of
young people were alienated by the tremendous
surge in disco music and the seemingly endless
narcissism of the "Me Decade." But until the
rise of the Outlaws, Willie and Waylon, there
was no viable alternative. Suddenly there was
not only an alternative, but a mean, threatening
male alternative. With a single word, the new
cowboys could define both their style of music
and their attitude toward life, establish a readily recognizable uniform (denims and leather),
tap a virtually bottomless obsession with the
Old (and largely mythological) West, and give
the new young audience a handle to grab onto.

"I never did take it too seriously," Waylon
says. "I laughed at it. I never did call myself no
outlaw . . . Play your music and forget that."

Before *outlaw* really hit, Waylon had been following Willie's example, struggling to carve out a calm in the center of the shambles that was his personal life. Willie had married Connie in 1971, and his life had seemed to take a swing up. Waylon had coproduced and worked with a singer named Jessi Colter, former wife of Duane Eddy. He asked her to go out, but she'd already heard the outlaw stories.

"I could picture orgies going on in his motel room," she says. "But he kept after me, and one night he said, 'Would it make any difference if I told you I studied for the ministry once?'"

She thought the idea was so funny that she agreed to go out with Waylon. They were soon married, and she quickly served to counterbalance the worst self-destructive impulses running through Waylon's life.

Although she'd been married to Eddy and had been a part of the Los Angeles music scene, she had trouble believing what she saw around her in Nashville.

"What I couldn't believe," Jessi Colter said, "was that people would try to hold back a man's music because they were afraid any change in the music would cost them their jobs. I still don't understand that."

Although Waylon was a solid artist, the outlaw undercurrent was causing RCA, his record company, to shy away from heavily supporting him. There was a time, remembers Hazel Smith, when one of the heads of RCA said, in response

to a reporter's question, that should Waylon
Jennings sell as many records as Charley Pride,
another RCA artist, well then RCA would promote and hustle Waylon Jennings records with
the same enthusiasm lavished on Pride. Waylon
asked for an accounting. He was selling *more*
records than Charley Pride.

"I was just misunderstood there," Waylon
says. "They thought I was out to change and
destroy . . . to kill their music."

Having hired Neil Reshen as his manager as
well, Waylon watched the career of Willie Nelson very closely. Without a doubt, whatever
Willie was doing seemed to be working. The
next year, 1974, Willie was back in the studio
working on *Phases And Stages*, the concept
album, for Atlantic. He and Wexler were working in Muscle Shoals, Alabama, the site of some
of Wexler's biggest successes in soul music and
the home of some of the slickest rhythm and
blues pickers in the country. In many ways, the
album was closer to *Yesterday's Wine* than
Shotgun Willie. Critics compared it to a country and western *Sgt. Pepper's Lonely Hearts
Club Band*, a moving look at the relationship
between man and woman.

"The album is an excruciatingly universal account of the way one man and one woman deal
with their divorce," said one reporter, "but it
ends with one very significant song called 'Pick
Up The Tempo.' (The song) speaks of an affir-
mation of life and a determination to triumph
over its emotional problems."

The first part of the album is from the
woman's point of view; the second from the
man's. Again, Willie blended older songs in with
the new, and even critics who despised country
music took the album to heart. At the same
time that *Phases And Stages* was released, Atlantic began dismantling its country music division.
Ironically, Wexler's vision was accurate but too
early, a criticism frequently leveled at Willie
himself. Atlantic Records was ahead of its time.
Although the album was just tossed out to sink
or swim, it sold more than 400,000 copies—
about four times as many as a typical hit country album.

The snowball, though, had already started
rolling down the mountain. Although Nashville
was less than thrilled with the whole idea of
Willie Nelson, it couldn't turn its back on a
hitmaker. Willie struck a deal with CBS Records,
another Nashville monolith. The deal was,
however, that CBS would only put the records
out: Willie Nelson would have complete artistic
control. It would, in fact, be his own label,
Lone Star, distributed by CBS.

Period.

He'd record what he wanted where he wanted
with whomever he wanted. He even had control over the album covers. CBS chafed, but
agreed.

For Waylon and many of the other "outlaws,"
it was more than a war cry. The battle had been
joined, and the fort had surrendered without
firing a shot. Willie had won.

Almost immediately afterwards, Waylon went to New York City, over the heads of the Nashville executives, with Neil Reshen to renegotiate his contract. One of the executives there still had a huge portrait of Willie Nelson, late of RCA Records, hanging over his desk.

Waylon pointed at the photo and growled.

"You already blew it with him, hoss," he said. "Now don't blow it with me."

Waylon got what he wanted.

15

Tompall Glaser And Hillbilly Central

There's a tendency on the part of both the public, which can be excused, and the music business itself, which should know better, to see the changes in popular music as an overnight sensation, a chance happening that shook popular culture to its roots. The Beatles, for example, just . . . appeared, as if by divine intervention. No matter that their musical roots stretched across the ocean into the rhythm and blues of the Deep South. No matter that their fame was preceded by years on a grueling club circuit. For the audience, one minute they weren't there, the next minute they were. Overnight success. The same for Elvis Presley and the rockabilly explosion of the mid-1950s. No matter that a dozen Elvis Presley look-a-likes had been working the bars around Memphis and northeast Mississippi for years, searching for an audience for their blend of white-boy country and black-boy blues. No matter that Sam Phillips had been searching for months when he finally hit on Elvis Presley, then Johnny Cash, then Jerry Lee Lewis. Suddenly there was Elvis Presley, shaking his hips on the Ed Sullivan Show.

And so it was with the "Outlaws."

When Tompall Glaser came to Nashville in the late 1950s, the last thing in the world he planned to be was a revolutionary. What he came to be was a star, and being from the Nebraska outback—"I didn't even see anybody except family and friends until I was twenty-one years old," he says—that task didn't seem all that hard. He had heard the same myths as Willie Nelson and was drawn by the same dreams: Step off at the bus station one day, step on the Grand Ole Opry the next. When Tompall got to Nashville, all the greats were still there and working—Roy Acuff, Hank Snow, Lefty Frizzell, Ernest Tubb—all living proof that the end of the rainbow was still there for the taking.

For a while it seemed like the sky was indeed the limit. Within a few hard years, the Glaser Brothers—Tompall, Jim and Chuck—were one of the hottest acts in country music, one of the first groups to consistently cross over to the pop charts. One of Tompall's songs, "The Streets of Baltimore," had become a hit for Bobby Bare. Cotton was high; the living was good.

Tompall was, in fact, enjoying the very lifestyle that Willie Nelson wanted so desperately to achieve. The late 1950s were strictly party time, remembers Roger Schutt, "Captain Midnight" to his radio listeners and eventually to everyone else.

"Everybody just roared, you know," Midnight says. "Everybody was hanging out at Tootsie's for real . . . it was really loose. You could stay out and roar for two or three weeks."

Midnight became increasingly involved in the music business, especially with his friend Tompall. Record production was cheap and simple, summed up basically by saying spend as little money as possible and crank the thing out. Work the Opry, play the honkytonks and peddle records off the back of the bus—if, that is, you could afford a bus. Nobody was getting rich, but nobody was starving, either. It was funky, but the times were getting ready to start changing.

"When we first got here," Midnight remembers, "the music business was like a brotherhood . . . Everybody did hang out together and nobody did have offices and there was a certain pride."

It was in the middle 1960s, according to Tompall, when the music business started to change. The continuing success of rock and the rise of the Nashville Sound had taken their toll.

"Everyone got into a business-type thing," Midnight remembers. "People started having office hours and secretaries and wearing coats and ties and suits and things. They took the fun out of it, you know. You couldn't walk into somebody's office, jump up on somebody's desk, kick their door in as a joke . . . They started taking that shit seriously."

The changes in country music went a whole lot deeper than not being able to kick someone's door in for a little recreation. The shift to the Nashville Sound left not only Willie and Waylon out in the cold, but groups like the Glaser Brothers as well. Country music was veering away not only from honkytonk sounds, but from honkytonk *reality* as well. The song "The Streets Of Baltimore" was almost not recorded because it was about a country girl going to the big city, leaving her husband and deciding—on her own—to walk the streets of Baltimore. Real country girls, Tompall was informed by the powers-that-be, would never go off to the big city and become *whores*. Nashville had the same reaction to a song Tompall discovered by a new writer named John Hartford. Tompall's company published the song, then faced an almost total boycott in Nashville.

The song was "Gentle On My Mind."

"Everyone turned it down because it was too radical a song," Tompall says. "Because it was about *shacking up* ... Well, a lot of kids were *shacking up*, and the song touched a lot of chords ... When something becomes such an important part of society that it has its own definition and its own character, then it must be faced."

Tompall had been fascinated with English textbooks—fascinated because he thought the poetry he was reading in the textbooks was definitely inferior to the poetry he was reading from the best of Nashville's songwriting community. He also noticed that if a song was called a *folk* song, it was reprinted in college texts. If it was called a *country* song, it was ignored.

" 'The Streets of Baltimore' was written about the time that women were realizing they didn't have to put up with all that shit," Tompall says. "So a lot of these little gals started showing up around the Grand Ole Opry, country chicks about nineteen years old who had gotten married when they were fourteen or fifteen. And they had this poor boy they were married to. There were a lot of them: This old boy, you could tell by looking at his hands that he'd worked his ass off, tell by his clothes that he didn't have much money left to spend on himself. And there was his little darlin', just eyeing every cowboy who came through."

But there were two things that Nashville didn't want anymore: controversy and hillbillies. Controversy didn't sell, and hillbillies were just plain embarrassing. If you liked *country* country music, Tompall says, "you were automatically provided with someone to harass and degrade you for liking such utter garbage. It didn't matter one bit whether, the year before, you and your brothers had been named the top vocal group by the Country Music Association. Nor did it matter that the song you discovered, "Gentle On My Mind," had made a star of an unknown singer named Glenn Campbell, turned the songwriter, John Hartford, into a cult hero, and had gone on to become the most recorded song in the history of popular music. It didn't mean a damn that you were *right*, only that you were out of step.

"People use musical tastes to assign social status," Tompall continues. "For a long time people who really liked country music never had a socially sophisticated reason to. There was a certain amount of pride in a hillbilly or a cowboy or a farmer living their own lives. They owned themselves. People wouldn't give up much to do that, but they liked looking at it. The hillbilly singer represented those kind of people."

But the big business of Nashville no longer represented the dirt-poor farmer or the prosperous rancher. Country music wasn't sure who it represented, who it was singing to.

At that point Tompall made a discovery that would make the Outlaw movement possible. Working independently, he discovered much the same thing that Willie and Waylon would discover with Neil Reshen.

Record companies weren't really willing to talk with most artists. Artists were hillbillies and didn't understand the fine points of deal-making. They fretted too much about music. The big hold the record company had over the artist was that the artist had to go somewhere and record, and the record companies owned the studios. Most of the producers were either on the record company payroll or tied somehow to a specific company. Then a strange thing happened—RCA decided to fire a producer but keep using him. "Cowboy" Jack Clement had been producing one hit record after another for Charley Pride, but his freewheeling ways grated on the nerves of RCA's management. The solution was to fire him, then contract him back for Charley Pride albums. Between those albums, Clement was free to do whatever he wanted, including producing other albums for other record companies.

Tompall saw a tremendous opportunity. More than any other single factor, having the record company *assign* a producer to an artist perpetuated all the problems of Music City. When the producer was assigned, the artist had to struggle to do what the producer wanted, which might or might not be what the artist originally intended. Furthermore, why record at a major label's studio at all? Differences in studios can have a major effect on the sound that comes out; an artist like Willie Nelson might work better in a small, intimate studio setting, rather than the clinical environs of a bigger studio.

Tompall Glaser decided to try an experiment. He called a major record company and asked for the president of that company. Then, instead of saying it was Tompall Glaser calling, he said it was the president of Glaser Productions, representing Tompall Glaser. The company's president quickly came to the phone.

"That was when I first began to know the power of business," he says. "I talked to this person at a record company (about money) . . . went home, formed a production company, called myself president, went back and talked to the *same* person and got an additional $100,000. I thought, 'Whattaya mean! So that's what I've been missing.' "

For Tompall, the whole scope of what had been happening in Nashville became crystal clear. While the hillbillies were worrying about music, the record companies were worrying about control.

"Imagine taking Hank Snow's and Lefty Frizzell's band away from them when they recorded," he seethes. "They quit programming Ernest Tubb, so they made him 'obsolete.' . . . But he's not obsolete. There's still a market for him."

Like a kid with an Erector Set, Tompall began tinkering with the idea of being a businessman. He discovered that one of the things that was negotiable was total artistic control. He could get it, and not just for name acts like Waylon and Willie. He also discovered that another negotiable point was money. He would pore over rock-and-roll fan magazines, taking note of the money being paid to new rock stars. Each time the president of Glaser Productions called a record company, he upped the ante a little more.

Tompall Glaser is not a calm person; at least, he was not a calm person in the early days of the 1970s. He believed in his heart that country music could be as big as rock and roll, just as he believed the poetry of Willie and Waylon was every bit as good as—in fact, even better than—the stuff he was reading in his wife's English textbooks. He and his brothers already owned a recording studio on one of the back streets near Music Row, and he began fixing it up like there was no tomorrow, pouring money into the facilities.

What Tompall built was a first-class recording studio without *rules*. More and more, Glaser Studios was replacing Tootsie's as *the* hangout. A whole new generation of songwriters—Lee Clayton, Shel Silverstein, "Funky" Donnie Fritts, Guy Clark—as well as some of the best of the old Tootsie's crowd found their way to Tompall's.

His great obsession, however, was pinball, and in that he had found a soul brother in Waylon Jennings. Night after night they played pinball in any one of Nashville's all-night pinball emporiums. One night they got into a good-natured argument about a song. Tompall thought Waylon should cut "Loving Her Was Easier," a Kristofferson song. Waylon thought it was a good idea, but remained skeptical.

"Who's gonna produce it?" Waylon asked.

"Me," Tompall replied, "or you wanna do it?"

It caught Waylon off-guard. You can call a recording session right now? he asked. In response, Tompall walked over to a pay telephone, called the studio and set up a session. Waylon went into the studio and for the first time learned what complete artistic control could mean.

That's nice, Waylon said, just pick up the phone and call a session in the middle of the

night, just like that. Don't pay a producer—do
it yourself and get what you want.

"I ain't good enough to be terribly big,
anyway," Tompall recalls Waylon saying at that
first session. "But that ain't what I want. I just
want to be terribly good."

"Well," Tompall said, "you're just going to
have to hang around."

Waylon moved his offices into Glaser Studios.
They were called cowboys; some people called
them assholes. Then the small radio station in
North Carolina called for some advice. After
the phone call, Hazel Smith went into Tompall
and Waylon's office and told them what she'd
done.

"Outlaw!" Tompall screamed, and Waylon
did the same thing, but with a whole lot less
enthusiasm. But something clicked for Tompall.
He didn't like labels, but he could put up with
them if they helped him prove a point. Maybe
"Outlaw" was just the ticket in dealing with
the burgeoning new country music audience,
the new audience that Tompall, Waylon and
Willie were courting. Waylon wanted to stop
the whole thing right then and there, but Tompall
counseled caution. A label, he said, means only
as much as you want it to mean, and this particular label might just make both of them a million dollars. He was, of course, right.

About then a journalist from New York came
to the studio, in search of the new Tootsie's.
After a few days at Tompall's studio, he announced that it was like being in the middle of

Hillbilly Central, a name that the people at Tompall's had always used to refer to the Pancake Man restaurant down the street. Needless to say, the name stuck.

"Up 'till that point, the guys were just not having a good time making records," Captain Midnight says. "They were having creative decisions made for them by people who weren't in tune with what they were doing or what they wanted to do, since they weren't exactly doing what they wanted to do. Exactly who or what was responsible for it, who knows? It just got to the point where something *had* to happen. If it hadn't happened, we'd all probably be in the insurance business."

When the full impact of the Outlaw movement began making itself felt in Nashville, Glaser Studios really started smoking. By 1974 the studio with no windows near Music Row had become Hillbilly Central with a vengeance. Waylon and Tompall were hot, and Willie had returned to Nashville with the adulation usually reserved for a visiting deity. Cowboy hats and boots were springing up like mushrooms after a warm rain, and one critic described Nashville as "Dodge City, East." Swapping Willie and Waylon stories became the latest craze; the more hip you were, the closer to the flame you could claim to be. Outlaw Chic had arrived.

For Willie, it was about time. While Nashville seemed to be picking up the tempo at last, Willie was busily carving out an empire in Austin, Texas. The barriers that were standing when

Willie stepped on the stage of the Armadillo fell with a crash, and Willie Nelson was welcome everywhere.

"When you say Nashville," he says, "what you are really talking about is a lot of people from Texas and Oklahoma and the rest of the world who have gone up there. The powers-that-be in Nashville are not people who were born in Nashville, so you really can't geographically put the blame on Nashville. It just happens that's where folks wound up, that's where all the promoters and thieves from all over the country went when they found out that was where the action was."

It was, Willie continues, just like when a younger Willie Nelson in Houston figured he had to move to Nashville to amount to anything.

"So there were lots of people doing the same thing at the same time I was," Willie says. "When I found that out, they were already there . . . they already had their plans set in Nashville, the way they wanted things to be, and I didn't fit into them too well."

Even with Atlantic Record's country division down the chutes, Willie charted two singles, "Bloody Mary Morning" and a duet with folksinger Tracy Nelson, "Nothing's Cold As Ashes After The Fire's Gone." A few months before, Willie had decided to resurrect the Dripping Springs Reunion, only he would try to do a few more things right than the original promoters. One of the first things he did was change the date—even the most diehard country music fan didn't appreciate getting cold and wet. Willie reasoned that the best time for the reunion was the Fourth of July, since it almost never rained on the Fourth of July, and when it did, it was a blessing rather than a curse, given the blast-furnace heat. He called it, grandly, "Willie Nelson's Fourth of July Picnic," and invited Waylon, Kris Kristofferson, Leon Russell, John Prine, Charlie Rich and all sorts of other people, the idea being to play one day and get the hell out of Dodge.

It remains for history to decide whether the second Dripping Springs Reunion, a.k.a. Willie Nelson's Fourth of July Picnic, was any better organized than the first. It certainly didn't appear to be.

"Those goddammed hillbillies," one of the organizers snorted.

Aside from a backstage scene that resembled the Sack of Rome, no ice, not enough rest rooms, an unlimited quantity of wine, whiskey and various chemical substances, enough sunshine to smelt lead and a security force who seemed to think they were in a Dirty Harry movie, the big problem was that there wasn't enough electricity.

As soon as it got dark and the biggest stage lights came on, the Picnic was plunged into total darkness. Eventually, Tom T. Hall came on, thanks to someone's portable generator.

The amazing thing was that when everything was totaled up, Willie broke even. Everyone was up in arms. There was lots of shouting and blame-throwing, none of which seemed to phase Willie.

The first Picnic established him as the undisputed godfather of Austin, Texas, and for him that was the ideal situation. Because unlike many other cities of its size, Austin had begun to develop its own music community, with studios, pickers and all the necessary impedimenta of the business.

It was a made-to-order power base for Willie, a power base from which, whether he liked it or not, he'd challenge the supremacy of Nashville.

16

The King Of Austin, Texas

Some say it was blind luck; others say Willie Nelson was always a better businessman than anyone, himself included, ever gave him credit for. While Nashville seethed, Willie was quietly but methodically consolidating a power base in Austin, Texas.

"I don't believe in the Austin Myth," he said later. "I don't believe in the Nashville Myth or the New York Myth. I think there are good musicians all over the world making music. Now, there might be some towns where good musicians gather more than they do in other towns. Austin is that place, for sure. There's probably more good bands playing live music in Austin than any other city in the country."

For a while, that statement might have been literally true. While the music city of Nashville was trying to figure out what was going on with all these cowboys, the music city of Austin was coming into its own. The decision to bypass Houston and move to Austin had momentous consequences for Willie Nelson and for country music.

Like Nashville in the late 1950s, Austin was a magnet for pickers and songwriters around Texas. Much of Austin's attraction was that the city itself was something of a melting pot, sort of Texas in miniature. Aside from all the various musical influences that rampaged around the state, Austin also had the University of Texas, a convenient repository of long-haired kids with money. The first roots of the Austin music scene came at a folkie bar run for years by Kenneth Threadgill. In the early 1960s Threadgill befriended a young and already roaring Janis Joplin, then garnered modest success at the Newport Jazz and Folk Festival.

Like the rest of the country, Austin suffered through the divisive years of the Vietnam war. It was a time of "us" versus "them," which was strongly reflected in the music community. Country music had always been a strong part of the Austin musical mix, but not in those grizzly days. White boys sang *blues*, brother; only rednecks listened to country music.

The first signs of a thaw came in 1970 when Eddie Wilson discovered an old armory for rent next to a Chicano skating rink a few hundred yards from the Colorado River. Wilson, manager of a local group called Shiva's Headband, rented the auditorium, named it the Armadillo World Headquarters and was quickly in the music business.

The Armadillo quickly became a vortex for music in Austin, mainly the hippie-freak standard-issue musician. But Wilson and his partner, Mike Tolleson, were looking for something a little different. They weren't afraid to book anybody who might sell. When things were at their grimmest, in fact, they got a beer license and opened a beer garden, an act that would shake a true hippie to his mystical core. Rednecks drank beer. They brought in Bill Monroe and the Flying Burrito Brothers, Bette Midler and John Prine. The soft-drink machine dispensed Lone Star Beer in long-necked bottles for a dime.

All this musical cross-fertilization resulted in an off-beat—and wildly enthusiastic—audience. Acts who'd toured Tennessee and Alabama for years came back from Austin with a bemused smile and began spending more and more time in Texas.

The Armadillo also focused the attention of Austin on *music*. An area can have a lot of clubs and still not have a good audience. The success of the Armadillo spawned a number of other similar clubs, and Austin's reputation as a music city grew. The big risk, though, came in 1972 when Wilson and Tolleson decided to introduce Willie to the Armadillo crowd.

"We thought we could promote a kind of fusion and see different types of people come together so that Austin could be a total community," Tolleson says. "We also brought in Waylon, Tom T. Hall and several others; what emerged was a pretty different image—people became something more than just hippies or rednecks, and it was a very satisfying thing to see it happen."

Practically overnight, Willie became the center of the Austin musical universe. He was already a honkytonk saint, The Record Men being one of the biggest concert draws in the state. His unorthodox style and looks attracted the young people, who sensed, quite correctly, that Willie Nelson was a rebel.

"It is a strange and energy-filled convergence of folk/rock musicians, singers and songwriters who have come to the country life for their inspiration and to country music for a musical base on which to build their own individual styles," wrote historian Douglas B. Green. "It has been happening in the middle-sized, middle-classed, middle-American, middle-Texas town of Austin, the latest, hippest place to be in the music business."

By Willie's thinking, Texas had been at fault for letting the music slip away. There were always recording studios in Texas, but Nashville had the mystique. The Austin revolution wasn't the first time Texas had risen to prominence as a music center. Ironically, there was a point in the early 1950s when Dallas actually challenged Nashville for supremacy in country music. A producer named Jim Beck had a state-of-the-art studio in Dallas where Lefty Frizzell, Ray Price and even Marty Robbins recorded. Beck had a special relationship with Columbia Records, and his studio was clearly better than anything available in Nashville. Around 1955, one of the other major record labels in Nashville, Decca, intimated that they might be willing to move their recording to Dallas. Nashville recording pioneers Owen and Harold Bradley went out and purchased a building on 16th Avenue South and completely outfitted it to beat Beck's Dallas studio. The recording industry in Nashville was saved.

"We let it slip out of Texas," Willie says, "and go up to Tennessee."

Willie Nelson wasn't the only musical attraction in Austin. Perhaps the most famous part-time Austin resident was Jerry Jeff Walker. Strangely enough, Jerry Jeff Walker was born in upstate New York. He was possibly the last traveling minstrel to leave home and ride his thumb around the country. Early on, he wrote "Mr. Bojangles" during one of his periodic passes through Austin, and the multitude of cover versions was enough to keep him in guitar picks. Unlike most of the glut of folk singers in the early 1960s, Walker was drawn first to Nashville, then to Texas.

During another of his passes through the state, Walker found himself in the near-ghost town of Luckenbach. Luckenbach had been dying since the late 1800s, when it was a trading post with the Comanches. In 1970, the town made the news briefly when two local ranchers bought the whole town. The two, Hondo Crouch and Cathy Morgan, bought the place on a lark—

how many people could own their own town,
after all? Quickly they opened the most important aspect of any town, a bar. The biggest
event since the late 1800s was when CBS corre-
spondent Charles Kuralt came by for his "On
The Road" program. Luckenbach was nowhere
and proud of it. Hondo Crouch became famous,
and all sorts of folks went to Luckenbach, Texas,
just to get away from it all.

Jerry Jeff Walker went there and liked it so
much he recorded an album there. The album
was *Viva Terlingua*, released in 1973. It included songs that would become standards in
the outlaw repertoire: "Up Against The Wall
Redneck Mother." "Desperadoes Waiting For
A Train," and "London Homesick Blues," which
would eventually be adopted as the theme song
for the immensely popular syndicated television
show, "Austin City Limits." Unfortunately for
Jerry Jeff Walker, like Atlantic Records, he was
about two years too early. Most rock fans
thought Jerry Jeff had probably finally fried his
brains on the road and Jack Daniels Black Label.
Rock stations wouldn't play the record because
it was too country; country stations wouldn't
play it because it was too rock. The general
consensus outside of Texas was that nobody,
but *nobody* cared about Luckenbach, Texas.

Born in Dallas, Michael Murphey originally
planned a career in the church. He moved to
Los Angeles to study at UCLA, but things didn't
work out. He drifted to Austin after a five-year
stint in Los Angeles as a staff writer for Screen

Gems music, where he ground out 400 songs before chucking it and heading back to Texas. His function in Austin was that of intellectual; a phrase he coined during an unhappy period in New York City—cosmic cowboy—eventually came to symbolize the fusion in music that the Austin scene seemed to be heading for.

Murphey's songs were mini-classics. "Geronimo's Cadillac" and "Cosmic Cowboy" made Murphey a star in Austin; a few years later a song called "Wildfire" would make him a national star.

Early on, Murphey put his finger on the pulse of the area. The music of the whole Southwest, he said, from Texas to San Diego, was deeply rooted in the mythology of *cowboy*—and not just on a shallow level. In fact, he said, it was getting deeper all the time. In Austin, Murphey found a place to work without getting totally wrapped up in a music business community.

"I don't encourage the idea that there's any music scene in Austin," Murphey told Jan Reid. "There are a lot of good musicians in this town, but I don't think anyone should ever come to Austin because there's a scene here. Because any time you start relating to a scene, you're in trouble. Scenes have destroyed an awful lot of places."

Austin wasn't so much caught up in a scene as it was a whirlwind, all centered around Willie Nelson. Other Austin acts like Steve Fromholz and Marcia Ball and Rusty Weir found themselves dragged along like bits of debris in the twisters that eat their way across the plains in the summer. *Everybody* loved Willie, from University of Texas coach Darrell Royal to rawboned old men who spent their best days on a tractor. The scene grew and expanded.

One of the early additions was also one of the strangest. Doug Sahm was as Texas as armadillos, but when the flower-power 1960s hit, he headed for San Francisco. His band there was called the Sir Douglas Quintet, and it was pretty good—but in the mid-1960s being "pretty good" didn't cut it; to be successful, an act needed to be *English*. It was the height of the British Invasion, and even Willie Nelson in Nashville was feeling the effects. For the Sir Douglas Quintet from Texas, the effects were disastrous. The solution came from another Southwestern legend, promoter Huey Meaux. Huey reasoned that nobody would know they were from Texas unless somebody spilled the beans. The first Sir Douglas album had the band facing backwards, and subtle publicity suggested they were an unknown but terribly English group.

Sahm cut two classic hits, "She's About A Mover" and "Mendocino," before the gloss wore off. His personal dilemma was summed up in the title to one of his lesser-known songs, "Lawd I'm Just A Country Boy In This Great Big Freaky City." He moved back to Austin and made it a point to encourage new local talent.

"Our music is countrier than ever," Sahm told an interviewer at the peak of Austin-mania. "I can't 'splain it."

"If you believe the press releases about the Armadillo," wrote one caustic journalist, "it sells more Lone Star Beer than the Astrodome, and is the hot center of something called the 'Austin Scene'—which makes it the Grand Ole Opry of something called College Kid Country or Red Neck Rock, depending on your point of view."

The only thing that Austin lacked, in fact, was a solid connection with one of the major record labels, virtually a necessity for any area to become a recording center. Although studios popped up in the wake of Willie like fleas on a blue-tick hound, the link to the majors never materialized.

By 1974, Willie Nelson figured he had it made. Newspapers in Texas were trumpeting that Austin's favorite son was at the peak of his popularity. Nashville had acknowledged that he could sing—a little—and Willie's records were selling. He was still packing them in everywhere he played, as long as he played in Texas.

It was hard to imagine how things could get much better.

17

Red-Headed Stranger

The pieces were all in place, the players all set, when Willie Nelson prepared to cut his first album for CBS Records. The one thing Willie knew for certain was that it was going to be a concept album, like *Yesterday's Wine* or *Phases And Stages*.

"If you're sitting in your living room and you're listening to an album," he says, "you have a certain mood going, you don't want that trip broken. You want to keep it all the way through."

There was a song that had been gnawing at him his whole life. He sang it to his kids in the old hard days in Texas, and he sang it for honkytonk heroes and college kids. The song was "The Red-Headed Stranger," an old ballad by Carl Stutz and Edith Lindeman.

"I used to sing it to my kids when they were growing up," he says. "At night at bedtime I used to sing the song . . . they loved it. We sang

179

'The Red-Headed Stranger' and my kids used to sing it word for word."

It was a ballad of the Old West—*cowboy*, but, as Michael Murphey had pointed out, not some shallow shoot-em-up. It was, rather, the Old West of mythology, a man with a hidden pain and a dark past, headed toward an uncertain future. The red-headed stranger from Blue Rock, Montana, rides into town on his raging black stallion. With him is a bay horse, a horse that once belonged to his beloved wife. In an encounter, he kills a saloon girl when she grabs at the bay horse. She is buried and he rides away, since everyone knows horsethievin' is a killin' offense. Like some dark figure of death, the red-headed stranger rides on. It is the plot of a thousand cowboy movies, the substance of a million dreams.

"The little kids liked it so much that I knew the big kids would, too," Willie says.

Willie had wanted to record it for a long time, but there just seemed to be too many verses, too much to cram into a single song.

"I never quite got around to it the way that I wanted," Willie says. "First of all, it was too long to be commercial, too many verses. And it was just a long time before time came around to do the song, 'The Red-Headed Stranger,' right."

Right after the CBS deal was signed, Willie and Connie were driving back to Austin from Steamboat Springs, Colorado. The conversation drifted from what Willie was going to do with his artistic freedom on "The Red-Headed

Stranger." Again, Willie lamented his inability to get the song on record. Connie suggested that instead of just a single, he design a whole album around the song.

"By the time we got to Denver," Willie says, "I had most of the album in my head."

As soon as he got home to Austin, he got out his guitar and a tape recorder and laid down a rough version of *The Red-Headed Stranger* album. Like Willie's other concept albums, *The Red-Headed Stranger* blended elements of old and new into a single, fluid storyline.

There was, of course, "The Red-Headed Stranger." There was also an old song written by Fred Rose, Hank Williams' sometimes mentor and one of the great songwriters in Nashville history, called "Blue Eyes Crying In The Rain;" Eddy Arnold and Wallace Fowler's "I Couldn't Believe It Was True," T. Texas Tyler's classic "Remember Me," Hank Cochran's melancholy "Can I Sleep In Your Arms" and a moving piece to close the album, "Hands On The Wheel," by Billy Callery. In between those songs, Willie wove the story of a preacher and an unfaithful woman, of revenge, retribution and, ultimately, redemption.

He knew that to work, the album had to be simple; theme and mood needed to carry the album, not musicianship. He also knew that there was no way on earth he could cut such an album in Nashville. The pressures would be great, and Nashville flatly did not understand simplicity.

The band now included a harmonica master named Mickey Raphael, one of the floating group of Austin musicians who played on many records, including Jerry Jeff Walker's *Viva Terlingua* album. Raphael had been hanging around a small studio in tiny Garland, Texas, Autumn Sound Studios. Autumn Sound had originally been a commercial studio for advertising agencies, but had gone through a substantial upgrade at the hands of engineer Phil York. In late 1974 Willie cut a single there, "Bonaparte's Retreat," and liked it. It was, said a picker familiar with the place, "funky, a good place to work." In early 1975 Willie and the band went to Garland to record the album, *Red-Headed Stranger*.

Much to the chagrin of engineer York, who had worked on such big sessions as Helen Reddy's "I Am Woman," Willie had his own way of making an album. Instead of being isolated in the sound booth, Willie insisted on being out with the band to give the music a more live and natural feel. It also created more nightmares for the engineer, who was struggling to keep each musical part separate. The final version of any album is the result of a "mix," where each individual instrumental or vocal track is mixed together to create the ultimate version of the song.

Willie retained an almost gospel simplicity, relying on guitar, harmonica and Bobbie's understated piano to blend the themes together. At one point, when the entire band was playing on "Blue Eyes Crying In The Rain," Willie stopped the session, played through the song with just his guitar and vocal, then asked the band to play only what was necessary. Several of the band members, realizing there was no need for them to play at all, voluntarily got up and left.

In Nashville, something like that could never have happened.

The album was finished in three days at a cost of less than $20,000—peanuts.

When the recording was finished, York invited Willie to help with the mixing, and for the very first time Willie Nelson had a chance to control what was going out under his name. Like Waylon Jennings pressing the red button to record the final mix at Tompall's studio in the middle of the night, it was a first for Willie.

In the entire careers of the two men, they'd never had that privilege.

With *The Red-Headed Stranger* in the can, Willie Nelson, at peace with himself, went on the road.

18

Pick Up The Tempo

To say that Nashville was less than enthused by *The Red-Headed Stranger* would be kind. CBS Records reacted with something akin to panic. They'd sunk a lot of money into Willie Nelson and this . . . this . . . *gospel* record wasn't what they'd expected at all.

"Well," Willie says, "they expected more *Shotgun Willie,* something more up-tempo."

Waylon and Neil Reshen played a tape of *Red-Headed Stranger* for one of the powers-that-be at CBS, who listened intently and then offered the opinion that the album was probably a good demo tape, but certainly not anything that CBS records would want to *release* for public consumption.

Couldn't Willie at least put some *strings* on it?

Waylon and Reshen stormed out of the office, and the story quickly made the Nashville gossip rounds.

Against its better judgment, the record company released *Red-Headed Stranger* exactly as Willie recorded it. They also released a single from the album, "Blue Eyes Crying In The Rain." Willie originally had lined up two songs for the album slot occupied by "Blue Eyes Crying In The Rain," which was his second choice. Connie, however, convinced him to keep "Blue Eyes . . ." at the last minute.

Much to the surprise of not only the CBS executives but Willie Nelson as well, "Blue Eyes Crying In The Rain" began soaring up the charts. By July, it was Number One; Willie Nelson's first Number One record.

To be fair, not everyone at CBS had agreed with the first executive's appraisal. Many of the mid-level executives were taken with both Willie Nelson and the album. To their credit, they worked it like crazy, seeing to it that not only people who wrote about country music, but rock critics as well got copies. Their pitch went something like, "Listen to this, then call us and tell us what you think."

All of a sudden, twenty years later than he figured, Willie Nelson was becoming the star he always dreamed he would be.

"In the hands of a less talented artist," wrote one critic, " 'artistic freedom' means the freedom to indulge in excess. Willie Nelson has been pursuing artistic freedom for his recordings for some time, and when he gets it, he never comes away with less than a masterpiece.

It goes without saying that *Red-Headed Stranger*, his first Columbia album, is a masterpiece."

Rolling Stone, which had never evidenced any great love for country music, wrote, "Willie Nelson . . . has recently recorded an album so remarkable that it calls for a redefinition of the term 'country music.' . . . The world that Nelson has created is so seductive that you want to linger there indefinitely."

Willie took the success with a calmness that had become his trademark, almost as if he was unwilling to give himself over to any sense of relief. He had, after all, traveled this road before.

The success of *The Red-Headed Stranger* was the straw needed to break the back of the old power structure in Nashville. The fact was that Willie Nelson and his buddies were right and the Nashville heavyweights were wrong. They had made a wrong call of such drastic proportions that it cast doubts on all their other calls, on all the accepted business-as-usual truisms that Nashville had comfortably functioned by for years.

Moreover, the biggest week of the year, the Disk Jockey Convention and the nationally televised Country Music Association Awards, were coming up, and Willie Nelson wasn't nominated for anything. Waylon Jennings was, but the rumor around Nashville was that Waylon was fed up with the whole thing and wouldn't be attending the event. Frantically, the Country

Music Association invited Willie Nelson to appear and sing a song.

Willie happily agreed. Of course, he wouldn't be wearing a tuxedo. He'd be in jeans. And he'd have his own band, of course.

At that point, the CMA would probably have agreed to let him perform nude just to have him perform.

Willie Nelson came back to Nashville in triumph, a conquering hero, the star he'd always dreamed of becoming.

The mood in Nashville was ebullient, the parties wilder, the celebrations louder and longer. Willie seemed to be everywhere at once—dropping by Hillbilly Central, paying an obligatory visit to the big CBS party, speaking at the BMI party for songwriters. He never said an unkind word about Nashville, but he left no doubt who the victor was.

He had done what the record companies, the very record companies who were courting him now, had spent almost twenty years telling him he could never do.

The hottest rumor at the convention was, "Willie's coming." That alone was enough to draw a huge crowd of Willie-philes, whether the location was Opryland or Ernest Tubb's Record Store, right across from the Sugar Shack Massage Parlor and the crumbling shell of the Ryman Auditorium.

Willie was going to play Ernest Tubb's, in recognition of the tremendous influence old ET had on both Willie and country music. One of

Willie's inflexible rules has been to always give
credit where credit was due, to thank and wherever possible help the people who helped him.
Later, when he had his own studio in Austin, he
would open that studio up, free of charge, to
many of the old Western Swing musicians in
Texas; when he wasn't on the road, he'd join
them and play for the sheer joy of the old
music.

"These guys," Willie says, "are all my heroes."

ET's Record Store was an institution in itself.
After the Opry on Saturday night, he'd host the
Midnight Jamboree, a chance for the diehard
Opry fans to glimpse a few more of their heroes
before heading back to Ohio or Michigan or
Kentucky for Monday morning at the factory.
The old honkytonker opened his stage to both
Opry greats and newcomers, especially newcom-
ers who had something to say.

The crowd this Saturday night was restless.
Something was clearly going on, but the people
in front of the crowd, mostly tourists who'd
been waiting a couple of hours, didn't know
what it was. Speculation was rife. The rear of
the store and out into the street began filling up
with people who were nothing like the regulars;
longhairs in pre-faded coveralls, people with
brand new Stetsons and unscuffed boots, skinny
short-haired people in record company t-shirts,
talking like New Yorkers. In the middle of the
crowd, a tow-headed boy craned his neck to see
what was happening. He wore a Future Farmers Of America jacket over his coveralls, which,

judging by the frayed edges, got faded the natural way. He was about fourteen. Suddenly he began to laugh.

"Mama, Mama!" he cried with an accent thick enough to cover biscuits. "Mama, lookit them hippies!"

He took his mother, who looked tired and faded, and turned her toward the door. The hippies in question acted like they owned the place, gently pushing their way through the packed crowd toward the stage.

"Mama, wouldja lookit them *hippies*!" the boy said, as delighted as if he'd seen a dancing bear. But when the hippies climbed on stage, the boy's delight turned to bewilderment. The hippies pumped old ET's wrinkled hand, then turned and picked up a guitar, launching into a song. The song was "Blue Eyes Crying In The Rain." The Future Farmer's bewilderment turned into genuine joy as it dawned on him.

"Gol-durn, Mama," he said, pointing at the stage. "Gol-durn, Mama, that's ole Willie!"

For the rest of the evening, dividing lines and all kinds of labels went out the window. Willie played and played, old standards and new songs, Bob Wills, Johnny Bush, Lefty Frizzell and, of course, Willie Nelson. All the while Ernest Tubb, the veteran of a thousand honkytonk wars and a one-time outlaw himself, looked on like a proud father. To half the audience, "progressive" meant half of *Progressive Farmer*; to the other half, "farmer" meant the dumb character in a traveling salesman joke. But all of them knew

Willie Nelson, and all of them understood the emotions that made up the bedrock of Willie Nelson's life and material.

Outside, Nashville crept toward a cool, clear dawn, but inside the plate-glass storefront of Ernest Tubb's Record Shop, magic was in the air. There are times, few times, when music becomes something more than *music*. That night in Nashville, across the street from the dead hulk of the Ryman, Willie Nelson wove a powerful spell. For an evening, the Red-Headed Stranger was real, the trail was endless, the burdens heavy, the glimpse of salvation distant indeed. People might have come to Ernest Tubb's for a lot of reasons. They all left Willie Nelson fans.

On the nationally televised awards' show, Willie, complete with long hair and omnipresent red bandana, and his band drew a seemingly endless standing ovation. For most of the audience, here was a workingman's hero, a man who had been there, seen it and done it, now singing about it in a way a workingman could understand. The music business audience saw something more. They saw the man who didn't compromise, the one who wouldn't bend, wouldn't sell out. Every songwriter who'd ever been told his work was noncommercial, every singer who'd spent years working Holiday Inn lounges, looked at the stage and saw that country music was still a music of the people. That, as producer "Cowboy" Jack Clement once said, the friends and neighbors had spoken, and the friends and neighbors

were always, *always* right. Even Waylon came
and accepted his award as Male Vocalist of the
Year. When the show's host, Glenn Campbell—
who had seen his career take off when Tompall
Glaser published a raunchy song—handed Waylon the award, he said, loud enough to be heard
across the country, "About damn time, Waylon."

The ovation was deafening.

In a little side note, it wasn't all peaches and
cream in Nashville. Later, at the Grand Ole
Opry, Roy Acuff came on stage and told the
capacity crowd that he was going to do a song
that had been written by his late partner, Fred
Rose. That song, Acuff said, was a hit right
now, but Roy was going to do it right. He
launched into a high, lonesome version of "Blue
Eyes Crying In The Rain" that sounded strange
after Willie's carefully phrased version. When
Acuff finished, he lowered his fiddle and said,
with gruff affection, that Willie wasn't a bad
boy, if he'd just get rid of some of that hair.

"I think a lot of people got to thinking that
everybody had to do the same thing Hank Williams did, even die if that was necessary," Willie Nelson says. "And that got out of hand. I
used to think that George Jones got drunk because Hank Williams did, like he really thought
that was what he was supposed to do."

Nashville seemed at times an endless cycle of
"The Way Things Were Done," and there was
an exuberant feeling in seeing them flaunted. As

the week wore on, Willie decided to stay on in Nashville for a while to do a little recording with Waylon Jennings. They never got together and plotted, Willie remembers. That was a misconception.

"We both had legitimate gripes and when we got together, we'd talk about them," Willie says. "We felt we were being ignored, for whatever reason. I'm sure one was because we didn't particularly dress the way an established country musician was supposed to. They were a little angry with us for that, but I still didn't see that we were doing anything wrong. When we did get together, we'd play music together. We found we were pretty good together, and that there was safety in numbers."

Perhaps the biggest point of the whole week was that all of a sudden, country music was fun again. Like the golden days of the late 1940s or late 1950s, Nashville seemed alive, reborn.

Ole Willie's magic really worked.

19

So You Think
You're A Cowboy

Beneath all the cowboy boots and Stetson hats that sprouted overnight in Nashville, Jerry Bradley could smell the sweet scent of money. Bradley was Chet Atkins' replacement as the head of RCA's Nashville operation, and ever since he'd taken over, he'd been looking for a way to turn Outlaw-mania into cash. RCA was, after all, in the business to make records and money. It was not in the business to make a philosophical stand for or against any segment of country music. He began to hatch a scheme.

Bradley had noticed the obvious evidence. Aside from all the denim and boots, *Red-Headed Stranger* had made fools out of CBS, RCA's biggest competitor; the head of CBS had even walked out of a room where the album was being played. However red its face was, CBS was making a lot of money off Willie Nelson. Then Waylon Jennings' wife, Jessi Colter, found herself on the FM *progressive rock* stations with

"I'm Not Lisa." Jessi Colter was on Capitol, another of RCA's major competitors.

Bradley realized that in Waylon Jennings he had potentially the hottest thing since Willie Nelson. The only problem was how to break him into the new audience.

"Waylon was booking out as The Outlaws, he and Tompall and Willie occasionally," Bradley told interviewer Martha Hume. "Willie had just had a hit; Jessi had just had a hit. Waylon had been having all kinds of hits, but none really as big as Willie or Jessi. So I told Waylon we ought to do this 'Outlaw' package and make his picture a little bit bigger and boost his image a little bit."

Waylon agreed, as long as Tompall could be used on the album.

"In my mind—I didn't scratch it out on a piece of paper—I had a mezzotint brown poster, you know, and *Wanted: The Outlaws!* and the pictures," Bradley said. "I think that's the way we wound up doing it. He (Waylon) liked it and started working to get it out in November 1975, and got it out in February."

Jerry Bradley always knew *Wanted: The Outlaws!* would sell, but even in his wildest imagination he couldn't imagine how much it would sell. It sold like crazy, the very first album out of Nashville to ever go platinum—sell one million units. It sold to country fans; it sold to rock fans who'd just heard "Blue Eyes Crying In The Rain"; it sold to laid-back hippies who thought Jessi Colter had a neat voice; it sold to pop and easy-listening fans who wondered what all the hubbub was about. It sold to just about everyone and his dog.

"It's unfortunate that there still has to be a sampler, or primer, or golden book of some of the best singers working everywhere," wrote Chet Flippo of *Rolling Stone*, on the back of the album. "But apparently not everyone has gotten the message yet . . . Call them outlaws, call them revolutionaries, call them what you will. They are just some damn fine people who are also some of the most gifted songwriters and singers anywhere."

The irony of it was that the album wasn't particularly good, certainly not the best collection of work from such talented people. The album consisted of previously released tracks or out-takes from recording sessions, some of which were cleaned up in the studio. Its biggest flaw was one that Willie Nelson would be quick to recognize—there was no continuity. The album lurched from track to track, neither setting a tone nor developing a mood.

The best cut on the album was one Waylon had recorded the year before, "Good-Hearted Woman," the song he and Willie had written years before. Waylon had recorded the song live at the Texas Opry House, then Willie went into the studio and added a duet part. "Good-Hearted Woman" became the runaway hit song of 1976, quickly topping the country charts and rising high on the pop charts later that year.

In fact, if there was any single point that country music turned on, it was the two minutes and fifty-six seconds of "Good-Hearted Woman." The song is a curious blend of Willie and Waylon. It has Waylon's beat, Waylon's drive, but the lyrics have Willie's sensibilities, his feeling for the Third Law of Karma, "What goes around, comes around." It remains one of the best single statements about the music of Willie Nelson and Waylon Jennings.

For Willie's work, RCA chose two excellent songs from *Yesterday's Wine*, "Me And Paul" and "Yesterday's Wine." They were particularly good choices, because they were classic Willie Nelson. "Me And Paul" remains one of the most powerful statements about friendship and the road, the travels of Willie Nelson and Paul English.

"We got a few bad reviews," Bradley says. "Willie was selling four or five hundred thousand records (before *Wanted: The Outlaws!*) and wound up selling a million. So there were five hundred thousand people Willie got to he hadn't been able to before. So definitely it helped everybody. But to the diehard Willie, Waylon or Jessi fan, I think they might have been a little offended. But if they could understand that it maybe brought more people to accept them all, it was a good album. It served a purpose."

Like Willie and Waylon, Jerry Bradley dismissed "Outlaw" as a marketing concept, a way to sell records. Waylon is just his music, Bradley said. So was Willie.

When Outlaw-mania hit Nashville, all hell broke loose, doomsday at the OK Corral. The local sport changed from softball played at the Opry to pinball, played mean and dirty and half-drunk in places like the Wooden Nickel or the Burger Boy. The working day began around 8 p.m. and wrapped up when the sun made a belated appearance over the Nashville skyline. Jack Daniels Black Label became the common denominator, and when the bucks started rolling in, the scene shifted to cocaine and little white pills to keep things rolling until dawn. You couldn't be an Outlaw, after all, without a coke stash.

Everyone in Nashville began looking like bit players in a remake of *The Wild Bunch*, walking bowlegged and spitting on the Music City sidewalks. Executives grew beards and receptionists shucked most of their clothes, and each day it got a little worse.

The money was rolling in. Willie and Waylon had broken the bank at Music City. The success of *Wanted: The Outlaws!*, following close on the heels of *Red-Headed Stranger*, changed the way the country music business worked. If Willie Nelson could sell a million, two million, three million records, then a lot of the old tried-and-tested methods that had held Willie back for years were simply obsolete.

20

Waylon & Willie

In contrast to the year before, the 1976 Dee-jay Convention and CMA Awards show was a love fest, all directed at Nashville and Austin's favorite son, Willie Nelson. One critic went as far as noting the rumor that Willie had been appointed "Interim Supreme Being" for all of Texas, Oklahoma and much of New Mexico.

Willie and Waylon swept the CMA Awards. *Wanted: The Outlaws!* was named Best Album of 1976, and "Good-Hearted Woman" was named best single. Willie and Waylon were named Best Duo of the year for "Good-Hearted Woman." This year, however, Waylon Jennings flatly refused to come. The year before, Jessi had badgered him into showing up, but in 1976, he stayed home to watch "Jesus Christ Superstar" on television. Willie accepted each award, bounding onto the stage and accepting on behalf of "me and ole Waylon."

Afterwards, Willie announced that he had

had his quota of awards shows, since he didn't want to be placed in the awkward position of competing head-on with Waylon.

"Most of the awards that one of us is in, the other is in," Willie said, "and I just don't want that, and he doesn't either, so we're just both taking our names out of the pot. Because we don't want to be in competition with each other—we never have been—especially not on national television. Just to sit there and look dumb while Waylon wins or I win, either way, it's not right."

It was quickly obvious that some kind of follow-up would be necessary. Willie had released his own album, *The Sound In Your Mind*, also recorded at Autumn Sound Studios in Garland, Texas. That album represented a transitional period for Willie. It lacked the coherent theme of *Red-Headed Stranger*, but included a medley of "Funny How Time Slips Away," "Crazy," and "Night Life." It also featured Willie doing some of his favorite songs from his youth, a theme that he would return to again and again. To keep things from slowing up too much, the album included a rollicking version of Lefty Frizzell's "If You've Got The Money, I've Got The Time." *Billboard* Magazine named it the best country album of the year. Waylon released his *Ol' Waylon* album, which featured a single titled "Luckenbach, Texas (Back To The Basics Of Love)." Jerry Jeff Walker's secret was out of the bag with a vengeance. Willie Nelson sang the last verse, and the song entered the country charts higher than any other song in history. "Luckenbach, Texas" was a bigger hit than "Good-Hearted Woman."

Jerry Bradley wanted a replay of *Wanted: The Outlaws!*, and both Willie and Waylon agreed. This time, however, instead of tinkering something together, they'd cut new stuff, or mostly new stuff. The album was titled, appropriately enough, *Waylon & Willie* (it was, after all, an RCA album, and the RCA artist got top billing), and it shocked the music world by debuting at Number One.

"I humbly submit that the world needs a lot more Willie & Waylon right now," wrote critic Chet Flippo on the rear jacket of the album, "and a whole lot less of that other crap."

"Waylon picked most of the songs," Willie said at a press conference. "There wasn't a lot of research in this album."

It was, however, a much better effort than the earlier "duet" album. The premier song on *Waylon & Willie* was Ed and Patsy Bruce's "Mamas Don't Let Your Babies Grow Up To Be Cowboys," already a top hit for Ed Bruce. Bruce, a veteran songwriter who later had a part on the "Bret Maverick" television series, wrote the song while stuck in traffic in downtown Nashville. The original lyrics were "Mamas, don't let your babies grow up to be guitar pickers," but it just didn't have the right feel. "Cowboys" did.

The two began touring together, and it quickly became obvious that there was a critical differ-

ence in style. Willie loved the road, thrived on
it. Given the opportunity, he'd play until dawn
night after night, ride the bus day after day.
Instead of getting tired, he just got better. Willie
would never turn down an autograph seeker,
and he had a kind word for practically everyone.
For Waylon, though, the grind on the road
began grinding him down. Always a very private person, he took the incessant demands of
the fans poorly. He drove himself harder and
harder, and by his own admission it showed in
his attitude and his music.

The Willie/Waylon tours were major productions, outdrawing every touring act in America except Sha Na Na. For the first time, security was tight—perhaps too tight. One night in
Louisiana, Waylon's security people refused to
let several major rock stars backstage to pick
with Willie and Waylon.

Once a person got backstage, the feeling was
different, subtly *wrong*. Usually the backstage
scene generated a certain amount of togetherness,
an I-don't-know-what-we're-doing-back-here-
but-we-all-must-be-friends. At a Willie Nelson
concert, that feeling used to be particularly
strong. There was also the feeling of being in on
the ground floor of a particularly pleasant
revolution, and of being genuinely welcome there.
Then there was the old neighborly feeling that
always existed between a country star and the
audience.

The Willie and Waylon tours weren't like
that. The size, the sheer overwhelming popular-

ity of the two performers did away with all that. Instead, the backstage areas were crawling with security, ex-bikers slapping multi-cell flashlights against their palms and looking for an excuse to kick ass; hangers-on lolling in open doorways demanding to know what business any and everyone had there. It was more like doing time than making music.

But for the crowds out front, the music was great. Sometimes the crowds were almost totally young people, newcomers riding the outlaw wave. At other dates the audience was older, more subdued, come to hear the author of "Hello Walls" and the guy who sang "Cedartown Georgia."

The outlaw "movement" began getting a little out of control. In fact, the outlaw movement began getting *a lot* out of control. The only two people in the country who claimed not to be outlaws were Willie Nelson and Waylon Jennings.

"The outlaw thing to me is a big joke," Willie told interviewer Stacy Harris in 1978. "I'm just *not* an outlaw. There may be one or two things I do illegally. I speed occasionally. I go past fifty-five miles-per-hour, but not intentionally. I mean, I don't go around breaking laws all the time. I pay taxes. I pay rent . . . So how they figure me an outlaw, I don't know. It must look good in print. It may sell some magazines. I don't really care. If they want to call me that, I'll go along with it."

The problem was that once Nashville sensed a buck to be made, and once they had the hot breath of Austin on their back, they were perfectly happy shifting from the Nashville Sound to the Austin Sound. If America wanted outlaws, by God Nashville would give 'em outlaws. Every record that came out of Nashville was billed by clever promotion men as "outlaw," every second-rate singer in denims got a recording contract. In one particularly wretched performance, one second-rater walked out on stage and announced that he'd just been in Texas (pause for shouting) with Willie (pause for screaming, shouting and general rowdiness). Whenever things calmed down, he'd just shout "Willie!" to get the crowd roaring again.

"Outlaw" seemed to take on a life of its own. RCA even carted Willie and Waylon to the prestigious Rainbow Room atop Rockefeller Center in New York City. Willie and Waylon were seated with their backs to the wall, fending off well-wishers and the hordes of record company people. Waylon was distracted and annoyed, like an animal backed into a corner. He picked at octopus salad, spoke when spoken to and left as soon as he could. Willie, on the other hand, took it all in stride, pausing, to the chagrin of record executives and hangers-on, to talk with a young journalist.

Willie even arranged for the release of the gospel album he recorded for Atlantic, *The Troublemaker*.

"I've been trying to get that album out for a

long time," Willie says. "They kept putting me off from label to label. RCA wouldn't let me do one. They thought I needed to be a more established artist before I did a gospel album. I've done thirty-two albums and only one gospel album."

Predictably, even the gospel album sold.

After a show in Washington, D. C., Willie was met backstage by Jody Powell, press secretary to President Jimmy Carter. There was someone, Powell said, who really wanted to meet Willie, and could Willie be at the White House the next day for lunch? He had come, truly, a long way from Abbott, Texas.

About that time, cracks began appearing between Neil Reshen and Willie. The IRS was after Willie for some $71,000 in back taxes. There were further rumors of problems between Willie and Reshen over the handling of the Willie Nelson Picnics. Although there was no public announcement, Willie soon had a new manager. Waylon retained Reshen, and the gossip-mongers began discussing the split between Willie and Waylon—although both parties denied it.

"I don't know," Willie says. "Everybody seems to be, if not causing trouble between me and Waylon, to at least say there is trouble between us. But as far as I know, there's not. Some people don't like it when people are too good friends or are too successful. It doesn't matter whether you're in music or whether you're two good plumbers with the most business in town."

Part of the problem was probably that Willie Nelson simply kept getting bigger and bigger. Just when Willie seemed to peak, he took another step up, to another plane. Music, movies, television—nothing seemed beyond Willie's grasp. But for Waylon, things began going sour. Concerts weren't drawing as well. His money disappeared. His career seemed, for a while, to be in danger of totally self-destructing. It had to grate.

There was, happily, a reconciliation that is still going on. Willie and Waylon are on the charts again, and Waylon's career is once again on the upswing.

For Willie, there was always the road, an escape hatch when all the publicity got too much to stomach. He kept touring, pushing the Family Band to do 200, 250 dates a year, unheard of for a star of his caliber.

"Everybody likes to take a few days off now and then," he says. "But any more than a week and you, uh, start getting restless. You want to go out and do it all over again . . . I've got lots of friends who are doing the same thing. Guys like Ernest Tubb, Faron Young, Jimmy Dickens—these guys are still going up and down the highway, still enjoying what they're doing, and as long as I enjoy it, I'll keep doing it. As long as I'm able."

21

Healing Hands Of Time

One of the things always cited by the "Willie, The Canny Businessman" school of thought is the continuation of the Willie Nelson's Fourth of July Picnics. After the 1973 Picnic, where Willie just scraped by, breaking even, odds were that Willie Nelson would never become involved in something that crazy again. Odds were wrong, of course.

The Picnics became part of the Willie Nelson mystique, a sort of rock concert for the post-Woodstock generation. Some of the Picnics did indeed resemble Woodstock, although slightly drunker; the worst, the 1976 Picnic at Gonzales, Texas, was more like Altamont, the flip side of peace, love and flowers.

Organization was never the strong suit of any of the Picnics.

"I glimpsed Willie once," says journalist Patrick Carr, Editor of *Country Music* and veteran of several Picnics. "As I remember, the last one

206

I attended was incredibly hot, and we spent all our time looking for a Winnebago. It was your basic endurance contest."

Unlike the huge music festivals of the previous decade, Carr says the emphasis at the Picnics was never on the music, although the music was extremely good.

"The Picnics were more a celebration of Texasism," Carr says. "They were very much Texas events."

The Gonzales Picnic managed to incorporate everything that was bad about rock concerts—blistering heat, drugs, drunks, storm-trooper gate security, slipshod organization and, in general, bad Karma. There were fistfights, stabbings, reported (but never verified) rapes and heaven knew how many overdoses. Rumor reported that Willie was furious, storming around a suite in a nearby hotel room and demanding to know what on earth had happened. Even before the Picnic had ended, Willie and Connie flew to Hawaii, away from the eye of the storm. Willie was reported to have lost $200,000 on the event.

The next year, in 1977, the Picnic was more organized. Then, after a brief hiatus, the Picnics returned in 1983 as mobile parties, the biggest of which was held at, of all places, The Meadowlands stadium in New Jersey, within spitting distance of New York City.

One of the biggest problems with the Picnics (and any of the larger concerts) was the entourage that surrounded Willie. Willie's magnetic personality attracted all kinds. Like the early days of his career, when perfectly normal people would throw away their own careers to travel with Willie, the "family" grew faster than a pile of iron filings next to a magnet. CPAs or Hell's Angels, it made no difference to Willie. But the whole idea of "outlaw" had a huge appeal to genuine outlaws, people who had seen the darker side of life. And, frankly, like New York writers drawn to tough convicts, the Outlaws developed an affinity for outlaws. Both Waylon's and Willie's concerts sometimes resemble a biker reunion. Willie, in fact, is one of the featured performers in a recent movie presenting a positive image of the Hell's Angels.

"I have no idea who will walk down the hall next," Willie told interviewer Mike Reynolds. "It could be a politician. It could be a Hell's Angel. I have friends everywhere. I'm not ashamed of the people I'm around. Even though some of them are probably what some people would call, uh, disreputable characters."

Of course, the problem looks much worse than it is. Music journalists routinely report that they've seen someone in Willie's or Waylon's party running around with (shudder) a *gun*, overlooking the fact that many concerts are *cash* operations. Somebody ends up walking around backstage with many thousands of dollars in a briefcase. Besides, after two weeks on the road with a major country act, Gandhi would probably go out and apply for a pistol permit. Weirdness prevails.

"I don't really know anybody who considers

himself normal," Willie told *Country Rhythms* Magazine, echoing a common Willie Nelson refrain. "I doubt very seriously if there's any such thing . . . When you start expecting everybody to be normal, that's when you have problems."

Willie appears unconcerned with it all. Some of his friends are undoubtedly low riders, which is understandable for a man who's spent most of his life in barrooms—"You never heard of a church brawl," he quips.

When you mix liquor, drugs and honkytonks, violence is never far below the surface, and if you hang around enough honkytonks, you're eventually going to meet the broken end of a longneck beer bottle.

"We really have a lot of sayings in Abbott, where I grew up, like, 'A hard head makes for a sore ass,' " Willie told *Country Rhythms*. "A lot of those little sayings are designed to keep your temper from getting you in all kinds of trouble, because if you think you're mean and tough, there's always somebody a little bit meaner and tougher. There's just no future in thinking you can go around and whip the world every time somebody makes you mad."

The other thing that a life in the honkytonks will do is strip an intelligent man of any illusions of his own invulnerability. After years of sporadic practice, Willie Nelson has a good grip on karate. He once told an interviewer that he could crush a board and a brick with karate, which would come in handy if he was ever jumped by a board and a brick. In the event of tire irons, beer bottles or .357s, all bets were off.

"I'm pretty cantankerous at times," Willie says. He recalled one time in a Phoenix 'tonk when he stepped out the back door of the club to sign an autograph and ended up in a silent, bloody fight for half an hour, Willie swinging a two-by-four, the other guy with an equally awesome piece of wood, until somebody came and broke it up.

There is a pervasive myth that weaves throughout popular music, something to the effect that suffering and ultimately death are the prices an artist must be willing to pay. Along about the late 1970s, Willie looked back and saw at least some parts of the myth gaining on him.

"I could see myself disintegrating before my eyes," Willie told Roy Blout in *Esquire*.

He began jogging, eventually working up to five miles or more a day. He exercised regularly, practically gave up drinking, gave up almost everything except marijuana.

"I've been smoking it since I was a boy," Willie says, casually dismissing the question. "Mexicans across the street from where we lived grew it in their yard. In Abbott, Texas, nobody cared. And Abbott is probably one of the quietest, sanest places in the world."

And, in truth, it would be hard to tell the difference between Willie Nelson straight and Willie Nelson stoned; odd, since the dope he smokes is usually powerful enough to fuddle a rhino at fifty paces. He has little use for other drugs, including ultra-trendy cocaine—although he admits to having tried probably everything at least once.

"I'm my biggest enemy," Willie says. "Once I realized that, it was easier."

In 1979 the Country Music Association ratified what everybody already knew; Willie Hugh Nelson was named Entertainer of the Year, the highest award country music can give. Of the five nominees—Kenny Rogers, Barbara Mandrell, the Statler Brothers and Crystal Gayle—Willie was probably the dark horse. The clear favorite was Kenny Rogers, riding the huge success of "The Gambler."

After sitting through the entire awards show and watching Kenny Rogers grab every award in sight, Willie figured he was off the hook.

"I thought Kenny was about to clean sweep," Willie says. "So I was surprised. I was *shocked.*" He was wearing his usual jeans and a neat cowboy shirt, his long hair pulled back in braids. He took the microphone and thanked the audience modestly, started to turn away, then turned back to the audience.

"When you talk about entertainers," Willie said, "entertainers of years, not just one year, but entertainers over the years—I like to think about people like Little Jimmy Dickens, Faron Young, Ferlin Husky and all those people, and, ah, I'd like to see these guys up here one of these years, because they certainly deserve to be."

The applause was deafening.

Afterwards, Willie spoke again about his heroes, country music stars from the 1950s who had a tremendous influence on the country music stars of the 1970s. If Willie Nelson had his way, they would never be forgotten.

Later, he was asked if he thought he was singing with more confidence. He paused for a long time before he answered.

"Yes, there's a lot to that," Willie said. "There were a lot of years when I felt like I was singing to myself. A lot of times I was. There was me and two couples out on the dance floor, and that was it. The crowds have gotten bigger, and as the crowd gets bigger, your confidence grows. Maybe you're doing it right."

Again, it seemed that Willie Nelson's career couldn't get any bigger. Even *The New York Times* gushed the praises of the leather-tough singer from Texas.

"He plays with the vibrant enthusiasm of a Fats Waller," wrote Al Rheinhart in the *Times*, "with the gleeful fulfillment of an artist who has finally found his audience, and through them, himself. He is truly happy to be there, playing his music, and it shows."

"An objective look at the present state of Willie Nelson's nearly three-decade-long career indicates that he not only learned from the error of his ways, but he's in fact gone a step farther and turned them all into triumphs," wrote Willie-watcher Bob Allen in *Country Music* Magazine in 1980. "For at least the last three years, some journalists have been predicting that his career was bound to peak any second now, and that it would all be downhill from there. But the fact is it just seems to be gaining more and more momentum—almost by the day."

Willie, as usual, was philosophical—"I feel like I've made all the mistakes," he says, "and I hope I've learned from them."

22

Stardust

"I've got," Willie Nelson says, "about a thousand things I want to try."

With outlaw-mania at its very peak, when the mere mention of the words "Lone Star Beer" would send the crowd into a frenzy, Willie went back into the studio to record again.

He wasn't, however, going into the studio to record his own songs.

"Professional songwriters," he says, "are just like everyone else. They get tired, too. They like to take time off, especially if you've written a lot of songs and have a pretty good catalog built up . . . That's what most Americans want to do, get a little nest egg set aside where they don't have to work anymore. Everyone else retires at forty or fifty, but people expect a songwriter to write until he's one hundred and seven."

Besides, the musical evangelist in Willie Nelson had an idea. All his life he'd been singing the old songs, the ballads he'd listened to growing up.

"When I was a kid," he says, "Bobbie used to buy these songbooks. She was taking piano lessons, and she'd buy these World War Two songbooks—everything from 'Stardust' to 'Don't Sit Under The Apple Tree With Anyone Else But Me.' That's what we would do all day. She would read the music out of the books, and I would sit there with my guitar and play along with her. I couldn't read the music, but I learned the chords to most of them through playing guitar while she played piano."

If Bob Wills was the main character on which Willie Nelson would base his life, there was still another character he both admired and felt a growing kinship with. The character was Hoagy Carmichael.

"I liked Hoagy Carmichael personally," Willie says. "I liked the character I saw in the movies . . . the character that he portrayed in the movies—the lazy, laid-back type of guy that he was. I'm sure that's the way he must have been in real life. Even as a kid growing up, I could see how good he was."

Willie was captivated by two of Carmichael's greatest songs, "Georgia On My Mind" and the classic "Stardust." "Stardust," written by Carmichael in 1927, shares the honors with W. C. Handy's "St. Louis Blues" as one of the most recorded songs of all times, with over 1,000 *American* versions of the song.

Willie decided to do an album of his ten

favorite songs. Not being one to do much research, Willie picked the songs off the top of his head.

"(I wanted) the songs I thought were the best songs ever written by anybody," Willie says. "The classics. The masterpieces. The first one I thought of was 'Stardust.' 'Georgia' was number two."

His other favorites were "Blue Skies," "All Of Me," "Unchained Melody," "September Song," "On The Sunny Side of the Street," "Moonlight In Vermont," "Don't Get Around Much Anymore" and "Someone To Watch Over Me."

It wasn't the first time Willie had turned to the standards he knew best. *The Sound In Your Mind* featured the 1949 Frankie Laine hit "That Lucky Old Sun," and as far back as the early 1960s he'd recorded "Am I Blue?" from the 1929 musical *On With The Show*.

While Willie's record company wasn't exactly overjoyed with their top artist producing a record that didn't even mention Texas once, they held their peace. CBS Records had already had one run-in with Willie the year before, in 1977, when Willie decided to release a tribute album to the ailing Lefty Frizzell.

The album was important to Willie. Growing up in Texas, Lefty had been a big influence, sharing the honkytonk pantheon with Ernest Tubb. Lefty's songs—"If You've Got The Money, I've Got The Time," "I Never Go Around Mirrors," "She's Gone, Gone, Gone," "I Love

You A Thousand Ways"—were dear to Willie's heart.

The album, however, seemed to stall after Willie finished cutting the tracks. CBS was uncomfortable with the title, *To Lefty From Willie*, conceived by Willie as a simple and honest explanation of the album.

In product meetings, where record executives met to discuss the marketing and sales of the record, the title was met with disdain.

"That title is just so *blah*," said one record exec. "So we want to title it *Songs For A Friend*. Less specific, you know? We think it's a great title. I mean, who the hell knows who Lefty Frizzell is anyway?"

When *Songs For A Friend* got back to Willie, the legendary Nelson temper flared. The title of the album was *To Lefty From Willie*; it was not a negotiable point. It came out that way, *or else*. CBS was unwilling to find out what the *or else* might be.

Willie didn't get mad a lot, but when he did, it was violent, like a mirror cracking of its own accord. Small things would touch off his temper. A particular irritant was closed doors—sometimes he kicked them in even when he had the door keys in his pocket. One small record company put out a copy of Willie's early tapes, of which Willie was not particularly proud. Willie went to visit the offices, and although no one would confirm things one way or the other, the company president's office no longer had a door.

"I don't get mad a lot," Willie says. "I don't

like to get mad, and I hope I'll never get mad again. It makes me feel terrible, and I'm not pleasant to be around. People actually get up and leave the room. My wife goes away. Anytime you get angry, it lets the poisons out and makes you feel bad, if you can't justify it."

Willie cut the *Stardust* album with famed producer Booker T. Jones at the helm. The album became one of the biggest selling of Willie's career, with "Georgia On My Mind" becoming one of his most memorable single hits.

"Mr. Nelson is the one American popular singer who gives the impression of being part of both the counterculture and the mainstream at the same time," wrote Robert Palmer in *The New York Times*. "What one sees *is* an outlaw—a cowboy gone wrong. What one hears, especially on Mr. Nelson's recording of "Stardust" and other standards, is a weathered but reassuring voice singing the old songs as if they mattered to him."

Because, of course, they did.

23

Honeysuckle Rose

The successes of the records, the touring and the Picnics presaged even greater successes for Willie Hugh Nelson. At the peak of his popularity, as writers are quick to note, Willie attended a party given by CBS honcho Billy Sherrill. The party was in honor of actor Robert Redford, who was collecting money for his environmentalist Citizen's Action Committee.

Both Willie and Redford were heading to California, and the two shared a plane. On the way out, Redford asked if Willie had ever considered being in the movies. The fact was that movies had always been at the back of Willie's mind, ever since the early days of growing up in Abbott.

"When I first saw Gene Autry when I was a kid," he says, "Roy Rogers . . . all those guys. There was no doubt in my mind that was what I wanted to be—a cowboy movie star. I was five years old at the time."

More than childhood aspirations, Willie saw his concept albums as soundtracks to a movie. *Red-Headed Stranger* was a good example. The back cover of the album features a series of watercolor panels telling the tale of the Stranger, "Like it was a movie." Turning *The Red-Headed Stranger* into a movie had been a persistent, if elusive dream. Willie had been offered other movie roles, but had turned them all down—"I wasn't sure whether either one of us knew what we were doing." Now Robert Redford was offering Willie a pathway to follow his early dreams.

The project was Redford's *Electric Horseman*, the story of a one-time rodeo champion named Sonny Steele, reduced to plugging breakfast cereal in a Porter Wagoner-style suit that shines with twinkling lights instead of rhinestones. In response to the insanity of his life, Sonny Steele has become something of a hopeless drunk.

Willie's role was that of Sonny's manager and friend. It was a small role, but Willie took to it surprisingly well.

"It wasn't," Willie says modestly, "a hard part.

"I thought I was great," he adds.

He wasn't alone. One critic wrote that Willie was "the bonus" in *The Electric Horseman*.

Besides, Willie says, acting isn't as hard as it's cracked up to be.

"It's not all that different from being on stage," he says. "Except you've got to memorize your part instead of songs, and songs are usually longer."

After the success of *Electric Horseman*, it seemed for a while that the next film project Willie was likely to become involved in was the filming of *The Red-Headed Stranger*. A production company to film the album had been formed by Willie and two actors, Gary Busey, fresh from his success in *The Buddy Holly Story*, and Jan-Michael Vincent, a very successful character actor in such films as *Big Wednesday* and *Hard Country*. Robert Redford was interested in the role of the Stranger himself. That project, though, got shunted aside for a starring role in a major movie, *Honeysuckle Rose*. That film would be produced by Sidney Pollack, the director of *The Electric Horseman* and the director of such films as *Jeremiah Johnson* and *They Shoot Horses, Don't They?* Pollack was so impressed with Willie's acting debut that he couldn't wait to line up another project, this time with Willie as the star.

Honeysuckle Rose is about a country music singer and his life on the road. He's married to Dyan Cannon, but falls for a younger singer played by Amy Irving. It was Willie's first starring role.

"The musical part of the character's life certainly parallels mine," Willie says. "Everything he goes through, I've been through at one time or another. The movie covers thirty days in the life of a bandleader."

The screenplay was written by fellow Texan

William Wittliff, also author of another Willie Nelson film, *Barbarosa*. Wittliff had written the screenplay for *Thaddeus Rose And Eddie*, a made-for-television movie featuring Johnny Cash. When Willie saw the movie on television, he was so impressed that he asked around and was finally introduced to Wittliff.

"Willie and I hit it off," Wittliff says. "We have a lot in common, I think . . . if one listens between the lines of *Red-Headed Stranger*, it's real powerful stuff. It's about losing grace, and redemption. I'm moved by that album."

Not surprisingly, the first joint project between the two men was Wittliff turning *Red-Headed Stranger* into a screenplay. Willie was so happy with that screenplay that he asked Wittliff to rewrite the screenplay to *Honeysuckle Rose*. The movie is something of a distant remake of the 1939 Ingrid Bergman hit *Intermezzo*, where it's a famous violinist who gets trapped between the real world and the performing world. One thing that *Honeysuckle Rose* had to have was a lot of music.

"One person who saw *Honeysuckle Rose* when we first screened it came up to me afterwards and said, 'I think it's got too much music in it,' " says Jerry Schatzberg, director of the film. "I told them, 'You must not have been listening to the music, because the music *is* the story.' I wanted to tell a love story, and tell it mostly through music."

One thing everybody told Willie: If the film was to have a shot at an Oscar for the best soundtrack, there was going to have to be some original Willie Nelson music written for the film. At first, that seemed to be a problem, since Willie hadn't been writing a lot of songs. When the dam broke, on the airplane from Atlanta to Austin, there were no more problems.

"I surprised myself in writing several new songs for the movie," Willie told *Country Music* Magazine. "We hadn't planned on that at first, but once we got into it, some ideas came to me."

The problem with writing songs was a bit deeper than Willie let on. He was used to songs coming easily.

"It used to be that songs came to me all the time and it was just a matter of writing them down," he says. "I wrote a lot of songs, hundreds of songs, that way. But now sometimes one will come and I'll just write it down, and sometimes a situation will come up that will require me considering to write another song. The movie was a good example of that. I had to decide whether I was a songwriter or not ... whether I could write any more songs."

Not only did he prove that he could still write songs, Willie Nelson proved conclusively that he could still write *hits*. "On The Road Again," the song he'd quickly jotted down on the plane, became one of his biggest sellers. "Angel Flying Too Close To The Ground" also became a hit, as did the *Honeysuckle Rose* soundtrack album itself. Predictably, Willie made sure that some of his oldest and dearest friends shared the billing and the profits. The double album included songs by Hank Cochran, Johnny Gimble, band-member Jody Payne—and Kenneth Threadgill, the man in Austin who helped start the whole ball rolling.

Co-stars Amy Irving and Dyan Cannon had nothing but good words. He was nervous, Dyan Cannon said, but he covered it up well.

"You've got it rough, Willie Nelson," Amy Irving said. "For a guy who's just become an actor, you've got three movies in the works, and in between you just keep making records and winning awards and going on national tours. Shucks, be sure to write if you get work."

Predictably, the gossip mills quickly linked Willie and Amy Irving, which Willie, equally predictably, shrugged off.

"Amy Irving's a beautiful lady," he says. "It wasn't hard to imagine myself running away with her."

He was bitter about the pain those reports caused Connie. Amy and he were friends, he said, nothing more. Anything more was just something somebody made up.

The only discordant note in the filming came when Amy Irving inadvertently came between Willie and his fans. Late one night in a Texas restaurant, Willie was signing autographs. Irving, who had a very early call the next morning, tried to get Willie to leave. The legendary Nelson temper flared. First and foremost, before everything else, came his fans. They were there, he told her, before she was, and they'd be there when she was gone.

"Country people," Willie says, "have a certain hominess about them, and that's what they told me it takes to make a good actor—honesty."

"He is less insecure, less temperamental than most actors," Director Schatzberg reprises. "I'd tell him what to sing or do, and he'd sing or do it. He really wants to be good, so he listens, and he listens well."

Honeysuckle Rose became Willie's first hit movie.

After a small but critically well-received part in the movie *Thief*, Willie began work on *Barbarosa*.

Willie, Wittliff told *American Film* Magazine, had called him a few months after he'd begun working on *Honeysuckle Rose* and asked if the screenwriter had any other scripts lying around. Wittliff offered Willie his very first screenplay, a mythic Western about an aging gunslinger.

"Willie literally stuck his finger in the middle of the script, opened it, read two pages, closed it and said, 'I want to be that guy,'" Wittliff says. "Then Willie suggested we talk to Gary Busey for the other guy."

The film was directed by Australian Fred Schepisi, one of the finest talents in Australian filmmaking. What Willie, Wittliff and Schepisi were trying to do was redefine the American Western, the movies Willie loved so well growing up. The advantage of having an Australian director was that Schepisi could see beyond the cowboy and gunslinger stories into the kind of mythic quality Willie was looking for.

Although *Barbarosa* was not the huge box-office success that *Honeysuckle Rose* was, it was very much a critical success.

"The best western in a long while is *Barbarosa*, a film which uses one American legend, Willie Nelson, to create another," wrote Janet Maslin in *The New York Times*, "and Mr. Nelson has more than enough grace, grandeur and magnetism for the job."

Another critic claimed Willie Nelson had the "best face since Humphrey Bogart."

Film projects immediately began stacking up as Willie Nelson became a "bankable" star, a star the studios were certain could pack the theaters. He starred in a special CBS television presentation of "Coming Out Of The Ice," the story of two Americans imprisoned in Siberia. Journalists on the set in Finland reported there was no sign of Willie the musician. "There will be no 'Coming Out Of The Ice' polka," Willie quipped.

He then began work on another major project, a film with old friend Kris Kristofferson called *Songwriter*.

Although he stars in them, Willie doesn't seem to have time to go to the movies. His favorite stars are Bogart and Robinson and Raft, maybe Marlon Brando in *On The Waterfront*. No matter how successful he is, though, movies are not the road, and the road is what Willie Nelson is *still* all about.

"Mainly I'm going to play music," Willie says, "because that's what I really know how to do and what I enjoy doing more than anything else in the world . . . Movies are fun, but they're confining. You can't get up and go somewhere every day. You have to get up and stay somewhere every day, and that goes against my grain a little bit."

24

An Interview With
Willie Nelson

MB: We'd like to talk a bit about your budding movie career, Willie.

WN: Okay with me.

MB: You seem to be well on the way to becoming another movie sex symbol, *à la* Kris Kristofferson, that other country boy who made it big.

WN: Yeah, I guess so. In spite of everything I can do.

MB: What's it like, being an actor instead of a singer?

WN: Actually, not that much different. Instead of learning songs, you just learn what you're supposed to say for that particular scene. Which is usually not as long as the songs you've got to learn. It's really not hard; you've got plenty of time to learn everything. Most of the people who make movies are unhappy about sitting around all that time waiting for one shot, but it was really good for me, because it gave me plenty of time to see what was going on.

MB: How did you get involved with Redford and *Electric Horseman*?

WN: Redford and I were together in Nashville at Billy Sherrill's house. Redford was down there to try and get some guys to do some benefits for his Citizen's Action Committee—I think that's what he calls it. Charlie Daniels, Marty Robbins, Charlie Rich, Waylon, me—a bunch of people were there. That was the first time I'd met him. Anyway, we hit it off pretty good. We flew together out to California, and on the plane he asked me if I'd ever thought about getting into movies. I told him I thought I could probably do it. Several months later, he called me and told me he had this project that he thought I'd be interested in doing.

MB: I read somewhere that acting in movies was only the beginning for you; that you had some ideas about directing as well. Do you want to become the first country-and-Western John Ford?

WN: Oh, I'd like to learn everything there is to know about movies. I'm not sure I ever will—I haven't learned everything there is to know about the music business, even after all these years. But I am interested in all aspects of the movie business—

you know, even the cameras and stuff. I might be a cameraman one of these days.

MB: Was it some sort of movie deal you were discussing with Burt Reynolds last time you were in New York?

WN: Actually, it was nothing at all. We were just hanging out, you know. Of course, if Burt asks me to be in a movie with him, I'll say yes. And if he ever wants to come up onstage and sing with me again, I'll say yes to that, too. He came up and sang with us in Lake Tahoe or Vegas or somewhere, you know.

MB: Yeah, I saw the pictures in some gossip magazine. The caption was something like "A beery Reynolds joins Willie Nelson onstage . . ."

WN: We sang "Up Against The Wall, Redneck Mother" and "Luckenbach, Texas", I think.

MB: Seriously, your life does seem to have shifted gears since the old days in Austin. Now that you're hanging around with the likes of Reynolds and Redford, do you feel that's affected you at all, or are you still the same lovable Willie?

WN: Oh no, not him! No way! Not after spending an evening with Candice Bergen and Jane Fonda. There's no way to ever be the same again. I think it'd be a mistake to even go around telling people you were the same. They'd know you were lying!

MB: But you've always been such a populist—such a man of the people, if you will. Don't you feel different up there on that plateau?

WN: Well, to be perfectly honest with you, I really don't feel all that much different. I'm still hustling every day. Instead of paying $100-a-month bills, we're paying $1,000-a-month bills. The income has gone up, but the bills have gone right up with it. It really doesn't ... nothing's changed that much.

MB: Are you still trying to do two hundred and fifty nights a year on the road?

WN: I hope we do that many this year, but with the movies I don't know if we'll be able to or not.

MB: But why, Willie? You're obviously making all the money in the world (laughter), so why do you—or why does anybody, for that matter—want to spend eighty percent of your time on the road? You must love it an awful lot.

WN: Sure we do. We all do. Everybody does.

MB: But look at your contemporary and singing partner, Waylon Jennings. Each year he cuts the number of dates he does in half.

WN: I mean, everybody in my group—I wasn't talking about Waylon or anybody else. I just mean all of us. We all enjoy playing music, and so it's not really that hard work. It is hard when you're playing too many nights in a row and you're not getting paid enough, you know. I mean, you might like to take a few days off for a change of pace or to rest a little bit. Everybody likes to take a few days off now and then. But I think any more than a week, and you start to get . . . uh, restless. You want to go out and do it all again.

MB: Don't you think that you'll wake up one morning and just shout "Whoa!"?

WN: No, I don't think that. I've got lots of friends who are doing the same thing. Guys like Ernest Tubb, Faron Young, Jimmy Dickens—these guys are still going up and down the highway, still enjoying what they're doing, and as long as I enjoy it, I'll keep doing it. As long as I'm able.

MB: One of the most important things to happen in Nashville that eventually changed the whole music industry was the rise of the songwriter as an artistic force in his own right, as opposed to the conventional idea of the songwriter being some gnome on Tin Pan Alley. You were one of the first.

WN: Yes. Me and Mel Tillis, Wayne Walker, Roger Miller, Harlan Howard . . . Like you say, there were a lot of writers. The whole industry depended on the writers, and the writers finally realized that. They finally started banding together, or else

getting farther apart—one of the two—
where they couldn't be put in any kind
of mold or categorized. I think we all
ran from that in Nashville. We ran from
the labels. We didn't want to be included
in whatever the industry wanted us to
be included in.

MB: There was a whole lot of time spent
writing songs which the industry didn't
(and still doesn't, sometimes) think of as
"commercial."

WN: There was such a big argument over the
word "commercial." And it became, I
don't know, a word that was hated by
the writers. We hated to hear the word
"commercial," 'cause there was some guy
who didn't know anything at all about
songwriting and, we felt, didn't know a
fucking thing about the music business,
was standing up there telling us what
was "commercial!" They were trying to
tell us what the people wanted to hear,
when we had just come from the people.
We had just sailed into that town. We
knew what the people liked where we
came from, and maybe we didn't know
what people liked everywhere. But when
all of us got together, coming from
everywhere, we realized that people were
liking pretty much the same thing—good
songs—and they were having trouble
finding them. 'Cause the good songs were
being stopped—if they weren't "commercial," they never got out.

MB: That was the case across the board?

WN: Look, a good song had very little chance. If it had more than three chords in it, it wasn't commercial.

MB: Why is that, do you think?

WN: It's idiots, really. They say ignorance is no excuse, but it's got to be the only excuse. Ignorance has got to be the only excuse for anything like that to go on. The people simply do not know, and will not learn. And will never learn. And yet they're in a position to hurt a lot of people who are trying to make their way as whatever—a singer or a songwriter. And there's people there, at the top, who have lost contact—if they ever had contact—with the people and don't know what's going on.

MB: Lost contact with all the friends and neighbors?

WN: Really. I mean, they sit behind a desk for so long and answer the telephone, and pretty soon they become telephone salesmen. And they don't know anything at all about what's going on out there. "We've got something in this town," they say, "that we want to sell you out there." And the people out there say we don't want it; we want something else. "Well," they say, "you'll just buy what we send you." And people had to for a long time.

MB: How do you think the country-music audience has changed since those early days in Nashville?

WN: Well, a whole new audience has grown up. A new, more progressive audience—progressive thinking, liberalized thinking. Liberalized to the point where they don't believe everything that they're told. If someone sends out a record to them, just because it's a name artist on a name label, that doesn't mean that it's a good song. For a long time, disk jockeys' and radio stations' hands were tied—maybe they still are—where they had to play a major artist from a major label. A new guy had no chance at all because of the formats.

MB: There's two schools of thought about your move to Texas. One says that you were the right man arriving in the right place at the right time—blind-ass luck, if you will. The other is that you had it all scoped out, and you cannily decided to move back and take advantage of a budding music "scene." You have any thoughts on that point?

WN: Well, I felt I could no longer make any progress in Nashville. I felt like I had gone as far as I could go with my record label there. I had gone as far as I could go with the town. I was already established as a songwriter, and I didn't feel that I was ever going to be able to sell any records as an artist in the environment I was in. I'd been going down to Texas and living there off and on for years, so I knew what was going on. I knew that the Armadillo World Headquarters was rolling. I would work Big G's (an old country hangout), and then I'd go over and see what was going on at the Armadillo Club. I got up and picked at the Armadillo one time, and there was this brand-new audience! I discovered that there were young people who liked what I had been singing all my life to people my age or older! There was a whole new audience there, and I felt like Texas was where I could come and, if worse came to worse, I could still make a living singing around Texas and singing for the people I've been singing for all my life, except I'm singing for their children. Sing the same songs I've always sung, and sing them the same way I've always sung them.

MB: Waylon once told me that when you first invited him to Texas to play, you didn't bother to tell him that it was to a "bunch of hippies." He said he walked out onstage and was scared shitless!

WN: (Laughter) Well, it was singers discovering audiences and audiences discovering singers!

MB: It seems that there are two distinct kinds of songwriters. One is a craftsman, and he builds a song like someone would build a house, a brick at a time, and to be sure, they write some great songs. But the other—like Hank Williams, say—sort of plucks the song out of the air, like magic. You seem to be that kind of a songwriter.

WN: I think all my thoughts, or most of my thoughts, that are songs are surface thoughts. They're not anything that I've laid awake thinking about for years to write down on the paper. It's just . . . I write off the top of my head, whatever I'm thinking at the time. So, being a shallow thinker (laughter), I'm not going to be saying anything too heavy.

MB: If that's the case, Hank Williams was a shallow thinker, too.

WN: Right! I think simplicity is the secret to communications. You get too-big words, and then you've lost the third-grader, which I think we all are, mentally, until we die.

MB: Are you able to do that much writing anymore?

WN: I do as much . . . No. Let me say no, first. As much as I've been working, I haven't been able to get into the writing, so I've been blaming my work.

MB: Boy! Have I heard that one!

WN: Yeah, yeah. Whether that's true or not, I don't know. It seems like when I take off a few days, rest a while, I'll usually start back writing.

MB: Since some of your greatest songs—"Hello Walls," "Night Life," "Ain't It Funny

How Time Slips Away," "Crazy," a lot
of *The Red-Headed Stranger*—seem to
spring from the depths of your depression, could it be that you're too happy
to write songs? Are you waiting around
for depression?

WN: Well, uh, no. I'm waiting to have some
time to get my mind clear where I can
start thinking about what I was depressed
about before.

25

The Man Who
Beat The System

In light of his past accomplishments, it would probably be premature to say that Willie Nelson's career has reached its summit.

He is producing albums like they are going out of style—in fact, Willie suffered a collapsed lung in Hawaii in 1981. Doctor's orders were to stay off the road for a while. Willie followed his doctor's advice to the letter. He stayed off the road and began work on five—count 'em, five—albums.

The albums he's produced in the last few years have been an eclectic bunch, a mixed bag of the thousands of songs that Willie Nelson seems almost compelled to record.

In 1979 he recorded a wonderfully off-beat album with Leon Russell, *One For the Road*.

"We (Leon and I) spent about a week together out in California a while back," Willie says. "We did several songs—they're old standards; you'd know them all—everything from 'Riding

Down The Canyon' to 'Tenderly' to 'Heartbreak Hotel.' Leon and I did a hundred and three songs in one week. Leon would sit down at the piano and I'd sing, and we did eighteen songs in one night. It was kind of just flowing real good. We'd just go through the books and find a song we both knew, and then we'd cut it. Most of those cuts are just one take."

The scene must have been reminiscent of the first Atlantic sessions, with Willie and his hymnal in hand, cutting every gospel song he knew. *One For The Road* is one of Willie's most exuberant albums, a tribute to two of the most knowledgeable souls in popular music.

There followed a procession of "tribute" albums. After *One For The Road*, Willie cut an album of Kristofferson songs.

"Suddenly I had 'artistic control,' " Willie says. "So I had to come up with some album ideas. I started thinking of some of the easiest ones, and one of the easiest ones was songs I'd known for years and that I like to do. Kris Kristofferson's songs were easy; that's one of the reasons I did it. It didn't require a lot of teaching of the band or anything. We'd known those songs for years."

Willie the Bandleader remains a constant, as does the Family Band. The band now consists of Bobbie Nelson on piano, Paul English on drums, Bee Spears on bass, Jody Payne on guitar and Mickey Raphael on harmonica. More often than not, guitar great Grady Martin, one of the most important influences on Willie's early picking style, plays with the band. Master fiddler Johnny Gimble is another regular.

The albums continue in a steady procession—an album with Ray Price and Roger Miller, another collection of old favorites, an album with Merle Haggard, another album with Waylon Jennings. The *Take It To The Limit* album with Waylon marked a return of the famous duo to the charts, laying aside the long-running rumors that there was any bad blood between them. Typically, the two "outlaws" decided to record songs by the Eagles, Simon and Garfunkle and George Jones.

A second concept album, *Tougher Than Leather*, was the culmination of a project Willie had on the back burner for years, a Western legend built around the theme of reincarnation.

"It's (reincarnation) a positive way to look at life," says Willie, who has delved deeply into the teachings of Edgar Cayce and others. "Everything moves in one direction; you either go up or back; you're either progressing or regressing, one of the two. You never stay in one place. I don't believe anything ends, 'Pow!' and it's all over. That just doesn't make sense. You can't destroy matter; if you stop it here, it comes to life over there. You can't destroy energy."

Success rests easily on Willie Nelson's weathered shoulders. When he first returned to Nashville in 1975, *Country Music* Magazine ran an article titled, "The Man Who Beat The System." Willie Nelson beat a lot of systems, shattered a lot of myths and changed a lot of people's views about both country music and American heroes.

"To be perfectly honest with you," Willie Nelson says, "I don't feel that all much different. . . . Nothing's changed that much."

He has just about all the material things he might want for. When he's not on the road, he lives with Connie and their two kids, Paula, thirteen and Amy, ten, on his 122-acre spread north of Denver. He still owns the farm in Austin, which he left after it became a Mecca for country music fans around the world. His oldest daughter by first wife Martha, Lana Fowler, lives on the ranch with her husband and four kids. He also owns the Austin Opry House, a 1700-seat concert hall; the Pedernales Country Club, complete with golf course, clubhouse and Olympic-sized swimming pool, a few condominiums, an apartment building and a bar and restaurant, not to mention his own recording studio. His son Billy lives on the 200 acres in Ridgetop, Tennessee.

In Texas, Willie was barely able to step out of the house before he was swamped by friends, fans and well-wishers, and it just wasn't in Willie's heart to turn the people away. In fact, he was even unable to avoid giving his unlisted phone number away to anybody who asked. The solution to the first problem was to move to Colorado; the solution to the second was to have a phone number that changed every six weeks.

Willie Nelson is clearly one of the highest-paid performers in all of the entertainment field. He still tries to get in 200 nights a year, at up to a staggering $500,000 per show. A dozen of Willie's albums have gone gold, and six have gone platinum—one million sales. *Stardust* has sold two million copies, double platinum. Of course there are song royalties and the movies—at one point, it was reported that Willie's fee for acting in a movie was a cool one million dollars.

He bought a $1.7-million Learjet to help him get home more often.

"I still like riding on the bus," Willie told *Country Rhythms*. "It's just that this gives me a chance to rest a lot between shows, and I figure I can go a lot longer by doing it this way than I can by going up and down the highway in a bus."

He remains a fitness addict, even jogging with then-President Carter. Over the years, he's lost thirty pounds and is in much better shape than most of the people who come to his shows. The shows, by the way, are still four hours long.

"People respond basically to the same things," Willie Nelson says. "Once you find out what they respond to, then you can put on a pretty good show."

There's a certain satisfaction in knowing that dreams occasionally do come true. Willie Nelson has come a long way from the small boy in Abbott, Texas, leaning over the huge Philco radio, listening to the Grand Ole Opry and dreaming of being a honkytonk singer. It has been more than years and miles since a small red-haired boy sat in the darkened movie theater, dreaming of being a cowboy star.

So far, in fact, that you'd swear the life of Willie Nelson would make a damn good country song.

26

Ain't It Funny
(How Time Slips Away)

It is a very special premiere night at New York City's prestigious Bottom Line Club. Instead of the usual rock act, tonight's premiere performer is none other than Dolly Parton, the queen of country music. A few years before, such a premiere would have been unthinkable. But country music has taken the U.S. by storm, and the Bottom Line is packed to capacity.

The young journalist, not so young anymore, sits waiting for the show when a new crowd of celebrities is shown in.

"It's Willie," the packed crowd murmurs. "Willie's here."

A smiling Willie Nelson comes in and takes his seat with four of his guests.

Before the show starts, the journalist walks over to Willie's table. Willie introduces him around to his guests—Burt Reynolds, Carol Lynley, Candice Bergen. They nod greetings.

The young journalist and Willie talk for a

few minutes, about recording sessions and up-coming movies. Willie talks about one of his pet screen projects, *Songwriter,* starring close friend and fellow "outlaw" Kris Kristofferson, an epic of the bad old days of boozing and drugging and honkytonking that was the real life of country and Western musicians and song-smiths, not excluding Willie and Kris. The young journalist stands to leave, then bends down and whispers to Willie, "It's not like the good ole days, is it?"

Willie Nelson smiles his famous Willie Nelson smile. His hair is tied back in a bandana, and he is wearing jeans and sneakers.

"No," Willie says, "thank God, it isn't."

INDEX

BE SURE TO READ

LIVING PROOF
THE HANK WILLIAMS, JR., STORY

By Hank Williams, Jr.
with Michael Bane

"THE HANK WILLIAMS, JR. STORY
WILL GRIP YOUR HEART"
— George Vecsey
co-author of LORETTA LYNN: COAL MINER'S DAUGHTER

NOW A MAJOR NBC-TV MOVIE
STARRING RICHARD THOMAS

LivingProof

An Autobiography
HANK WILLIAMS, JR.
with Michael Bane

Standing in the shadow of his father, legendary Country and Western singer Hank Williams, young Hank, Jr., hit the top and then the bottom—booze, drugs and the wrong women—until the horrifying moment when he nearly died, and was reborn

Hank Williams, Jr., was three years old when Hank Williams, Sr., died of drugs and alcohol en route to a show. The public—and a star-struck widow—refused to let go of the legend who wrote and sang "Your Cheatin' Heart," "Hey, Good Lookin'," "Lovesick Blues" and many other Country and Western classics.

At age eight, Hank, Jr., carefully coached in his father's style and mannerisms, walked onto a stage and sang his father's songs. He was, his mother said, the "living proof" of his father's immortality.

LIVING PROOF is the powerful story of a gifted young man, trapped in a legend that became a hell on earth, as the demons that destroyed his father reached out for him. . . .

RAVES FOR
LIVING PROOF
The Hank Williams, Jr., Story

"LIVING PROOF appealed to me as a gutsy tale of physical and emotional survival. It has the combined qualities of a psychological whodunit and a roller coaster ride."   —Richard Thomas

"I was not expecting the kind of depth or honesty found in LIVING PROOF. Honest to Pete, I kept finding tears in my eyes . . ."
—John Lomax
Country Music Foundation

"More than any other country singer, Hank's life has been public property—ever since he was three years old and his Daddy died at 29 in the back seat of a Cadillac . . . Hank, Sr. was a hard act to follow, especially for his son . . . Spurred on by an aggressive mother, he lived on the road . . . He quickly learned how drugs and liquor and casual sex could ease the pain of living on the road, and by 16 or so he was a veteran, wise beyond his years . . . He was on a downhill slide in 1975 when he took a real downhill slide—500 feet down the side of a mountain in Montana . . . His face was destroyed, and it was months before his ordeal was over and he knew that he would survive as a normal human being . . . It's an intense, brutally frank look at country music and the price that's paid by those in the business, as told by a survivor."

—Smiley Anders
New Orleans Sunday Advocate

"Truth is stranger than publicity . . ."

—Chet Flippo
Rolling Stone

LIVING PROOF—A DELL/BRYANS BOOK ON SALE
WHEREVER FINE PAPERBACKS ARE SOLD—
OR USE THIS HANDY COUPON FOR ORDERING:

"Tell me what's going on," Tate demanded.

Stephanie didn't look at him. "Bittman wants something from me." She turned her face to his, and he saw for the first time the gleam of tears there. "He drove my brother off the road and took Dad."

"I'm sorry." For one crazy moment, he wanted to wrap her up in an embrace. "How does it fit together? What is Bittman after?"

"I can't tell you any more."

He folded his arms. "I want to know what's going on, and you're going to tell me."

Her eyes glittered. "I wasn't supposed to get anyone involved, or he'll kill my father."

"Too late. I'm involved."

Her eyes grew cold. "No you're not, Tate," she said as she pushed by him, leaving a tantalizing whiff of the cinnamon fragrance she always wore.

Why, he wondered, could he pass through his day without remembering so much as what he had for lunch—but he could recall every detail of Stephanie's face after seeing her for only a few moments in the past four years?

Books by Dana Mentink

Love Inspired Suspense

Killer Cargo
Flashover
Race to Rescue
Endless Night
Betrayal in the Badlands
Turbulence
Buried Truth
Escape from the Badlands
Lost Legacy
Dangerous Melody

*Treasure Seekers

DANA MENTINK

lives in California, where the weather is golden and the cheese is divine. Her family includes two girls (affectionately nicknamed Yogi and Boo Boo). Papa Bear works for the fire department; he met Dana doing a dinner theater production of *The Velveteen Rabbit*. Ironically, their parts were husband and wife.

Dana is a 2009 American Christian Fiction Writers Book of the Year finalist for romantic suspense and an award winner in the Pacific Northwest Writers Literary Contest. Her novel *Betrayal in the Badlands* won a 2010 *RT Book Reviews* Reviewers' Choice Award. She has enjoyed writing a mystery series for Barbour Books and more than ten novels to date for Harlequin's Love Inspired Suspense line.

She spent her college years competing in speech and debate tournaments all around the country. Besides writing, she busies herself teaching elementary school and reviewing books for her blog. Mostly, she loves to be home with her family, including a dog with social anxiety problems, a chubby box turtle and a quirky parakeet.

Dana loves to hear from her readers via her website at www.danamentink.com.

DANGEROUS MELODY

DANA MENTINK

Love Inspired

Recycling programs
for this product may
not exist in your area.

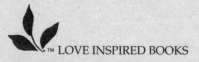

™ LOVE INSPIRED BOOKS

ISBN-13: 978-0-373-67534-0

DANGEROUS MELODY

www.LoveInspiredBooks.com

Printed in U.S.A.

Brothers and sisters, I do not consider myself yet to have taken hold of it. But one thing I do: Forgetting what is behind and straining toward what is ahead, I press on toward the goal to win the prize for which God has called me heavenward in Christ Jesus.

—*Philippians* 3:13–14

To my dear friend Patsy in Waxahachie.
You are an encouragement and a blessing to me.

ONE

The piercing ring of the phone made Stephanie Gage almost drop the box she was carrying. Her mind jumped to a horrible conclusion. Bittman had found her. Again. Now it would start all over, the phone calls, the flowers left on her doorstep, the feeling that she was being watched. Stephanie felt a flush of anger and shame. Her decision to work for Joshua Bittman had been disastrous. For her it was a job, for Bittman, the beginning of an obsession—and he'd stalked her steadily since she'd quit his employ two years before.

She tried to rein in the rampaging fear, to remember the courageous woman she used to be. How had he found her so quickly? Her new number was unlisted, her small Victorian, a quiet retreat from the hustle and bustle of the Mission district, quiet and anonymous—or so she'd thought.

She was about to snatch up the phone and let the fury fuel her words when she recognized her older brother Victor's number on the caller ID. Chagrined at her own paranoia, she answered.

"I'm in the car," Victor said. "Took the scenic route along Highway 1. The view is spectacular and no traffic. Guess what, sis?"

Stephanie heard only joy in his voice. It reverberated through her like the cool breeze of the San Francisco morning.

"Brooke and I set a date for the wedding," Victor told her. "And our hard-to-please dad has given his stamp of approval, now that he's finally met her."

"Not that it matters," her father chimed in. "No one listens to me anyway."

She laughed, pushing back her messy black hair. "I'm listening, finally." Though she could force a brave tone, the mental scars would never fade, even if the memories did, if and when the fear finally abated.

"I don't think you've given up your rebellious side yet, little lady," her father added.

Little lady. She'd just celebrated her twenty-sixth birthday.

"Did you call Luca?" Her other brother had been close to marrying a few times, but now he was immersed in their activities at Treasure Seekers, the private agency run by the three Gage siblings dedicated to finding treasures for select clients. Luca would be just as pleased that Victor was tying the knot with Brooke, a woman they'd met during their last treasure hunt, whose father Victor had wrongly believed was a criminal.

"I'll call him next. He's probably busy trying to find our next case," Victor said.

"Hard to top securing a twenty-million-dollar painting."

Victor chuckled. "He was blabbering about an emerald collection when I left for southern California."

She marveled at his voice, so light and joyful. Somehow knowing Victor's heart was mended made her own broken relationship easier to endure. Pushing the image of Tate out of her mind, she forced a happier tone. "I'm thrilled for you." She spoke louder, over the background noise, which seemed to have edged up a notch on his end.

He started to laugh but broke off suddenly. "Hang on. What is…?" The noise swelled into a screech of tires.

Fingers suddenly icy, Stephanie clutched the phone. "Victor?"

Her heart fractured, along with the sound of shattering glass. "Victor!" she screamed. "Dad. What's happening?"

A hideous scraping tore at her ears. She yelled something into the phone, incoherent syllables, fear and helplessness making her words shrill. Tinkling glass, the protest of distressed metal, a massive thunk and the sound of tires sliding over gravel.

She thought she heard her father cry out, and she squeezed the phone in a death grip.

"Answer me," she screamed, heart thundering against her ribs.

Then the noises faded into a soft crunch of gravel. Quieter, softer until there was no sound at all. No sound, except the violent hammering of her own heart. Her mouth would not form the words for a long moment. "Victor? Dad? Are you all right?"

Metal creaked, the sound of a door opening. Hope rose inside her. "Tell me you're all right," she whispered.

A voice came on the line. Cold, musical and chillingly familiar. "Stephanie, I have your father. There's something I need you to do for me. I will call you back in exactly four hours," Bittman said. "Mention me to anyone, and Wyatt Gage will die." The phone clicked off.

Her frantic call to the police revealed that a passing motorist had reported the wreck and a Lifeflight helicopter was transporting Victor to the nearest trauma center. Another call to her father's cell phone went unanswered. With numb fingers, she dialed Luca.

Joshua Bittman could not have her father.

Because if he did...

"Hey, sis. What's up?"

She pictured him, a bigger, blonder version of their dark-haired older brother, his green eyes sparkling with mischief.

What's up?

She knew Luca. She knew without question that if she told him the truth, he would summon the police and personally storm Bittman's Hillsborough mansion. But she also knew Joshua Bittman. He would not hesitate to kill Wyatt Gage and Luca in a heartbeat to get whatever it was that he wanted. "Victor was on the phone with me and he crashed," she said, stomach twisting. She gave him the details, leaving out any mention of their father being in the car.

Luca exhaled, voice tight with emotion. "Did you call Dad?"

There's no use, she wanted to shout. *Bittman has Dad.* The words stuck in her throat, but she finally choked out a reply. "No answer."

"My buddy's on duty today, he's a Lifeflight nurse. I'll call him on my way to the hospital and call you back."

He hung up, and she began to pace in frantic circles. The minutes slowed to a crawl as she tried to decide what to do that wouldn't make the situation worse. After what seemed like an eternity, Luca called again.

"My buddy said they admitted Victor and took him in for emergency surgery. He's...been badly hurt."

The words lanced through her. Brooke and Victor were supposed to be starting a new life together, and Brooke deserved it as much as Victor, having

seen her ailing father narrowly escape false im-
prisonment for a robbery. The Treasure Seekers
Agency had recovered all manner of rich prizes,
but their last adventure to locate Brooke's father's
missing painting was far more treacherous than
any they'd undertaken. Floods, tunnel collapses
and a murder seemed like distant memories now.

Victor was the backbone of the agency. She
flashed on a memory of him and their father, knee-
deep in piles of old books, hunting out references
to a priceless stamp. Terror about Victor's progno-
sis and her father's whereabouts made her hands
ice cold, her breath short.

She realized Luca was talking.

She jerked. "What?"

"I said I'll call Brooke and meet you at the hospital." He paused. "Keep it together, Steph. You're
strong. Remember that."

"We both know that's not true." She'd collapsed
when Tate Fuego had walked out of her life, de-
scending lower and lower until she found herself
fully entwined in Joshua Bittman's nightmare
world.

"Steph? Are you there?"

She heard the edge of a deeper concern written in Luca's voice, underneath the calm exterior.

Could it be that her father had been injured but
made it out of the car? Was he wandering around
the crash area in need of help? Her heart leaped.

Maybe Bittman was bluffing. Maybe he hadn't snatched him after all, and she was wrong.

The hope lasted less than a minute before it dried up and disappeared. The truth left a sour taste in her mouth.

Bittman did many things, but one thing he did not do was bluff.

He also did not threaten.

He punished. He was a billionaire many times over, and she'd suspected he'd paid officials to look the other way on his business dealings. Worse, she'd known people who'd crossed Bittman to simply disappear with no evidence on dirty Bittman's well-manicured hands—vanished as if they'd never existed.

She checked her watch. Three-and-a-half hours to go. As the little hand ticked away the seconds, something shifted inside Stephanie. The fear coursing through her body coalesced into another emotion, white-hot and razor sharp. She would not sit by while Bittman turned her life upside down again. She was done running, done hiding. He would pay for what he had done to Victor. He would deliver her father unharmed.

"I have to go somewhere," she said.

"Come again?"

She braced herself. "Go to the hospital. I'll call you when I can."

"Steph," he said. "You're in trouble. I can hear it in your voice. Whatever it is, let me help you."

Not this time, big brother.

A few minutes after two o'clock, Tate Fuego pulled his motorcycle to a stop in the shelter of massive trees lining the gate that circled Joshua Bittman's mansion. The building itself was a domed-top monstrosity of white stone, flanked by stretches of impeccably manicured lawns and a rectangular pond that reflected the building. A long driveway was empty except for a mint condition Mustang GT 350 and a black Mercedes.

Tate saw no sign of his sister Maria's car, though he knew she'd been a regular at Bittman's place. Her phone call three days prior scared him. Her normally upbeat personality was gone, and the woman on the line sounded irrational and unsteady, though she would not tell him why. Then nothing. No response to his texts, and no one answering the door at her apartment. He ground his teeth. She shouldn't have gotten involved with Bittman in the first place, and if he ever got a chance, he'd take Stephanie to task for introducing them.

The breeze teased ripples into the water of the pond, mirroring the discomfort in his own gut at the thought of Stephanie. Her dark eyes flashed in his memory, and he blinked away the pain. At the sound of an approaching engine, he rolled his bike farther back into the shadows. A van rumbled slowly by with *American Pool Company* printed on the exterior. When it pulled to a stop at the intercom, the driver, a stocky, crew-cut man with a face corrugated by wrinkles, leaned out to speak into the box.

"Pool service," he heard the driver bark, with a Spanish accent.

Tate grabbed the handle to the rear doors of the van and eased it down, wondering if he would be caught. In a moment he was safely inside. The guy parked the van and headed for the pool with a water test kit. Tate slipped out the back and ran for the nearest side entrance. In a place this ritzy, he knew interior security cameras would pick him up quickly, but he didn't need much time. One minute with Bittman, he thought grimly, was all he'd need.

He found himself in a gleaming kitchen, which was thankfully empty. The place was quiet, eerily so. Not one housekeeper in sight? No butlers or maids? Strangest of all, no burly security personnel barreling toward him.

His instincts prickled.

Muscles taut, he crept up the stairs and heard a murmur of voices. Heading swiftly along the hall, he came to a large window that looked down on an atrium. Trees that had to be at least twenty feet thrust upward toward the enormous skylights that bathed the space in pale sun. He was startled when a blue blur whizzed by his face. A parrot with feathers the color of the sky and intense yellow eyes peered at him from a branch. Below, through the screen of foliage, something else moved, this time of the two-legged variety.

Tate retraced his steps downstairs, skirting the lower floor hallway until he found the entrance to the atrium. The glass door was closed but not locked. Opening it as quietly as he could, Tate entered the warm, humid enclosure.

The parrot noises were varied and loud. Shrieks, raucous squawks and even some words rang through the space. An Elvis song, Maria's favorite.

Teeth gritted, he ducked between the spiked leaves and headed deeper into the bizarre tropical room. Branches crackled on his left, and he froze. Bird or Bittman, he could not tell. He passed a long metal pole with a mirror affixed to the end, leaning against the wall. Some sort of device so Bittman could check on his nesting birds? He turned to head back to the door when he felt a cold circle of metal pressed to his neck.

"Turn around," a voice growled.

A burly man, a head shorter than Tate, held a gun level with Tate's chest. He spoke into a radio. "I've got a guy in the aviary, and the girl is breaking down the door on the second floor."

Breaking down the door.

His brain filled in the rest. His sister. Kept here. That explained why she didn't return his calls, why she was no longer using her cell. The man was

pointing him toward the door, and Tate could see
the muscled arms under the suit coat.

He stepped back and raised a hand. "I don't want
trouble. I'll go."

After I find my sister.

He moved toward the door, Suit Guy a couple of paces behind him. Tate edged closer to the
glass wall until he was alongside the pole he'd seen
earlier.

"Get going," the man grumbled.

Tate did, as he grabbed the pole and swung it in a
wide circle, knocking the man to his knees. When
he completed the turn, Tate raced to the door. Pole
still in his hands, he cleared the doors and pushed
them closed, wedging the pole through the double handles. He made for the stairs at a dead run,
ignoring the pain shooting up his leg.

The pole wasn't strong, and the guy was burly.
He'd be through in a few good pushes.

Clearing the stairs, Tate charged toward the
sound of splintering wood.

Stephanie raised the upholstered chair again,
part of her brain noting that the legs of the nine-
teenth century Danish piece were starting to come
apart. She quickly scanned the richly appointed
sitting room. She knew Bittman must be watching
via the extensive network of security cameras. He
was playing some kind of sick game, allowing her
to walk in past all the security she knew he had in

place. The mansion itself made her nauseous, recalling how she had played into Bittman's schemes,
been tricked by his combination of massive intellect and complete indifference to anyone but himself. And her.

Shutting her mind to the memories, she turned
again to the locked door at the far side of the room
and pushed to see if she had weakened it. After a
thorough search of all the other rooms on the floor,
this was the last. It also housed the only door she'd
found locked, which meant there was something in
it she wasn't meant to see. It was now almost four
hours after the accident, and the mansion was the
likeliest place to have taken his prisoner. Only a
quarter of an hour remained until Bittman's promised contact.

Putting down the chair for a moment, she
slammed a palm against the wood door.

"Daddy?" she called. Ears straining, she heard
nothing. He could be gagged. Or worse.

She grabbed hold of the chair and raised it aloft,
knowing it could be a matter of moments before
Bittman or his lackeys stopped her.

Before she could smash it again into the locked
master bedroom door, someone caught her arm.
She shifted, turning to use the chair to strike at her
opponent, but whoever it was ducked and the blow
sailed over his head. Suddenly, she was pinned
face-first against the wall by a strong set of arms,

her cheek pressed against the wood. She struggled to free an elbow to bring it into her attacker's ribs when, just as abruptly, she was released. Knocked off balance, she readied a front-arm strike and whirled around, finding herself looking into the shocked face of Tate Fuego.

His hands dropped to his sides and he moved slightly back, as if he would turn away, but he didn't. Those eyes kept burning into her, taking in the scar on her cheekbone, churning her feelings into a tidal wave that threatened to overwhelm her. She kicked the ruined chair aside.

"What are you doing here?" Her voice sounded tremulous in her own ears, which infuriated her.

Tate didn't answer, instead turning around and shutting the double doors behind him, locking them and pulling a chair over to wedge against the wood. "Going to have company in a few minutes."

"What are you doing?" she demanded again.

He rounded on her. "Looking for Maria."

"I haven't seen her," Stephanie said.

Tate's broad shoulders tensed. "Why are you breaking down the door?"

"Because…" What should she tell him? She was searching Bittman's house? And what would be a reasonable explanation for that? She had to get Tate to leave. Bittman was clear that no one should know about her father, or there would be deadly consequences. "You've got to go, Tate."

He folded his arms. "Not until you've explained why you're bent on smashing down this door."

She sucked in a deep breath. "It's not your concern."

"There's a guy coming up the stairs in about another minute to throw me off the property. Bittman knows about my sister, and now I see you're involved with him somehow, so I'm making it my concern."

Stephanie's stomach tightened, and a sense of urgency nearly choked her. She moved to him, putting a hand on his solid chest. "Tate, please. You need to leave."

He gave her that slow smile, a shadow of the crooked, cocky grin from the time before everything had fallen apart between them. His hand touched hers gently. Then he moved off, sat in a high-backed leather chair and put up his booted feet on the pristine table. "I don't think so, Steph." He stretched his arms behind his neck, giving her that grin. "Fuego Demolitions is between contracts right now. I've got all the time in the world."

The outer door began to shudder as someone yanked the knob.

TWO

Stephanie felt a scream building as she ran to him and grabbed his wrist. His hands closed around hers, callused and strong. She knew it was going to be impossible to move him, but panic overrode her common sense. "Tate…"

A fist pounded on the door.

"Open up," shouted an unfamiliar voice.

She looked wildly at Tate.

He shrugged. "Bittman's security guy. I guess he made it out of the birdcage."

She had only moments. Tate or no Tate, she had to get to her father. Stephanie ran to the scarred door and screamed through it again. "Daddy," she yelled. "Answer me."

The words electrified Tate. He was on his feet and next to her in a second. "Your father's in there?"

"I'm not sure, but I've got to know."

He grabbed her arm. "Steph, what's going on?"

"Get out of my way." She shook him off and picked up the chair again.

He stopped her hand for the second time, pulling a pocketknife from his jeans. "Faster," he said, applying the blade to the hinge.

The pounding on the door was loud now, then it stopped abruptly. A crash of wood on wood made Stephanie jump. "He'll be through in a minute."

"Me, too," Tate said, popping loose the pin.

Stephanie saw the outer doors to the suite beginning to weaken under the assault of a foot or shoulder. With a crack, a booted foot came through a ragged gap.

Tate lifted the door free, and Stephanie tumbled in with Tate right behind her. There was a king-size master bed in disarray, sheets and blankets twisted. She ran into the adjoining bathroom, where she found a small basin and some bandages. Heart thundering, she returned to the bedroom to find Tate examining something.

He held up a pair of plastic restraints.

Her heart plummeted. The crack of wood in the outer room meant the security guy was nearly through.

She ran to the bed and felt the covers. "They're still warm."

His eyes locked on hers. "Got to be another way out."

Running into a sitting room that adjoined the master bedroom, they found it, a rear door partially ajar.

Stephanie didn't wait another moment; she

slammed through, Tate behind her. She heard him pull the door closed, but there was no way to lock it from the outside. Their pursuer would be right behind them.

She found herself running down a hallway that ended in a split stairwell. "Up or down?" she panted.

Tate pointed to a black scuff on the upper stair. "That way."

Both of them were breathing hard as they careened upward, finally coming to a door marked Roof.

"Wait," Tate called to her. "You don't know what's on the other side."

She didn't wait. She couldn't. Her father's life was on the line. She hurtled through and found herself on a flat rooftop, engulfed in a monstrous storm of noise. Wind whipped at her face and threw grit into her eyes.

She forced her head up anyway and saw a helicopter, rotors whirling.

The pilot in the cockpit gave her a startled look. In the back she could just make out a flash of silver hair—Wyatt Gage—and a familiar pale face beside him, an irritated Joshua Bittman.

The helicopter's engine whined, and it began to lift off.

"You can't take him!" she screamed over the roar. She took off running for the nearest landing skid.

"Steph!" Tate yelled. "No."

He made a grab for her, but she was too fast.

She increased speed and prepared to jump at the skid, which was now lifting off the ground.

Tate's fingers grazed her ankle and she lost her balance, rolling onto the cement roof, banging onto the hard surface, seeing in fleeting glances the helicopter well into the blue sky.

Getting to her feet, she ran to the edge of the roof, watching her father disappear. She whirled on Tate, tears streaming down her face. "You had no right."

"Would have gotten yourself killed," Tate said. His gray eyes were soft. "Your father wouldn't want you to risk it."

Fury, terror and grief rolled around inside, and she funneled them at Tate. "You shouldn't have done it!" she screamed. "You are not a part of my life anymore, Tate."

He flinched, but did not step back. "I know that."

She pressed her hand to her mouth to keep from shrieking, eyes drawn to her watch. Three fifty-nine. Thirty seconds until Bittman was supposed to have called. She'd blown it by coming here. She'd let her father down, let Victor down. She should have told Luca, let the cops know.

She struggled to breathe.

The door to the rooftop slammed open. The panting security guard stood there, gun drawn.

Tate raised his own hands and positioned him-

self in front of Stephanie. His face was hard, and
she knew he'd lost, too—lost the chance to find
his sister, if Bittman really was involved in her
disappearance.

The man with the gun drew closer and she
looked into the barrel, just as the phone in her
pocket rang.

Tate watched the guard as indecision crept across
his face.

"No phones," he barked. "Get inside."

Stephanie nodded obediently and started toward
the roof access.

Obedient? Stephanie? He tried and failed to recall a time when Stephanie genially obeyed a direc-
tive. Something was up, and he didn't have to wait
long to see what she had in mind. She stopped suddenly, sucking in a breath. Pressing a hand to her
side, she cried out, swaying until she went down
on one knee.

The guard let down his gun arm as he reflexively
moved toward her. Bingo. Tate dived, catching the
guy in the solar plexus, tossing him backward onto
the cement where he banged his head and blacked
out. The gun spiraled out of his hand, and Stephanie kicked it to the corner. She was on her feet
again in a moment, sprinting through the door and
down the stairs.

"Wait, Steph," he called, to no effect.

Tate took a moment to remove the man's belt

and use it to secure his hands behind him before he ran after her.

"What's the plan?"

"I'm going to the hospital, and then I'll find my father."

Tate saw the manic determination on her face. "The hospital? Tell me what's going on."

She didn't look at him, swiping her sheaf of dark hair behind her ears. "Bittman wants something from me." She turned her face to his, and he saw for the first time the gleam of tears there. "He drove Victor off the road and took Dad. We don't know if Victor's going to make it."

"I'm sorry." Her brothers, though they held nothing but animosity toward him, were her entire world. For one crazy moment, he wanted to wrap her up in an embrace. "How does it fit together? What is Bittman after?"

"I can't tell you any more."

He folded his arms. "We've been through this already so cut out the dramatics. I want to know what's going on, and you're going to tell me."

Her eyes glittered. "I wasn't supposed to get anyone involved or he'll kill my father."

"Too late. I'm involved."

Her eyes grew cold. "No, you're not, Tate." With that she pushed by him, leaving a tantalizing whiff of the cinnamon fragrance she always wore.

He followed behind her as she exited the mansion, got into the pristine Mustang and roared out of the driveway. When the dust settled, he made his way back to the motorcycle, still hidden in the trees.

Why, he wondered, could he pass through his day without remembering so much as what he had for lunch, but he could minutely recall Stephanie's face after seeing her, even only briefly, for the first time in four years? It was so unfair, especially when every detail—the full lips, the electric brown eyes, the determined set to her chin—reminded him of his greatest failure. Pain rippled through him again.

You are the worst thing that ever happened to Stephanie Gage.

He shook away the thoughts. He'd come to find Maria, and instead he'd fallen into Stephanie's life and that of the man he despised above all others, Joshua Bittman. They'd met enough times years before when Stephanie started consulting for him. Tate pegged him as an arrogant, condescending egomaniac with more than a casual interest in Stephanie. It might have been coincidence that, after a heated encounter with Bittman, whom he'd thought was trying to win Stephanie's affections, his business contacts had dried up. Fuego Demolition suddenly had regular clients canceling contracts without notice. He'd never been able to prove it was Bittman, but it gave him even more reason to find his sister and make sure Bittman hadn't done something to her.

He flipped open his cell and punched in Gilly's number. Gilly was an eccentric computer whiz he'd known since the sixth grade. "Need a favor. Can you find out which hospital Victor Gage was transported to? Car accident."

"What's going down?"

"I'll let you know as soon as I do."

Gilly provided him with the answer in moments.

Not involved, Stephanie said? He threw a leg over the seat of the motorcycle in spite of the ripple of pain. Not likely.

Kicking the engine to life, he roared off the property.

Stephanie was not aware of the miles unrolling under the tires of her car. Her mind worked and re-worked plan after plan as she hurtled toward the hospital. Each idea disintegrated into the anguished scream of her heart. *Daddy, Daddy.* She'd let Bittman take him. What had her father thought as he lifted off into the sky, looking down at the daughter who had failed to save him from a madman? Bile rose in her throat, and she fought the urge to floor the gas pedal, instead cutting around a driver in a van so closely that she could see his crew cut and the arch of his eyebrows. Tate had no right to interfere.

The call, the one at precisely four o'clock as she stared into the barrel of the security guard's gun, had been from Bittman. She phoned him back with no answer. She knew the unspoken message.

You didn't follow directions, Stephanie.
You told Tate Fuego.
Now your father will die.

Tate's interference might have cost her father his life. She fought to control the spiraling panic.

Focus, Steph. Figure out what to do.

Bringing in the cops would seal her father's fate. He would be found dead with not one shred of evidence linking Bittman to the crime, just a few phone calls. No menacing messages saved to voice mail. No incriminating texts. No one in his employ would dare testify that her father had been imprisoned at his mansion.

The picture of innocence.

And Victor might not live to identify the car that ran him off the road, or the person who removed Wyatt Gage from the car. As she parked and entered the hospital, heading for the elevator, she was a mass of indecision. She had no idea what she would say to Luca to explain her absence. As soon as the elevator doors opened, Luca shot to his feet from the waiting room chair.

She hurried to him. "How is he?"

"Stable, for the moment. Brooke's on a plane." He folded his arms. "Where have you been? And don't sugarcoat it."

"I'm going to see Victor, then we'll talk." Luca's thick brows drew together, but he didn't stop her. Victor's room was small. One tiny window looked into the San Francisco sky. He lay in the bed, dark hair shaved on one side and head swathed in bandages. Bruises darkened his face, and an IV snaked out from under the blanket.

Her eyes filled with tears. "Oh, Victor. I'm so sorry." Bittman was a plague set loose on the Gage family because of her. As soon as she'd accepted Bittman's offer of full-time work, he'd believed he owned her, and now her brother was paying for that horrendous decision. Her throat closed up, aching with grief. "I wish you could tell me what to do."

"About what?" Luca leaned against the doorway.

She kissed Victor on the forehead and followed Luca back out to the empty waiting area. Staring into her brother's troubled green eyes made her stomach clench into a tighter knot. "Luca…" She trailed off. Would telling him result in another accident? She couldn't risk it. "It's nothing. I'm going to do a computer search…to see who might have wanted to hurt Victor."

"I'm not buying it. Where have you been?"

"At Bittman's," came a voice from the far side of the room.

Stephanie's heart plummeted when Tate sauntered up.

Luca stiffened, hands balled into fists. "I should have known. Whatever trouble she's in concerns you."

"Not me. Bittman." Tate flicked a glance at her. "Tell him."

She glared back. "No, Tate."

"You don't have any choice, Steph," Tate said, eyes blazing. "You can't find him by yourself. Tell him, or I will."

Stephanie took a breath. Tate had backed her into a corner. Hands clenched, eyes on the floor, she told Luca everything. When she finally looked up, he was staring at her in disbelief. Then his eyes swiveled to Tate. "All right. This is family business, and we'll find a solution. Get out."

Tate shook his head. "Nope. My sister's disappeared, and Bittman has her or knows where she is. I'm staying until this plays out. Deal with it."

It happened in a flash. Luca had Tate by the shirt, and they went over in an angry pile of flying fists. Stephanie yelled and tried to grab Tate, but he wrenched away. Only a shout from an approaching police officer brought them to a standstill. The cop's name badge read Sergeant Rivers.

"What's going on here?" he demanded.

Luca and Tate got to their feet. Luca swiped at his forehead. "Sorry, officer. I lost my temper."

The officer looked from Luca to Tate. "That right?"

Tate nodded. "I egged him on. Wrong thing to do. Won't happen again."

He gave them another hard look before he turned to Luca. "I'm following up on our earlier conversation. I came by to tell you we've turned up nothing trying to ID the hit-and-run driver. How did you do coming up with any potential enemies?"

Stephanie caught Luca's eye. She sent him a pleading look and a shake of her head. Luca hesitated for an excruciating moment. "Nothing yet, but my sister's here now. We'll see if we can think of anything useful."

The officer's gaze flicked once more over the three of them. Then he nodded and excused himself to make a phone call.

Luca rounded on Tate. "Just so we're clear. You're no good for my sister, and you're not welcome here. You're involved only until we hand this over to the police or decide on a plan to get our father back."

"And my sister." Tate's lip curled. "You remember my sister, Maria, don't you Luca? You two have a history, don't forget."

Luca's face was a mask of rage. Stephanie stepped between them. "In light of the situation," she hissed, "can you two knock it off?" She felt the beginnings of an idea flash through her. "My files. I kept paper files when I worked for Bittman. Just odds and ends, bits that I found unusual in his business dealings. Maybe there's something in there that might give us a search direction."

She didn't want to go back to those dark days, the path she had taken that whisked her away from her family, from her faith. The twinges had been there when she first started doing some consulting for Bittman, a year before Tate's father was killed.

Tate hadn't wanted her anywhere near Bittman. Tate's words rang in her mind.

The way he looks at you...he wants you. You've got to quit working for him.

She'd brushed him off, chalked up his reaction to jealousy. Maybe she was even the tiniest bit flattered by it. In any case, her stubborn streak would have prevented her from giving up a job she enjoyed. The work intrigued her, challenged her, but she'd felt the odd sense every now and again that something was not right.

God had been talking to her even then, but she hadn't listened.

Luca nodded, eyes riveted to hers. "It's the last effort before we go to the cops, Steph."

She was already heading for the door. "I'm going home to look."

He shifted uneasily. "I don't want you going alone."

She smiled. "I'll be okay. You need to stay here until Brooke arrives."

Luca checked his watch. "She should be here in a few hours. Then I'll come. Let me call someone to go with you."

"I'll go." Tate's tone was casual, but Stephanie could hear steely determination underneath.

"No way." Luca took a step toward her.

Tate hooked his thumbs through his belt loops. "Doesn't matter what you want."

"She'd be safer alone." Luca's green eyes shone with anger.

Stephanie didn't want Tate around any more than her brother did. She also knew that every moment they wasted brought them closer to disaster. She went to Luca and hugged him. "I'll be okay."

He squeezed her. "Don't let him back into your life," he whispered in her ear. "He's trouble."

Trouble. Truer words were never spoken. She kissed his cheek and headed for the door, trouble following right along behind her.

THREE

Tate parked the motorcycle on the curb outside Stephanie's Victorian. She was already headed inside, the afternoon sun casting long September shadows over the neat yard, catching the gloss in her dark hair. The idiocy of his own actions came sharply home.

At worst, Stephanie despised him—and with good reason. He was, after all, a former drug addict who pushed her away, ignored her repeated attempts to get him help, and nearly ran her down while trapped in a cloud of painkillers. As for Luca, he'd just as soon take Tate apart one piece at a time. Not surprising. The Gages were tight and, in times of crises, impenetrable in their solidarity. They'd been just that way when he had descended into addiction. Guilt flared anew, along with the pain in his leg.

The Fuego family was an altogether different bunch, he thought with bitterness. They scraped for every opportunity, earned their living through hard work. Truth was, he'd been lost in a narcotic haze when his sister needed him the most, when she moved in with Bittman, six months after Stephanie quit working for him. Tate had been too addicted to painkillers prescribed after his leg was ruined in the accident that killed his father to do anything about it. Again the guilt stirred inside, but he fought it down.

His life had turned out scarily similar to his work as a demolitions expert. All the meticulous planning, endless mental rehearsal and the best of intentions was supposed to ensure that a condemned building would fall neatly, right on its footprint, with no overspray of deadly flying debris or partial failures that left structures tilting dangerously, still primed to explode. His relationship with Stephanie had turned out to be more like the time he'd witnessed the deadly power of a shock wave, a wave of energy and sound released when Fuego Demolitions took down a building. The massive wave traveled upward as was intended, before hitting a heavy cloud cover that forced the energy outward, exploding windows in the neighboring buildings. He could still hear the sounds of that shattering glass with the same perfect clarity that he recalled the end of his life with Stephanie.

He hesitated, trying again to steady his nerves. "Time to show some Fuego solidarity and do what you have to do to find Maria," he muttered to himself. It would be difficult because it meant sticking close to the most amazing woman he had ever known, a woman he could never have again, due to his own personal destruction.

Forget about your past with Stephanie. Find Maria. That's all you've got left.

He marched resolutely to the door and let himself into a small kitchen, painted in soft yellow tones. In the next room he could see boxes stacked in neat piles. "Nice place. Just moved in?"

"Couple days ago. I haven't made the time to unpack." She busied herself preparing coffee and pulling a plate of cheese from the refrigerator, along with a box of crackers, before she opened a can of cat food and put it on the floor. "Tootsie never misses a meal. She's like clockwork."

He watched her put the cheese and crackers on the table.

"There's bottled water in the fridge."

"You don't have to feed me, Steph."

She adjusted the crackers in the bowl, removing three broken ones and tossing them in the trash. "It's going to take hours to go through the files. You'll be on your own."

"Is this your way of keeping me out of your hair?"

She looked at him then, eyes like melted chocolate. Suddenly she was the sixteen-year-old girl he'd met while running the track in high school, eyes sparkling as she challenged him to a race. His stomach jumped. For a moment he thought she would say something, but her expression changed and she headed for the front room. "My files are in here."

He sighed. Stay in the kitchen and be quiet, was the unspoken command. She ought to know that *idle* wasn't his natural state. The kitchen window framed a view of the street, quiet and empty except for a few parked cars, two Prius and another one. He leaned forward. The other was parked a good block away, a streamlined black Mercedes. Something about it struck a familiar chord.

As he turned it over in his mind, another thought occurred to him. "Steph?" He poked his head into the front room. "Where's the cat?"

"What?" she said, blinking at him, a file folder in her hands.

"The cat. You said she was like clockwork about her food." He gestured to the kitchen. "Hasn't been touched."

Stephanie's brow furrowed. "I'll bet she's stuck in the upstairs bedroom again. The door swings shut and she gets locked in."

"I'll check." He eyeballed the front door before he left and made sure it was locked. Probably nothing but his paranoia in action, but he doubled back and locked the kitchen door, too, before he made his way quietly across the hardwood floor and up the creaking stairs, which emptied out onto the long hallway, with three doorways. Two were open, the one on the far end, which Tate surmised was the extra bedroom, was closed. He walked slowly, scanning the two open rooms: a bathroom and another small room filled with more boxes. One more door beckoned. He approached slowly, put an ear to the wood and listened. No sound.

He felt slightly ridiculous prowling the property, but if Stephanie was right, Bittman had nearly killed Victor and taken her father. He wanted something from Stephanie, and he would no doubt do anything to get it. Tate told her flat-out when she started working for him that something wasn't right, but she'd laughed it off, accused him of being the jealous type.

Not jealous, just perceptive. Bittman was crazy, and she should have trusted Tate. He felt a flash of anger followed by another surge of guilt. Who was he to blame her for not trusting him? He'd proven later that he was not a man she could count on.

Tate put a hand on the knob and turned it, inch by inch, until the door released. Pushing it open, he scanned the inside. A small bed, neatly made. Another door leading to what must be a bathroom, and one more, a paneled closet. He started with the closet, rolling it open slowly. Empty, not so much as a forgotten coat. The stack of three boxes nearby indicated she'd not yet gotten around to the spare room. This was odd for Stephanie, who was manically organized, a woman who arranged her books on the shelves according to size and color. It was not like her to leave anything half done, even after only a few days in her new space.

A soft thump came from the bathroom. He froze, listening. Another thump and a soft scuffling noise. The cat? Maybe. Maybe not. He crept closer to the door, which was pulled mostly closed. Since he hadn't turned on the light, the room was dim. Easing along one footstep at a time, he hoped the squeak of the worn floorboards under his feet would not give him away.

Drawing close enough to see through, he caught the flutter of movement. He did a slow count to three and threw open the door. It crashed into the wall behind as he leaped through. A pigeon with iridescent feathers around its neck fluffed in alarm from its perch on the rim of the old-fashioned bath tub. With an irritated flap of feathers, it flew back to the window and scuttled through the gap.

He watched the pigeon disappear through the open window.

It took only a moment for him to notice the scuff mark on the sill, a black heel mark that could only have come from a man's shoe.

Stephanie shoved the papers into the folder in disgust. What did she hope to find? How could she win against Joshua Bittman when he held the ultimate card? Her father's life. She tried to take a calming breath and offer up a prayer, but her mind was too scattered. She had to figure out a way, without Tate's help. His lazy smile replayed itself in her memory. His sister was so like him, though neither one would admit to it, except for one important difference. Maria led with her emotions, her passions and disappointments written on her face for all the world to see.

Bittman saw that need in Maria and exploited it, no doubt, after Stephanie quit his employ and tried to remove him from her life. Futile effort. Everywhere she went, he kept tabs on her, reminding her in the subtlest ways that he remained in her life in spite of her feelings. Phone calls, texts, jewelry delivered to her various apartments, even the smell of his peculiar cologne wafting through her car told her he was close, so close, with unrestricted access to her.

And now, it seemed, to her family and Tate's. Stephanie closed her eyes, thinking once again that the blame for Maria's relationship with Bittman lay squarely at Stephanie's feet. She did not believe, however, that Bittman had disposed of Maria in some violent manner. He didn't need to. With his wealth and enormous power, he could cut her out like a diseased patch of flesh. She would never get close to him unless he desired it. So Tate was wrong about the fact that Bittman made her disappear. If he would listen to reason, she could explain it to him.

Getting to her feet, she heard a soft meow from

the room earmarked for a guest room if she ever managed to put down roots.

She pushed open the door, calling up the stairs as she did so. "I found her, Tate."

There was an answering shout from upstairs, but she did not respond, her attention riveted by the man sitting ramrod straight in her grandmother's old rocking chair.

"Hello, Stephanie," Bittman said, stroking the cat curled in his lap. "You look breathtaking."

The folder slipped from her fingers, papers floating to the floor around her feet. She wanted to scream, to yell to Tate, but nothing would come out of her mouth. Bittman eased the cat from his lap and brushed at a few hairs left on his pants. His face was smooth and unlined, approaching his mid-thirties. Long, dark hair combed away from his high forehead accentuated the pale skin, brown eyes glinting through small angled glasses.

He gestured to the bed. "Please, sit down. I imagine your oaf of a boyfriend will be here in a moment."

He's not my boyfriend, she wanted to whisper. Instead she took a deep breath, fighting down the fear that clawed at her throat, anger rising along with it. "I don't know what kind of sick game you're playing, but I want my father back right now."

Bittman chuckled, his glasses glinting in the dying sunlight. "Impatient as ever. I will hold off until Mr. Fuego makes it down the stairs."

They didn't wait more than a few seconds before Tate crashed through the door. His eyes sought
hers, simmering with a mixture of anger and something else. "You okay?" he asked softly, pulling a
phone from his pocket.

She nodded.

Bittman sighed. "Mr. Fuego, put away the phone.
You will not be calling the police or anyone else.
Stephanie doesn't want you to do that."

His lips quirked into a smile. As much as she
wanted Tate to call the police, to have the supreme
satisfaction of watching Joshua Bittman go through
the demeaning process of being handcuffed on his
way to jail, she knew the cost was too high.

"Put it away, Tate. I have to know what he wants
from us."

"Where's my sister?" Tate demanded.

"I imagine this is why you intruded on my property."

"Where's Maria?"

Bittman's delicate eyebrows arched a fraction.
"Mr. Fuego, you bore me. Running all over town
like some Keystone Cop is not becoming. Stick
with your current job. Blowing up buildings is
more suited to your intellect."

Tate took a step forward. "Tell me."

Bittman gave him a cold stare. "Why would I tell
you anything? You are, in the common vernacu-
lar, a loser. Addicted to painkillers, barely able to
keep your father's business out of the red and, if

my information is complete, the very same man who almost killed Stephanie, a woman who is far too good for you."

Stephanie's heart twisted, and she grabbed Tate's wrist before he could go after Bittman. "Just tell us what you want."

Bittman nodded. "Nothing from Mr. Fuego. His presence is strictly an annoyance, and I believe he went so far as to upset my birds, for which a price must be paid at some future date. They are blue mutation, yellow-naped Amazons—very rare, you understand." He gestured to the other wooden chair. "Please, sit down, Stephanie."

Stephanie remained standing, Tate next to her. "Where's my father?"

"Right to the point. No catching up?" His eyes swept over her body, making her face flush.

Tate grunted. "Get on with it."

Bittman ignored Tate. "Your father is fine for the moment, housed at a location which you will never find on your own until we conclude a business transaction. I need you to locate something for me, and once you do, he will be returned to you in mint condition. Simple as that."

Stephanie tried to read the feelings in his eyes, but failed. There was never any emotion to take note of, not in all the years she had known him. Only when he spoke of his own father did she see a spark. "What is it? This thing you need me to find?"

Bittman folded his arms and looked out the window, scrutinizing the view. "A violin."

"A violin?" Tate snapped. "You're loaded. Go buy your own."

Bittman kept his eyes on Stephanie. "This particular instrument was my father's. It was made in 1741. It is unique, virtually a living thing and it is worth, to put a crude price tag on it…"

"Eighteen million dollars," Stephanie said with a groan. "It's one of only a few made by an Italian craftsman named Guarneri del Gesu."

"How do you know that?" Tate asked.

"Because it was reportedly destroyed in a fire at Bittman's father's shop." Her stomach tightened. "I read about it."

Bittman's eyes flickered. "That information is incorrect. The Guarneri was not burned, and I have recently acquired proof that it has surfaced right here in California. Someone has finally shown their hand by approaching a music store owner for repairs." His smile was terrifying. "I want my family's violin back. The person who possesses it can identify the arsonist who burned down my father's shop and killed my brother. I will be able to deliver the proper punishment, finally, after all these years."

Stephanie shivered. "There are plenty of other investigators and treasure hunters out there."

"I hired someone to gather information." His

tone hardened. "Until that someone decided to go after my Guarneri herself."

Tate sucked in a breath. "My sister?"

Bittman glared. "Yes. It seems rotten apples are common on your family tree."

"Why would she want your violin? What did you do to her?"

"Nothing at all. I suspect the eighteen million dollars was motive enough."

Stephanie felt a sliver of fear for Maria. "Has she found it?"

"I am not certain. She took my research, a small matter as I have it electronically archived, of course. I'll get it back, and she will pay." The words had barely left Bittman's lips when Tate was on him, hands wrapped around his throat.

"You're not going to touch my sister," Tate barked.

Stephanie pulled Tate away, using all her strength to pry at his arms, which felt like steel bands under her fingers. "Let him go. You're not helping Maria." She had to keep Bittman talking long enough to find out how to rescue her father and now, it seemed, Maria, before Bittman got to her.

Bittman stood, adjusting his clothing. "I want you to locate my violin and the person in possession of it before Maria does. She might scare him off, and that would make me very angry, which, I am told, is a frightening prospect."

Tate's breath came in short bursts, and Stephanie

worried for a moment that he would try to throttle Bittman again. She spoke quickly. "You could hire an investigator, a professional."

"But I want you, Stephanie. You have the Treasure Seekers' resources behind you and now, since your father's life hangs in the balance, you have the ultimate motivation to complete the mission for me."

Tate moved closer, and she felt his hand come to rest on the small of her back. It was the only thing that kept her mind from spinning completely out of control. For a moment, she thought Bittman was going to touch her, and she wondered how she would stand it. Tate tensed next to her, hand curled into a fist.

Bittman leaned close. "It is time for Treasure Seekers to go after the ultimate prize. Find it, and we will have everything we desire."

We? She pulled back slightly, her back pushed into Tate's chest. His fingers pressed her waist.

I'm here. He's not going to hurt you, the pressure seemed to say.

"And if I can't find the violin?" she whispered.

Bittman laughed softly before he whispered, "'I looked, and behold a pale horse…'" He gave her a smile that from anyone else would have been warm and filled with humor, but from him, held another meaning entirely. Icy trickles snaked up her spine in spite of Tate's reassuring touch and the fact that he moved her away from Bittman, inserting his own body between them.

Without a backward glance, Bittman was gone.

The room felt as if it was filled with tainted air, poisoned with a rank chemical that remained there even after Bittman's departure. She stumbled out of the room and back into the cheerful kitchen, which now brought no comfort.

Tate was speaking, but he had to repeat the question twice before it penetrated her haze of fear. "What's the business about the horse, Steph?"

She forced out the words. "We went riding a few times, back before I realized... He owns a stable full of the most beautiful horses you could imagine. So many to choose from, but he only rode one, a big stallion, completely white. The horse wasn't a good trail rider, too wild and headstrong. I asked him why he always chose that particular horse." She raised her eyes to Tate's. "He said he liked the imagery."

"Imagery?"

She swallowed hard. "It's from Revelation. 'I looked and behold a pale horse: and his name that sat on him...was Death.'"

FOUR

Stephanie sat next to Luca on the flight to southern California. A few hours before, Victor's fiancée, Brooke, had arrived from San Diego to stay with Victor, who was showing signs of improvement. Stephanie offered up another prayer of thanks.

Luca did not want to leave their brother any more than she did, which added to the concern written on his face. They'd both thrown some necessities in a bag and she'd arranged for a neighbor to feed Tootsie before they were off to the airport. Luca was not one to rush anything, which she suspected added to his stress.

At least Tate was not with them to add fuel to Luca's ire. He'd stayed with her at her house, combing through the research that Bittman emailed just after he'd left, until Luca arrived sometime in the wee hours.

"Tate's not with Treasure Seekers. It's better that he stays out of our way," Luca growled.

"He's not going to. He thinks Bittman's going to hurt Maria, or she's going to do something dumb trying to get her hands on that violin. Either way he's going to stick with it until he knows for sure. He's meeting us at the airport in Bakersfield. From there we go to Devlin's shop. The one who contacted Bittman about the Guarneri."

Luca shook his head. "Tate will be a problem."

She allowed herself a smile, in spite of her weariness. "Dollars to donuts that's exactly what he's saying about you."

Luca did not return the smile. "Steph, he's bad news. Guy's a pill popper and a hothead."

Stephanie looked away for a moment. "I think he's clean now."

"You think?" Luca took her hand. "He almost got you killed. Plus, if he hadn't shut you out, treated you like dirt, you never would have taken such a tailspin and started working full time for Bittman."

She pulled away her hand. "Let's be clear. I joined Bittman of my own free will, tailspin or not. What's happening to Dad now, to Victor—" She blinked back a sudden onslaught of tears. "It's my fault, not Tate's."

He took her hand again, his expression softer. "No blame games here. I'm sorry. I get overprotective."

"You don't say."

He squeezed her fingers. "Just don't let Tate back into your life."

"Don't worry, I won't." *Once was more than enough.*

He relaxed. "Run me through it again, sis. Bittman's father owned a music store and he inherited the Guarneri from a deceased uncle some twenty years ago. The violin has some special name, doesn't it?"

"The Quinto Guarneri." She nodded, glad to be in problem-solving mode. "It was given that name by the virtuoso violinist who once played it. There was a fire and the Quinto was presumed destroyed, though Bittman claimed someone set the fire. He further claims a second person was in the shop, a homeless man Hans Bittman allowed to stay there. Bittman believes while he was trying to get his father, Hans, out, the homeless man made off with the Guarneri before the store burned to the ground, but the cops could not substantiate any of it. Bittman's older brother, Peter, was killed in the fire. He was mentally disabled; Bittman believes he hid under the bed until the smoke was too much for him. Hans Bittman went out of business and died shortly thereafter of a stroke."

Luca's eyes narrowed. "So Bittman thinks this violin that surfaced is the one stolen from his father and the guy who has it…"

She nodded. "Is the one who took it from the shop. He's also the guy who saw the arsonist and…" She trailed off.

"And what?"

"And it's the only time I ever saw him show emotion, the few moments when he spoke of his father or brother. Whatever happened that night changed him forever." She chewed a fingernail. "Bittman went to a lot of trouble to involve us."

Luca's eyes roved her face. "I think he's got ulterior motives. He wants you, Steph, that's clear. He's never gotten over the fact that you quit working for him."

Her cheeks flamed. "He had to know I would, after I found out that he used me to break into that security system." He'd directed her to steal a car, a Bugatti Veyron, supposedly to test out the anti-theft system he'd installed. She'd stolen it all right, only it wasn't Bittman's car; it belonged to a man named Brown. The Gage family immediately rallied around Stephanie and appealed to Brown not to press charges. Brown was not swayed until suddenly, he dropped the charges with no explanation and sold the car to Bittman a week later. Stephanie had the suspicion Bittman had applied some excruciating pressure of his own. She also believed Bittman thought that by involving her in illegal dealings, he could blackmail her into staying with him. Blackmail was one of his specialties.

"You were more to him than an employee."

"Well, it wasn't mutual," she snapped. It was fun at first, consulting for a man with a genius intellect, and then after Tate broke her heart, she desperately needed a distraction. Treasure Seekers was in its infancy with not enough projects to keep her busy, so she'd accepted Bittman's job offer to be his security consultant and design software protection systems. In all her time with Bittman, never did she feel any stirrings of love for the man. Bittman did not seem capable of love even if she had been interested, any more than a mountain cares for the clouds that surround it.

The flow of memories was interrupted by Luca's next question.

"Can you get a look at the police report?"

She shrugged. "I don't know. The local police department there was flooded about fifteen years back, so a lot of the records were destroyed."

His eyebrow arched. "But you're still working on it anyway, aren't you?"

"What makes you think so?"

He laughed. "It's like waving a steak in front of a hungry Doberman. You've got to know. It's what makes you a great Treasure Seeker."

She wanted to return the chuckle, but darker thoughts prevented her from doing so. *If I don't find this treasure, we might never see Dad again.*

The plane descended through an oppressive gray sky.

She wasn't surprised to find Tate waiting at the airport, sporting a neat T-shirt, a softly worn pair of Levi's and a baseball cap. He nodded at her and ignored Luca as they headed to the rental car counter.

"How's your brother?" Tate murmured into her ear, sending tingles dancing along her ribs.

"Stable for now. Did you fly?"

He shook his head. "Drove my friend's truck."

She started. "You didn't leave my place until almost one. You must have been driving all night."

He shrugged. "Don't sleep much anyway. Called my friend Gilly. He's gone to Maria's place. Checking her computer."

"Hacking into it?" Luca said.

Tate shot him a glance. "You worried about Maria's feelings? You didn't worry about those before."

Luca jerked to a stop and faced Tate. "I didn't touch your sister. Get that into your fat head."

"You saying she's a liar?" Both men topped six feet, and now they were nose to nose, anger simmering between them.

"Stop it," she hissed. "We have to work together."

"Doesn't mean I have to like it," Tate said.

Luca snorted. "Don't worry, none of us like it, so you're in good company."

Stephanie was relieved when Tate sat down to wait while Luca rented a car. She caught sight of a vending machine at the end of a quiet corner of the terminal. Stomach growling, she realized she could not recall the last time she'd eaten. Not wanting to take time to order from the café, she headed for the lone vending machine.

Away from the terminal noise, she shouldered

her laptop strap and fished in her purse for loose bills, all the while wondering how she would keep Luca and Tate from killing each other long enough to find Maria or the violin. Her father would have told them both in that genteel way, "Cool heads, gentlemen." Thinking about him brought a lump to her throat. Had he been injured in the crash? Or worse? She only had Bittman's word that her father was unhurt. There had been bandages in the room where he had been held.

God, please, she whispered. *Please keep him safe until I find him.*

She felt off balance, useless, unable to locate her father and not there for her ailing brother. On impulse, she pulled out her phone and dialed, surprised when Brooke answered.

For a moment she could hardly imagine what to say to this sweet woman who loved her brother so deeply. "It's Steph. I'm so sorry, Brooke."

"It's not your fault. Luca told me a little about what's going on, and you have to know this didn't happen because of you."

The words were kind, but they did not change the truth. "How is he?"

Brooke sighed. "Still unconscious, but the doctors are easing off the sedatives so if all goes well he should be coming around."

If all goes well...

"I'm glad you're there with him."

Brooke must have heard the unspoken feeling in

her voice. "We both know you would be here, too, if you could. Just do what you have to do and stay safe. I'll stay right here with Victor, I promise."

Stephanie said goodbye and disconnected. What would happen when Victor did wake up? Would he remember the accident? Even more frightening, what if he was not himself anymore? What if he was damaged by the violence of the crash? The serious, steadfast brother whom she had relied on her entire life.

It was too much to worry about. Stepping around a man reading a newspaper, hat brim pulled down over his eyes, she continued to the machine.

Finally grasping some bills from inside her purse, she fed them into the slot. As her finger moved toward the button, the hair on the back of her neck stirred. Her subconscious knew someone was there before her ears detected the soft noise directly behind her. Before she could spin around, she was sandwiched against the machine by a man's heavy bulk, the breath forced out of her along with a cry. As she rallied to push him off, he jerked the laptop from her shoulder and ran down the darkened corridor.

She ran after him. He was strong and had the element of surprise, but she was fast and as determined as a lioness.

In a minute she'd caught up with him, his arms pumping as he headed toward the main terminal where she would lose him for sure. There was only one choice. With a surge of adrenaline, she leaped.

Tate was out of his chair as soon as he heard Stephanie's cry of surprise. He sprinted to the dim hallway in time to see a figure emerging with Stephanie's laptop under his arm. A moment later, Stephanie hurtled forward, catching the man by the ankles. They both fell, the man's hat flying through the air, along with the laptop. Tate ran to grab the man, but the assailant shook Stephanie loose with a vicious kick and leaped to his feet, running out the nearest exit door, grabbing his hat on the way.

Tate was paralyzed for a moment, wondering whether to pursue the laptop snatcher or help Stephanie. He decided on the latter. She was in a sitting position, blood oozing from the corner of her mouth, hair disheveled and cheeks pink with exertion.

He knelt next to her and a startled Luca joined them, along with an airport security officer who grilled them immediately.

"He tried to take my laptop," Stephanie puffed.

The security man answered a call from his radio. "No sign of the snatcher, but we'll keep looking." He gave her a quizzical stare. "I've been working here since the new terminal opened six years ago, and this has never happened before. Are you sure you don't know who that was?"

Stephanie shrugged. "He was wearing a hat."

"Uh-huh. Police will be here in a moment for your statement."

Tate and Luca helped her to a chair, and her brother gave her a tissue to apply to her lip. Another airport employee offered her medical attention, which she declined except for an ice pack.

"Are you sure you're okay?" Luca said.

She nodded. "Fine, just a bloody lip."

Tate shook his head. "You didn't think it would be nuts to try and tackle the guy?"

Her eyes opened wide in exasperation. "He tried to *steal* my *computer*."

Tate's stomach tightened as he looked at her, brown eyes glinting, outrage painted across her delicate features. Small woman, with courage as big as any man he'd ever met. He didn't love her anymore; there was too much anger and hurt between them to ever allow those feelings to take hold again. Still, he wondered why his heart beat unsteadily as he drank her in.

Luca sighed. "It won't do any good to tell her it was a dumb thing to do."

"Wasn't going to try."

Luca and Tate exchanged a look, probably their first that wasn't a hostile stare down.

"I'll go finish with the rental car then." Luca looked at Stephanie. "Can you just sit there until I get back?"

"I'll try," Stephanie said.

Tate reached over and picked a sliver of paper

from her hair, smoothing the dark silky strands into place. Soft and fine, just like he remembered.

She pulled back and finger combed her hair into some semblance of order. "I'm sure I look ridiculous after rolling around the airport floor."

"Nope. Same as always. Raindrops on roses." As the words left his mouth, his face flushed hot. Had he really said that? His mother always maintained that the most beautiful thing she could think of was raindrops on roses, and when he and Stephanie were together, it was his favorite way to tell her in his clumsy fashion how gorgeous she was. Gorgeous, perfect, different…and not his anymore. They were strangers, now and forever. He felt her eyes searching his face as he turned away, awkward as a teen boy.

He moved aside, pretending to look over the crowd, but inside blood pounded an erratic rhythm in his veins. *Go, do something, anything.* He pulled out his phone to check for messages he knew weren't there, then he strolled to the drinking fountain and sucked down some water. When he looked back again, he was relieved to see Stephanie deep in conversation with Luca. The slip hadn't meant anything to her. Nothing at all.

The cops arrived to take her statement. She didn't give them much. They were traveling on business; the would-be thief was a stranger. She provided a number where they could call with any follow-up questions, and that was that.

Luca and Stephanie retrieved their bags, and the three headed outside into the hot southern California air to pick up their rental car. Tate arranged to follow in the truck he'd borrowed from Gilly. After only a few paces, however, Stephanie stopped them both.

"I just figured it out."

"What?" both men said at once.

"The guy who tried to take my laptop."

"You said he was a stranger," Luca said.

"He is, but I've seen him before." Her dark eyes danced in thought. "I remember cutting around his van in traffic." She looked at Tate. "When we left Bittman's mansion, right after he flew off with Dad."

Tate's eyes widened. "I thought he seemed familiar." He snapped his fingers. "The hair. It was Bittman's pool guy. He followed you from San Francisco."

"Who is he?" Luca grimaced in thought. "Someone Bittman hired to keep tabs on us?"

Tate shook his head. "Seems like he wouldn't have his flunkies interfere. What good would that do? His pool guy might be working against him."

"Why?" Stephanie's expression was grave. "Who even knows the violin still exists?"

Luca's face was grave. "Is it possible Bittman was right about what happened all those years ago at his father's shop? About the arsonist?"

"Not just an arsonist," Tate said. "Remember, the fire killed Bittman's brother."

"He's returned and he's after the violin. The person who has it might be able to finger him for murder. He wanted my laptop to see if we'd found anything that could help him." Stephanie felt her pulse pound. "I think we'd better get moving."

Tate was already on his way to the truck. "I think you're right."

FIVE

Two hours after leaving Bakersfield, Tate guided the truck behind the rented Ford into a nearly empty parking lot, which served the music store and a sandwich shop in the minuscule town of Lone Ridge. The heat pressed in on them, making the asphalt shimmer in spite of the early fall color he detected on a few of the twisted trees. Tate wondered idly how Luca, who owned a car worth more than the trailer Tate lived in, felt about driving a regular vehicle. It was good for him to come down from his rich man's tower once in a while. *Might be a refreshing change,* he thought bitterly.

He shifted uneasily on the hard seat. Was that what had attracted Stephanie to him? He was a country boy who ate grits and drove a dinged motorcycle. Was he a diversion for her? A form of rebellion against her upper-crust family?

He rubbed at a spot on his jeans. He'd seen rebellion firsthand in Maria, becoming completely unmanageable when she turned eighteen, and then worse after their father died. The truth pricked at him.

How would you know, Tate? You were so strung out on painkillers, you did nothing to rein her in. He yanked open the door and plunged into the heat. Time for that to change.

Luca led the way into Devlin Music and Repair shop. The interior smelled musty, every square inch crammed with saxophones, trumpets, bins of neatly filed music and packages of reeds and guitar picks, old photos plastered to the walls with yellowing tape.

"We're here to see Mr. Devlin," Luca said to the short man who appeared at the counter. He was round and florid-faced, wearing a short-sleeved plaid shirt tucked into neatly creased pants. Around his neck hung a pair of reading glasses fastened to a brown cord.

Devlin looked closely at the three of them. "I'm Bruno Devlin. What can I do for you?"

Stephanie flashed a brilliant smile. "We're looking for an instrument—a very special instrument—and we were told you might have a lead on where we can find it."

Devlin's eyes narrowed a fraction. "You're not from around here." A German accent clung to his words.

"No, we came from San Francisco," she continued. "The instrument is a rare violin, a Guarneri."

His mouth opened and closed. "A Guarneri?" He

choked out a laugh. "Here? In this nowhere town? I am afraid you have the wrong information."

Luca frowned. "I don't think so. Our facts came from a reliable source. I think you probably know him."

Devlin's Adam's apple jerked. His response came in a low tone. "Joshua Bittman sent you, didn't he?"

Stephanie nodded. "You contacted him and told him that someone had been in your shop, looking for some repair advice."

He looked at his glass counter and buffed at a spot. "Yes."

"Why deny it?"

"Please," Devlin said, wiping at his forehead. "I don't know what is going on. I called Mr. Bittman because he contacted every music repair store in southern California asking for any information on a rare violin. I did what he asked as a courtesy, and that's that. Just business. I don't know where the violin is."

Tate shook his head. "It's more than business. You knew Bittman's father." Stephanie and Luca started slightly at Tate's statement, as if they'd forgotten he'd been standing there.

"I…" the man started.

Tate pointed to an old yellowed photo on the wall, a smiling Devlin outside a shop sporting a sign that read Feather Glen Music, with the year scrawled in marker on the corner. "Feather Glen's in New York." He looked at Stephanie. "In your files you said Bittman's father owned a music shop in New York around that time, not too far from Feather Glen. The instrument repair business is a pretty small world." He looked at Devlin. "You must have known Bittman's father."

Devlin scratched at his chin. "Yes, I knew Hans Bittman. Our families were neighbors in Germany once. We spoke from time to time. He allowed me to come and see the Guarneri after he inherited it." Devlin's eyes shone. "Never have I seen such an instrument. People say the Guarneris are second to Stradivaris, but it is not so. The sound is darker, more intense, and it would take years to master one, perhaps a lifetime."

Stephanie pulled the conversation back on track. "So you saw the Guarneri?"

Devlin sighed deeply. "Yes, the very day before the fire. Tragic, tragic. I helped him try to salvage his business after, but it was no use. He was ruined, his eldest son dead. His other son, Joshua, he became a different person then, too. Something switched off inside him when his brother perished in that fire. Something...died." Devlin pointed to his chest. "He went a little crazy. He always claimed that a thief made off with the violin and another man set the fire."

"Do you think he was telling the truth about that night?"

He shrugged. "He was a child, and he believed what he thought he saw. Maybe it was one of the bums Hans took in from time to time. He was a soft man, let them sleep in the workshop and fed them sometimes. One of them probably snatched it, and the fire started accidently. Maybe Joshua made up the story in his mind to make sense of his brother's death and the loss of his father's beloved Guarneri. No one will ever know."

Tate saw Stephanie puzzling it over. "So you told Mr. Bittman that someone came in with a Guarneri. Who was it?"

Devlin shrugged. "A wild man. Crazy hair and beard. He brought only a picture of the Guarneri, an old-fashioned Polaroid."

"Do you still have the picture?" Luca asked.

"No, but he said he would send me another so I could get a replacement string. He said he would return, but he did not say when."

Luca leaned forward. "Where did he live? Around here?"

Devlin shrugged. "In the desert, a town called Bitter Song."

"Sounds like a real tourist mecca," Tate mumbled.

"It's in the Mojave," Devlin said with a shake of his head. "No sane person would want to go there."

Stephanie gave Devlin a card and instructed him to call if the stranger returned. Devlin did not touch the card, but left it on the counter.

"Mr. Devlin, can I ask you one more question?" Stephanie said. "Has anyone else been here asking about the violin? A man with a crew cut or a dark-haired girl?"

"No, no one."

She pressed her palms to the countertop. "Then who are you afraid of?"

He blinked. "Afraid? Why would I be afraid? Mr. Bittman wants his violin, and I am helping him get it. You'll tell him, won't you? That I am helping him? Only him?"

Devlin didn't wait for an answer, but scurried away into the back room.

Stephanie stood staring after him. "*Only* Bittman? Do you think the pool guy or Maria beat us here and Devlin doesn't want to tell us?"

Tate's pulse quickened. "Let's ask some more questions around town. Maybe someone else will be more cooperative."

"And then—" Luca sighed "—we're headed to the Mojave."

"The place where only crazy people go," Tate finished.

"Then we'll fit right in," Stephanie said, leading the way back outside. "By the way." She pressed Tate's shoulder. "That was pretty good detective work in there, with the photo."

He shrugged, her fingers warm through his T-shirt sleeve. "Just trying to keep up with the real treasure hunters."

Luca gave him a quick nod of approval. "We

would have come up with that eventually, but you saved us some time."

Tate put a hand to his baseball cap. "Anything to help."

She smiled, but beneath the expression he saw the deep current of fatigue, and something else... fear.

He flashed back to his own feelings the moment he'd woken up in the hospital and asked about his father after the car accident that took his life. Was the terror still etched deep inside his own eyes? he wondered. One moment had been rich with laughter and teasing.

"When you gonna seal the deal and propose to that Stephanie gal? She needs a real man in her life."

He remembered his father's hand, thick and callused, waving out the window of the truck as Tate followed in a second vehicle until the unthinkable happened. Before Tate's unbelieving eyes, his father suddenly careened over the side of a cliff. After a moment of frozen shock, Tate was out of his car, panic propelling him down the slope. Flames spurted from the wreck.

I'm coming, Dad. I'm coming.

But he was still fifteen feet away when there was a boom that shook the ground. He could not get out of the way as a hurtling piece of metal barreled at him with missilelike intensity. There was a sense of something slicing through his leg, the feel of bone snapping and then…darkness.

The darkness had not gone away when he came to. In fact, it seemed to have burrowed deep down inside him, awakening pain so excruciating he'd believed the pills were the only solution. His own weakness disgusted him. He was sure, even though he was no longer the same person he'd been, that his weakness disgusted Stephanie, too.

"Tate?"

He blinked back to the present. "So what's the next step?"

Luca pointed to a small café, fronted in sun-parched wood. "I'm going to go there, ask around. I want to run Mr. Devlin through our computers and see what comes up, and give Tuney a call."

Stephanie explained that Tuney was a private investigator who had helped them find Brooke's missing painting. "We're going to have him look for Dad." Her voice trembled a tiny bit until she cleared her throat.

"Tuney's not conventional, but he's more tenacious than anybody I've ever met. If anyone can find a crack in Bittman's plan, it's him. Steph, see if you can find out if Maria's been sighted around here," Luca said.

"So what am I supposed to do while the Treasure Seekers are hard at work?" Tate asked.

Luca marched across the street. "Poke around," he fired over his shoulder. "Check in with your source and see if anything's turned up on Maria's computer."

Tate scanned the street, a wide swath of worn asphalt, bordered by a few storefronts standing on either side, interrupted by flat stretches of dusty ground and piñon junipers. The mountains rose in the distance, giving Tate an uncomfortable, hemmed-in feeling. The street was completely deserted. Not a soul to be seen anywhere. He sighed. "Poke around, huh?"

Stephanie shouldered her laptop. "Luca is focused. He knows how to follow a trail. That's what we do."

He didn't answer. His leg was stiff from the long drive, a dull ache throbbing above the knee.

"We're going to find Maria," she added.

The token effort goaded him. He rounded on her. "So you're concerned now? Why did you let her hook up with Bittman in the first place? If you were trying to punish me, you did a great job of it." It wasn't fair and he knew it, but there was no taking it back now.

She glared at him. "I introduced them before I realized what kind of a man he was. Then I tried to steer her away from him, Tate. I did everything I could."

"You knew the truth about Bittman. Maria was just a kid. You didn't try hard enough."

Fire sparked in her eyes. "I'm no substitute for

her big brother, and you weren't around. You can't blame me for that."

He wanted to snap off an angry reply, to meet her challenge with one of his own, but he found there was nothing to say. He turned away, determined not to limp.

"Tate, hold on," she called after him, voice contrite. "I know you had your own problems."

The shame burned through his good sense. He'd take her anger, her disgust, any emotion at all, but not pity. He stopped and spoke to his boots. "I took pills, Steph. Let's not soften it."

Her voice was soft. "You were in pain."

"Stop it." He whirled on her. "You don't need to make excuses for me. I'm clean now. I don't need your pity."

Her expression hardened. The gentleness in her eyes filmed over with something rougher. "You don't need me at all. You never did. You made that clear when you shut me out." She folded her arms across her chest. "I could have helped. That's what people do when they really love each other."

The words hung heavy between them. "I…" He ran a hand through his hair. "I'm going to check around."

Pain rippled through his leg, circling like a biting dog, along with more severe discomfort of another kind. He was wrong to blame Stephanie for Maria's predicament. Wrong. Shamed. Furious.

He pushed himself faster.

Ahead was the gas station, a run-down place sporting two pumps and a banged-up soda machine. Fighting to keep his mind off the conversation he'd just mangled, he passed a narrow alley between an empty warehouse and a storage locker facility. So lost in his own thoughts, Tate almost missed the muffled sound coming from the darkened alley.

Stephanie stalked back to the restaurant, her stomach in a tight ball of anger. When she forced herself to take some deep breaths, she realized she was furious with herself. Tate was history—whatever past they'd had was lost under a pile of disappointment and hurt. He was weak, because of the addiction he'd fallen into and his inability to accept the blame for his own failure toward Maria.

"Weak," she grunted to herself. She allowed herself a look back to confirm it, but her eyes saw something different than her brain. His wide shoulders were silhouetted by golden sunlight, head bent as if under some heavy burden. His limp somehow made him even more alluring. She exhaled loudly, certain that her mind was succumbing to pressure and worry. *Nuts, Steph. You're losing it completely.*

She slammed open the diner door so hard that the three patrons looked up in surprise. The waitress was the only one who did not look nonplussed. She smiled, her lipstick feathered slightly in the tiny lines around her mouth. "Table, miss?"

Stephanie pointed to her brother. Head ducked, she scurried to Luca.

"You look like you're ready to take on the world heavyweight champion. What's wrong? Did that idiot push your buttons?"

"He's not an idiot, Luca. He's a stubborn cowboy with a chip on his shoulder who wouldn't know a diamond from a doorknob, but he's not an idiot."

Luca blinked, smile held in check. "Whatever you say."

The waitress arrived, tucking a strand of silvered hair behind her ears. "Can I take your order, folks?"

Luca asked for a refill on his coffee.

"What kind of pie do you have?" Stephanie asked.

"Chocolate cream, banana, apple…" the woman recited.

"Whatever has the most chocolate in it, and make it a big slice," Stephanie said.

Luca waited until the waitress left. "I checked in on Victor. He's still stable, no change to report really."

Stephanie sighed, uncertain whether to be encouraged or disappointed at the news. "Tuney?"

"He's on board. He's going to work the helicopter angle, see if he can figure out where Bittman might have taken Dad."

She swallowed. "Do you think he'll be able to get a lead?"

"He's checking into the medical aspect, too, to see if Bittman hired a private nurse or doctor."

She tried to breathe out her terror. Tuney was a gruff character, crabby and volatile on the outside, but she knew him to be loyal, and most important, he understood what it was like to lose someone. "Good." She opened her laptop. "I'll keep working on the police report from Hans Bittman's store." It brought a surge of relief to be doing something. *One step closer to Dad,* she thought. She put her cell phone on the table. The waitress brought her a slice of pie that made her mouth water in spite of the mangled state of her nerves.

The laptop hadn't finished booting up when her phone vibrated with an unknown number. The hospital? She answered.

"Good afternoon, Stephanie."

Her breath froze in her lungs. "What do you want?"

Bittman laughed. "Is it unusual for a man to call and check on the progress of his employee?"

"We're not your employees, and we'll give you a report when we have some news," she hissed.

Luca gestured angrily for her to hand him the phone.

She mouthed the word *no*. Bittman did not want to talk to Luca; she knew that much.

"You've made contact with Devlin?" Bittman asked.

"Yes, and he's given us some info."

"Excellent. I'm confident that you will not have any interaction with the local police. They will only slow things down. No police whatsoever. That is clear, is it not?"

"Yes."

"Good. I have an update for you. It seems as though your father is determined to shed a few pounds."

She clutched at the phone. "What? What's wrong with him?"

"Nothing at the moment, but he is rejecting any food, even though we have provided him with some tantalizing fare. Ethnic food, I recall you said he enjoyed. Chicken mole? Prepared with the most exquisite care, and yet he refuses to touch it. He has not become a vegetarian recently, has he?"

Her head swam. He was not eating. That meant surely he was growing weaker with every passing minute. "You've got to let him go."

Luca was on his feet now, grabbing for the phone, but she fended him off.

"No, I'm afraid that would not work out well. He's very irate and stubborn, as are the rest of the Gages. If you don't want him to continue to starve himself, you need to retrieve my violin and the person who possesses it quickly."

"We will." Stephanie fought to keep both rage and panic out of her voice. "Let me talk to my dad. Just for a minute. Surely that won't hurt anything? I've got to speak to him."

"Perhaps another time."

"No, please." She hated the pleading note in her voice. "I..." She swallowed. "I would really appreciate it."

Bittman laughed. "Oh, Stephanie. A conciliatory tone does not win you any points with me. I admire you the way you are, fiery and totally unapologetic."

She gritted her teeth. "Let me talk to my father."

"Not right now, Stephanie. You have a violin to find," he laughed softly, "and a lovely slice of pie to enjoy. Goodbye."

Stephanie sat frozen, phone in her hand, staring down at the fat wedge of chocolate pie waiting for her on the scratched diner table.

SIX

Tate had the sensation of being watched as he sauntered along the sidewalk. Striving to keep his gait casual, shoulders relaxed, he walked by the alley, littered with stacks of boxes, the end concealed by a rust-blackened Dumpster. After a few paces he turned around, in time to see a figure ducking into the alley to escape detection.

Tate made his way as quietly as he could down the passage, passing by garish graffiti, trying to avoid breathing in the stench of rotting garbage. He stopped near where he was sure the man was hiding. "Come on out. Face me like a man," he called.

A figure stepped from the shadows. It was the man from the airport, the one who'd tried to grab Stephanie's laptop, the one who had driven the pool van onto Bittman's property. His graying crew cut glistened with sweat.

Tate looked him over. "Who are you?"

The older man raised an eyebrow. "Who are you?"

"All right. I'll play. I'm Tate Fuego. What do

you want with Stephanie Gage? I know you tried to take her laptop at the airport, and now you're following me. Why?"

He opened his mouth, eyes wide with surprise before they narrowed into slits. "I don't know what you're talking about."

"Yes, you do. You were working as the pool guy at Joshua Bittman's estate, and now here you are. How do you explain that?"

He smiled, showing yellow teeth. "Coincidence."

"I don't think so. Since you were hanging around Bittman's, you might have seen my sister, Maria. I'm looking for her." Tate saw no flicker of recognition cross the man's face. "Do you know where she is?"

"I don't know any Maria."

"What about Bittman? You're his pool guy, but something tells me you weren't just there to fix the chlorine."

"You're mistaken."

The lie ignited a slow burn in Tate's chest. "Know what I think?" He held his hands loose at his sides, ready. Considering the older man's crooked nose and battle-hardened face, he figured the guy would read the signs. He was right.

The man eased himself into position, ready for a fight. "What's that, boy?"

"I think you're a liar. I think you're going to tell

me why you're here, what you want with Stephanie Gage and what you know about my sister."

The man's hands balled into fists, instead of reaching behind him to his waistband. Tate felt relief. Fists he could handle—but a gun? Not so easily.

"Could be you're wrong about that," the man said.

Tate shifted his weight forward. "Maybe, but you're not leaving this alley until I find out why you're here."

The man dived at him, moving with surprising quickness. Tate managed to step to the side, but it didn't throw off the attack for long. The punches came in rapid succession, and took all Tate's powers of concentration to block them.

He ducked an incoming blow, which infuriated the attacker, who staggered as his punch fell short, glancing off Tate's shoulder. Tate used the moment to deal the man a violent shove to the side, sending him sprawling into a pile of plastic trash bags disgorged from the overflowing Dumpster.

Fighter that he was, the guy was on his feet again in seconds.

"How about you tell me your name?" Tate said, fists up and ready. "Since we're getting along so well and all."

A hint of a smile twisted his mouth. "Name is Ricardo, boy."

"I didn't catch your last name."

Again the smile. "Feel free to make one up."

"Are you here on Bittman's dime? Keeping tabs on us, maybe?" The eyes sparked, but Tate could not read an answer in the grim expression. A scent of cigarettes clung to the man.

A shout from the end of the alley drew both their attention. Before he realized what was happening, Ricardo dived behind the Dumpster and scrambled up a worn ladder that Tate hadn't even noticed bolted to the side of the building.

Tate followed, kicking aside bags of trash until he grabbed hold of the iron rungs. "I've seen this in movies," he called up. "It's no good climbing to the roof unless you've got a helicopter waiting for you."

Climbing was agony on his leg, but he forced himself upward, burning with shame that a man twenty years his senior could climb twice as fast. Teeth gritted, he continued, sparing only a quick look at the alley below.

Figures darted in and out of the shadows. One could have been Stephanie. He was glad he'd encountered Ricardo before Stephanie did because he knew from the kickboxing class they'd taken that she was a fierce combatant. She'd take Ricardo on in a heartbeat, especially after he'd tried to steal her laptop. He smiled, in spite of the fire in his thigh. Five feet to go before he crested the top. Ricardo might be waiting there for him. One good kick in the head, and Tate would find himself back in the alley the hard way. He pressed on, hands raw from the abrasion of the rough metal.

He stopped, head ducked two rungs before the top. He heard footsteps, but not close. Heaving himself up and over, he rolled immediately to the side and scrambled behind the nearest cover, a metal vent.

Ricardo was running toward the other side of the rooftop. Tate ran after him, catching up just as Ricardo came within a few feet of the ledge. Tate's heart pounded. The gap between the building and the lower storage unit next to it was no more than six feet, but the drop was a good twenty. It might not kill a man, if he landed feet first—but then again, it might.

Ricardo eyed the gap, and then Tate.

"This time I can read your mind, boy," Ricardo said, voice low. "You think an old man cannot make this jump."

"Not exactly," Tate said, edging closer. "I think an old man would be crazy to try it."

Ricardo smiled. "And I think a man with a crippled leg would be equally loco to consider it, eh?"

Tate kept his face neutral. "We can talk. Work together."

He didn't answer. Before Tate could react, Ricardo sprinted to the edge of the building and hurtled over the side.

* * *

Stephanie raced up the ladder as soon as she saw Tate following the crew-cut guy to the top. She had to get to the roof to help him.

Her fingers were still trembling from the phone call.

You have a lovely slice of pie to enjoy.

Had she been so naive as to think Bittman would let her wander off to find his treasure unsupervised? Was he even now watching her through some long-distance lens, tracking her every step? Paying the waitress to report back to him? And, she thought grimly, taunting her with the fact that her father was refusing to eat.

Another game. Showing you he owns you, controls you. He has all the power.

With a sick feeling, she realized that he did, in fact, hold all the power. What could she do except find his violin and hope he would keep his word to return her father? It was like trusting a cobra not to strike.

She pushed herself to the top, emerging onto a flat cement roof that shimmered in the heat. A blur of movement told her the crew-cut man had just leaped from that very rooftop. She read Tate's body language as he backed up, though she didn't believe what her brain was telling her. He was going to do the same—leap off the roof to the building next door.

"Tate!" Her voice came out in a shriek.

He started and turned. "It's the guy from the airport. Tell you later." He tensed to begin his sprint.

"Stop right there. You're not jumping."

He cocked his head. "I can make it."

"No, you can't, not with your leg." It was the wrong thing to say. Stubborn lines appeared around his mouth.

"I can do it."

She took a step closer and tried for a calm tone as she pulled out her phone. "Luca's down there. I'll text him." Her thumbs flew over the keys, though she didn't take her eyes off Tate.

Tate looked toward the edge, eyes calculating the distance.

Her instincts demanded that she yell, grab hold of his ankles if she must and keep him from jumping, but the truth was that Tate could not be forced—nor coerced—into anything. She took a breath, entreating God to help her find the right words. "I'm asking you not to do that, Tate. Please."

He cocked his head, eyes bright with surprise at her change in tone. "Why?"

Why? Common sense, of course. If Tate was injured it would slow them down, add to the difficulties they were already facing. Purely a practical reason, a counter to his irrational notion. She looked away from his intense gaze. "Because my brother is hurt, my father is missing and I can't take anything else." She hated the way her voice broke.

Her words betrayed an emotion that she would not voluntarily bare to Tate Fuego at any price.

He looked at her for what seemed like forever, though it was probably only a moment. Then his gaze slid back to the gap, and she knew that he was going to jump. He turned to the edge.

He was a hopelessly stubborn man who would run to his own destruction. She closed her eyes and imagined what it would be like when he was gone, too. Pain drove the breath from her.

When she opened her eyes, he was still there, only now he was close. So close he reached out a hand and eased the tears from her cheeks, tears she had not even known were falling. His face was tender, younger, the same face that she saw in her sweetest dreams before reality cruelly imposed itself. There was an odd questioning look there, too.

She let herself feel the gentle caress before she pulled away and angrily wiped her face. "I'm getting weak."

He chuckled, the remnants of the quizzical look still playing about his lips. "No, ma'am. Still the strongest Gage I know. Let's go see if your brother managed to accomplish anything."

She climbed down first, which allowed her time to grab hold of her fraying emotions. Crazy—she was becoming crazy. The longer this horrendous treasure hunt ensued, the closer she edged to complete insanity.

Luca was there the instant she touched ground.

"I found his car at the other end of the alley. He took off."

"You didn't stop him?"

Luca smiled. "As a matter of fact, I let him go."

Tate exploded, limping up to Luca as soon as he touched ground. "What? Why would you do that? What kind of game are you playing?"

Luca waved him off. "No game, just a tracking device I stuck to his car."

Tate did not relax. "We should have questioned him first, found out what the deal is with him and Bittman."

"Could be he's working for Bittman as some extra insurance in case we don't complete the job, but that doesn't explain why he went for Stephanie's laptop."

"Or he's the one who killed Peter, and he's going to try and get his hands on the violin and its current owner," Stephanie mused.

"All we've got are guesses," Tate snarled. "You're taking risks with my sister's life."

"We've got a life involved in this, too, Fuego, in case you've forgotten," Luca said.

Their loud exchange was drawing attention from the gas station attendant, who had emerged from his tiny office.

"Quiet, both of you," Stephanie said. "Let's get out of here before the police come around." Thinking of Bittman's earlier message made her shiver. It also reminded her that time was ticking away.

She pushed them both toward the car. "I'm riding with Tate. I want to know exactly what the guy said to him. We'll follow after you get a GPS signal."

Without waiting for his reply, she jumped into the passenger seat of Tate's truck. All business. No need to talk about her strange reaction on the roof.

"Get this relic started before Luca takes off without us." She felt eyes on her, Bittman's eyes, watching as Tate related the encounter with Ricardo. He gave her a strange look but eased the truck out onto the road after Luca's rental car.

"What happened that I don't know about?"

With a sigh, she told him about the phone call in the restaurant. He stared at her. "He's got tabs on you down here? What exactly is Bittman capable of?"

Stephanie wanted to close her eyes and avoid the question, but she could not. "Anything." She saw the muscles work in his jaw. "I finally realized that, when he used me to steal that car. I would have left anyway because it was becoming clear to me how he made his money."

Tate quirked an eyebrow. "I thought he was into communications systems."

"He creates billing systems, phone and internet, for big companies, only he tacks on a small charge to each bill, a few pennies in some cases. The surplus is routed to his accounts. The amounts are so small that they go undetected, and he makes millions. It's called salami slicing."

"You didn't go to the police?"

"I didn't have proof. Only suspicions and…"

"And?"

"And the day after I resigned, he sent me a photo."

"Of what?"

"My brothers and me at a family party, a private party in my father's backyard. I don't know how he got the picture."

Tate's mouth tightened. "Guy's got millions. He can buy whatever he wants."

"Not everything."

Tate was eyeing her closely. "So this is not just about the violin, is it?"

"He's…he's tried to get me back into his life. Everywhere I've gone, he's followed. Made phone calls, sent flowers." She swallowed. "Once I got home to find my neighbor had moved out suddenly. He was a nice man, a college student who used to bring me vegetables from the farmer's market." She looked out the window at the dust blowing along the side of the road. "To say Bittman's jealous is an understatement. He never liked it when I mentioned you as a matter of fact, back when I was just consulting for him. He said he'd known you weren't good for me. Made me think he'd been watching me for some time."

She'd had her proof later, after she'd left Bittman's employ. It came in the form of a photo

Bittman had sent, a picture of Tate entering a church-run drug counseling clinic. He looked terrible, worn out, cheek bruised by a fall, she'd guessed, eyes bloodshot and miserable. Her heart had broken all over again when she saw that photo.

Though it hadn't included a note, Bittman's message was clear.

You see? A loser, just like I told you.

"Did you have feelings for him?" His tone was sharp as glass.

She bridled. "That's not your business, Tate, but no. He was strictly an employer in my mind."

"You could have worked anywhere. Why work for him?"

Why him? Because he was interesting and smart and he distracted me from thinking about the man I really loved, the man who pushed me out of his life. "You don't get to interrogate me," she said, voice bitter.

Tate blew out a breath. "I told you when you first started consulting for him that he was a freak. You're smart and you're well connected. How could you ever have let that guy into your life?"

"Maybe because I don't like being told what to do. Your sister fell in with Bittman, too, remember?"

"Different story. My sister has always fallen for the wrong guy. She was impressed with his money, I'm sure, flattered to be hired by him to do his odd jobs. Never bothered to look deeper than the car and the fancy house."

"Maybe she just wanted someone to listen to her."

"I listened."

"No, you lectured." She sighed. "And so did I. I told her everything, but all she knew was that he showed interest in her."

His eyes flicked to her face and quickly away. "And I didn't."

She didn't answer. "Past is passed." But they both knew that wasn't true. As much as she wanted to leave their decisions behind, there were two people whose lives were precariously balanced on the shifting pile of past sins.

Her phone indicated a text from Luca. *Got signal. Buckle up.*

They followed Luca toward the blazing horizon. *Lord, please help us find them.*

Fast.

SEVEN

Tate pressed down the black feelings in his gut. Anger at Bittman, shame at his own failure toward both Maria and Stephanie and an unaccountable sense of betrayal that Stephanie had delivered herself into Bittman's world. He knew it didn't make sense. He'd been so desperate to keep her from knowing the truth of his humiliating addiction that he'd practically shoved her away, buried in his own grief at the death of his father.

The sound of the most horrible moment of his life echoed in his ears. He'd driven to see her, mind fogged on painkillers. Even in that altered state, his heart craved her, the need overriding common sense. After an incoherent ramble about how sorry he was, she'd begged him not to drive, pulling at his arm, trying to snatch the keys. He had to get away, to keep from shaming himself any further.

He'd wrenched free, floored the gas pedal, and then somehow she'd been there, in front of him and he couldn't stop in time. He remembered the soft thump of her body hitting the front fender, the blood oozing from her cheek. He'd managed one word, one agonizing plea. *Help.* And then it had all gone mercifully black.

He swallowed the nausea that came with the memory. God saved her from him, he was sure. Was He systematically removing all the people in Tate's life? His father, Stephanie, his sister? Where was the compassionate, loving guardian his mother always told him about? Once you accepted Christ, as he'd done as a teen, wasn't He supposed to help you, no matter what? Bring people into your life to mentor and guide you? When the addiction took hold of him with stunning ferocity, it seemed to drive away everyone close to him.

Now he was alone, and that's the way it would stay.

The miles unrolled in front of them. Stephanie remained busy on her laptop, and he dutifully tailed Luca. It was more comfortable for them both to be immersed in their own worlds.

"Guarneri made several instruments before he died in 1741, but the one that may or may not have burned at Hans's shop, the Quinto Guarneri, was unique. It was almost lost in a building collapse in the early 1800s, but amazingly it survived with only a slight scar on the scroll." She checked her messages again. Only one from Brooke, which she listened to attentively. "Victor's coming around," she relayed, relief shining on her face until a shadow of disappointment followed. "He can't remember what happened." She bit her lip. "He keeps asking for Dad."

Tate put a hand on her arm. "We'll get him back. Both of them."

She didn't look at him, but clasped his hand with hers. For a moment, hands twined together, it felt like old times. He was her rock, the rebellious love that would give his life for hers in a heartbeat. Her stomach let out a loud rumble, and her cheeks pinked. "I never did get to eat any of that pie."

"Under your seat there's a box of food. Take what you want."

She raised an eyebrow. "You never used to plan ahead much for road trips."

"Still don't. It's Gilly's truck. He doesn't leave home without a week's supply. He got trapped in an elevator during the Loma Prieta quake, and he vowed never to be without food again."

She slid open the compartment under the seat and grabbed a couple granola bars and a box of Oreos. "I'm going to give Gilly a kiss when I see him," she said, taking a big bite of the granola bar.

Tate chuckled. "I'm sure that will make his decade. He's had the hots for my sister for years, and she's never given him a second look. Too bad. He's geeky, but he'd treat her much better than the other guys."

He avoided looking at her.

"Tate, I know Luca would never take advantage

of a woman. He didn't touch Maria, and he certainly didn't try to force himself on her."

Tate's jaw clenched. "She says he did."

Stephanie tried to tread lightly. "She is...volatile. A week after she said that about Luca, she was involved with Bittman."

"I know she's made mistakes, but past is passed, just like you said. And we're supposed to be forgiven, right? That Christian thing?"

His tone was suddenly earnest, and something in his gray eyes was soft and tender. "Yes, that's right." She wondered again why it was harder to forgive someone you loved than a complete stranger. Her heart sped up a tic, and she realized she was actually pleased to have Tate sitting here next to her, clean of the painkillers that nearly destroyed him. Maybe he really had beaten his addiction. On impulse, she traced a finger across the toughened skin of his hand. He jerked, shooting her a look she could not decipher, but he didn't move his hand away.

He shifted on the seat. "There's water in my backpack."

She snagged it from the backseat and rummaged around inside, rifling through a clean shirt and a small travel case. Her heart stopped when she saw the bottle in the bottom of the pack. She read the label. Painkillers. Hating herself for doing it, she gently poked at it. The tiny sound of the pills shifting inside mirrored the crash of her own emotions. Half full.

He was still using. Maybe not at that moment, or even that day, but he would soon enough. The thought burned inside her.

"Find some?"

She'd always considered herself courageous, but in that moment she found she could not bear to confront him. She forced a smile and pulled a water bottle from the pack. "Yes, thanks." There were no tears forming in her eyes, no rage at herself for believing he'd gone straight. Only sadness and despair. She prayed silently that God would take away his burden because she now realized he did not have the strength to do it himself, and he probably never would.

"Something wrong?" he asked.

"Nothing that won't be fixed when we find my father and Maria," she said, turning her eyes out the windshield, watching the evening swallow up the day.

Tate finally followed Luca into a dark parking lot, home to a truck stop diner and a gas pump. They stayed at the far end of the lot, hidden by a screen of semitrailers. He'd kept a close eye on the rearview mirror and had seen no one tailing them, though the fact that Bittman was somehow keeping tabs on Stephanie's every move made a knot in his stomach.

Luca joined them, staying away from the parking lot lights. "Ricardo's stopped here. I saw him look around, check his watch. He's meeting someone."

Tate's hopes lifted. "Maria?"

"Or maybe the crazy man from Devlin's music shop. I think Ricardo paid Devlin a visit, and Devlin's afraid Bittman will find out and think he's double crossing."

"Let's go in and see for ourselves," Tate said, starting for the door.

"No, we wait here. We don't want to spook him."

Tate stiffened. "We've done enough waiting and following. We can't let him get away."

"He won't. His car is here. We wait." Luca's eyes glittered. "This is how we do things."

"You're a Treasure Seeker, Luca, not a private eye."

"It's oftentimes the same thing." Luca cocked his head. "We've found everything from paintings to a million-dollar stamp, so maybe you should step back and let us do our job."

They waited, the minutes ticking into hours until Tate was nearly ready to jump out of his skin. He was about to walk into the restaurant with or without Luca's consent, when Stephanie's phone rang. After a fleeting look of fear, she answered it. They watched as her eyes widened.

"But why don't you just tell me over the phone? What's the big discovery?" She listened, alternately cajoling and demanding. Finally she hung up. "The man mailed Devlin a picture of the violin. He's insisting we go see him in person."

"When?" Tate said.

"Now." She checked her watch. "It's an hour back to Lone Ridge, so we'll be there by ten if we leave right away."

"It could be a trap," Tate said.

"We don't have a choice," Stephanie shot back.

Luca's eyes danced in thought. "We'll have to split up."

"I'll go back with Steph. You stay on Ricardo," Tate said, retrieving his keys from a front pocket.

Luca hesitated, shooting a look at his sister.

She shrugged, and Tate felt a slice of pain at her obvious reluctance, but she acquiesced. "It makes sense since you've got the signal on him. If he does leave unexpectedly, you can track it."

"Be careful," Luca said to Stephanie.

I won't let anything happen to her, he wanted to say. It would have been false assurance. Besides, Luca would never trust him again after he'd almost killed Stephanie. Tate was not sure he fully trusted himself, for that matter.

It's just a drive. Take her, get the info and bring her back. He put a hand on the small of her back to guide her, wishing his fingers didn't relish the play of muscles there, wondering when the riveting movement of her dark hair would cease to mesmerize him.

Probably never, the same way he would never stop missing her, stop feeling the pain of his leg, which seemed somehow twined with the ache in his heart. The past is passed, but it was also unchangeable and unforgettable. He shut the door after her, which elicited an exasperated look from Stephanie, like it always had.

"I can shut my own door," she'd perpetually insisted.

"My mother taught me right," he'd responded a million times. A lady deserves that much, and she deserved so much more.

She was oddly quiet on the way back to Lone Ridge, tapping keys on her computer or gazing out the window onto the road, which was now only lit by a fat yellow moon.

A car zipped by going the other way as they approached the town, which was quiet and still.

"First car we've seen in miles," he said with a twinge of uneasiness.

"Mmm," she murmured.

He pulled the truck to a stop a couple blocks from the music store. "Best not to be too obvious."

"In case Bittman has someone watching, like he did at the restaurant? I don't trust him."

Tate drummed his fingers on the steering wheel.

Stephanie took a small pair of binoculars out of her pocket and trained them on the music store. "Looks dark."

"Could be we're early."

"It's ten-fifteen." She put a hand on the car's door release. "Let's check it out."

He stopped her. "Why don't we watch awhile first? Take our time."

Her mouth tightened into a luscious bow. "Because we don't have any time to spare. My father isn't eating, your sister is still missing and someone else is searching for the treasure that I'm going after."

She was out the door before he could say another word. He followed, trying to keep from stepping on the numerous small twigs that littered the walkway to the music store. The place was dark, windows shuttered.

He caught up with her as she knocked softly.

"Mr. Devlin?" she called. After a moment, she knocked louder and called again.

"Maybe he's gone home."

She shook her head, face pale in the moonlight. "He lives here, in a room in back."

He didn't ask how she knew, but he did manage to get ahead of her as she made her way toward the rear of the store. They saw it at the same time— the gleam of lamplight, showing from underneath a curtained window.

She tapped on the rear door and called Devlin's name again.

No answer. She dialed Devlin's number on her cell phone. They both heard it ringing inside, two rings, three, five before the answering machine came on. Stephanie pocketed the phone, her look mirroring the concern he felt.

"Something's not right," he whispered, mouth pressed to the delicate shell of her ear. "We should get back in the truck, wait and see what develops." He knew she wouldn't go for it, though.

Ignoring him, she tried the handle. It turned.

"Unlocked," she breathed.

"Breaking and entering," he retorted.

"Since when did you get all concerned with the rules? You're still the same guy who stole a pig from the high school ag department."

"The pig came willingly, and I borrowed, not stole."

Her grin sent his heart spiraling. He grabbed her hands and pulled her closer until her mouth was inches from his. Fighting a wild desire to kiss her, he shook his head. "Steph, this isn't a good idea."

She cocked her head but didn't pull away. "Devlin told us to come. He might be in there needing help."

"Or it might be someone else waiting. We don't know all the players involved."

She inched closer. "I'm going in there," she breathed, causing his body to tingle all over.

He held her tighter. "Let me. You stay outside with the phone. I'll yell if I need help."

She gave him an odd look. "I wish you would have told me you needed help before."

He felt confused. "I don't know what you mean."

"The pills," she said, eyes moist.

He stepped back. "I beat it by myself. I didn't need your help."

"And you don't need it now?" she whispered. She closed the gap and pressed her cheek to his. "Forget it. I'll go in and you stay in the truck."

He closed his eyes against the softness of her skin, the silken touch of her hair on his cheeks. Raindrops on roses. She was still the most beautiful thing he had ever seen, felt or come near to in his whole life. He pretended for a split second that she was his again, that his heart was whole and clean, cleaved once more with hers. When the feeling became too much to bear, he gently set her back.

Stop deluding yourself, Tate. Those are just memories of old feelings. Things are different now.

"Steph…"

It was a mistake. As soon as he released her, she turned the knob and darted into the silent building.

EIGHT

Stephanie tried to get her bearings. It was not the dim interior that confused her senses, but the way her body reacted to Tate's touch. He was an addict, and she could not allow him in her life again. That was clear, but why did her body seem so reluctant to get the message? She took a deep breath and willed her pulse to simmer down.

Tate stepped in behind her and they both stood still, listening. The soft hum of voices startled her until she saw Tate mouth the word *radio*. They stood in a minuscule kitchen, the sink filled with water and submerged cookware. A rickety table and chair stood off in the corner, littered with an untidy pile of sheet music and a plate smeared with something that might have been dried ketchup.

The kitchen had two exits. One led out to the store area, and the other must lead to Devlin's private room, where the light gleamed from under the slightly open door. She made a move toward the bedroom, but in a flash Tate was in front of her, crouched low, pushing the door open.

He managed to keep her behind him until he'd poked in his head. Then she pushed past and into the room which housed a cot and small end table, yet another stack of sheet music, an odd collection of hardware from various instruments and a chipped coffee mug. On the wall was a calendar of famous golf courses of the world, the page set to three months prior. In the corner, an old golf club and a bucket of balls were propped.

Stephanie was at the desk, sorting through the odd scribbled papers and moving aside piles of bills. "Nothing here of substance," she whispered.

He picked up a mug. "Still warm."

Her eyes widened. With an unspoken agreement, they left the bedroom and made their way toward the store. Once again they paused to listen before they pushed aside the door. The air was stuffy, the smell of mildew strong. Tate turned on the flashlight and beamed it around, looking into the spaces large enough for an intruder to hide. Large shapes covered with sheets gleamed back at them. Instruments, she imagined, but looking more like pale beasts in the gloom.

Tate was sidling around to the counter in the back corner, where they had first met Devlin. It would make the perfect hiding spot for Devlin, or someone else. There was no moonlight to help now, since long floor-to-ceiling drapes covered the front windows.

She wanted to call out, to ease Devlin's mind if he was indeed cowering on the dingy tile floor behind the counter. But there were others in the game. Maria was after the prize, and Ricardo was a player who was as determined to find the violin as the Treasure Seekers, a man who might be willing to kill in order to obtain it.

Tate was inches from the counter now, and she tugged at his belt loop. He looked over, face swimming in shadows. She opened her mouth to whisper…what? To be careful? Tate wasn't careful and never had been. It was part of the reason she'd loved him.

Past tense, Stephanie. He's history, and this is your investigation. She quickly danced around him and approached the counter. Grabbing a handful of music from a shelf, she tossed the sheets on the countertop. There was no startled movement, no sudden fluttering of a stranger hiding there.

She stuck her head over the top, Tate right at her side.

No one was there.

Stephanie sighed as Tate turned on a nearby lamp. "He's gone, but recently."

She went to pull aside the curtain and get a look at the street. Something solid met her fingers—a figure behind the curtain. She let out a cry as the figure, head covered by a knit cap, shoved by her, knocking her to the ground, heading for the back of the shop.

Tate rushed after, knocking over a wastebasket, which slowed him down momentarily.

By the time Stephanie made it to her feet, they had both shot out the back door and into the night. She took off after them, disconcerted when she exploded into the darkened yard, startling an owl from its perch on the limb overhead.

The yard emptied into a wild space behind Devlin's store, flat ground peppered with desert holly and folding down into a dry ridge straddling a gorge. It didn't provide much cover, or much of an escape avenue. The front would make more sense. She jogged along the pebbled stepping stones to the street, which was eerily quiet. The truck was still there, so Tate had pursued on foot. Ears straining, she could not decide which direction they had gone.

Her heart hammered in her chest, body frozen with indecision. The only reasonable plan was to drive the streets until she found them, but she had no keys. Had Tate left them in the truck? She scurried around to the driver's side. Just as she grasped the handle, she felt someone behind her.

She whirled to find herself face-to-face with a young woman. The girl's long hair was spilling loose from the knit cap, her dark eyes wide and scared. She clutched at Stephanie's forearms.

"Go home. Both of you. Go home and it will be okay, I promise."

Stephanie fought through her surprise. "Tell me what's going on."

She shook her head and looked around. "I can't explain it right now. Just get out of here before you get hurt. Tell Tate."

"No, you're going to tell him." Stephanie grabbed the girl's wrist. "If you're running from Bittman, it's a matter of time before he finds you." She tried to pull her toward the store but the girl resisted, yanking so ferociously that Stephanie lost her grip and took a step backward.

The younger girl stood for a moment in the street, eyes gleaming in the moonlight. "I know what I'm doing. You're putting us all in danger by being here. Go home," she hissed once more before she whirled and ran away into the darkness.

Tate sprinted into view, breathing hard. "Did you see which way he went?"

Stephanie swallowed. "Not he."

"What?"

"It wasn't Ricardo hiding behind the curtains, Tate. It was Maria."

They returned to the shop, Stephanie trailing Tate inside. She did not want to tell him his sister's message. It would only worsen his pain, but there was no way around it. He had to know. She related the conversation as best she could while he stood, arms crossed, taking it in. When she finished, he turned away, silent.

She went to him and put a hand on his shoulder, feeling the tension that turned his back muscles to steel. "We know she's safe for the moment. That's something."

He turned. "Safe? She's come here to steal from Bittman. How is that safe?"

Stephanie tried for a calming tone. "I know you were hoping it wasn't true."

He rubbed his hand across his face. "Yeah, I was hoping she was back home somewhere and Bittman was mistaken. Should have known."

She hated to see his helplessness. "We have to move forward, Tate, figure out what's going on and sort through it all. I'll call Luca and fill him in. See if there's been any movement from Ricardo."

He didn't answer. Instead he began to pace in restless circles around the periphery of the shop while she related the situation to her brother and learned that Ricardo was still inside the restaurant, though he had emerged several times to smoke a cigarette and make phone calls.

"So what happened to Devlin?" Luca demanded.

"That's the question of the day. He left here quickly." She lowered her voice. "Or someone took him."

Luca blew out a breath. "Maria must know."

"No doubt, but for the moment we don't know where she is, either. We'll drive through town, check around and then meet you." She disconnected and eyed Tate, who was now standing, arms folded, staring at the wall until he suddenly pulled out his phone and checked his messages.

"Text from Gilly. He says Maria hasn't touched her credit cards." Tate slammed the phone down on the counter and glowered. "Maybe Bittman is threatening Maria. She's trying to protect herself by running, not stealing his violin."

"Only one problem with that theory, Tate. Maria is here in Lone Ridge now, so she's involved all right—up to her neck."

His mouth tightened. "It's not what it looks like."

"Maybe it's not what you want to see. Denial is easy…" She broke off.

He blinked. "For an addict?" His words were soft, but they convicted her anyway. "I've done my share of denying, but this is my sister and I'm going to believe the best of her anyway, just like you'd do for your brothers."

She nodded. "I just hope you're not disappointed in the end."

"You need hope to be disappointed, and I lost that when I lost you."

The emotion came so quickly, she could not defend her heart against it. "I…"

"No guilt. My decisions, my choices. Right now, I've just got to look out for my sister." He moved away, scanning the walls of the shop, though she suspected his mind was far away.

I lost that when I lost you. She could not think of anything to say, staring at the tortured person before her, the remnants of the man who had been the anchor to her soul. *That was your mistake, Steph.*

Only God could be that anchor. No one was strong enough, not Luca, not Victor and not Tate Fuego, as much as she wanted him to be. She'd expected too much from him, invested too much in him and he'd let her down. Lesson learned.

She tore away her gaze. "I'll look in the back. Maybe Devlin left a note somewhere about where he was going." Without waiting for him, she marched into the kitchen, stomach still twisted in tight knots.

Devlin had been there recently, but so had Maria. If there was anything to find, she may already have snatched it. Recalling the dark look on Tate's face, she didn't think it would do any good to suggest it. She rifled the piles of papers again and sorted through Devlin's files, feeling more like a nosy relative than an investigator. A half hour later she was ready to pull the plug. It was nearly two o'clock in the morning, and the day was catching up with her. Fatigue and the tension between them seemed to weigh down her limbs. Her stomach felt alternately hungry and sick with fear. Time ticked away relentlessly. She mumbled a prayer for her father, for Victor... She cast a glance to the darkened store area and added a prayer for Tate and his sister.

Would Maria's bad decisions be too much for him to bear? Would it end this time in a tragic overdose? With fingers gone cold, she returned the pile of papers she'd been sifting through to their place and went back to the shop.

"Can't find anything," she said. "Let's go before someone calls the cops on us."

He nodded and moved with her, but stopped abruptly, staring at the wall.

"What is it?"

He pointed to the yellowed picture of Devlin's old shop, the one he'd noticed before that tied Devlin to Bittman's father, Hans. For a moment, she thought he was going to remove the picture and take it with them, but his fingers plucked something from behind—a stiff square slid behind the photo with only a small edge showing.

She crowded next to him as they shone a flashlight on the square. It was a Polaroid snapshot of a violin. Stephanie's breath hitched up a notch. "This must be what he called us about. Something in this picture was a revelation to him."

Tate pocketed the photo. "You were right before. We need to go now. We'll take a closer look, but not here."

She followed him out and they closed the door, making their way to the truck. Stephanie used her penlight to scrutinize the photo as they drove, but the light was poor. The silence between them lasted the whole hour's return trip until they met Luca, who was leaning against the side of the rental car.

Stephanie recognized the tension in her brother, tension that often arose after long periods of inactivity.

He straightened as they emerged, and Stephanie showed him the photo. "It's got to be the Guarneri."

"As near as I can tell. It's not a great picture and I'll need better light to examine it, but that's my guess. It's our first solid proof that we're on the right track."

"No more calls from Devlin? Maybe he got spooked when Maria showed up, stashed the photo and ran."

Tate shook his head. "My sister didn't threaten him. I think she was there looking, too."

"Maybe," Luca said slowly.

A dusty semi rolled onto the property, momentarily drowning out their conversation. They waited until it parked, the driver and passenger lost in shadow as they headed toward the restaurant.

"Ricardo seems to be getting more agitated. He comes out every ten minutes or so to look around. Whoever is meeting him is late." They continued to watch for another fifteen minutes until a banged-up Volkswagen Bug rumbled from the back parking lot and vanished into the darkness. "I'm going to take a look inside," Luca said. "I've got a bad feeling. Watch Ricardo's car."

Stephanie did not want to endure any more painful exchanges with Tate, but she knew making an obvious entrance might cause Ricardo to bolt.

A man with a thick black beard came out of the

restaurant as Luca went in. Stephanie pretended to talk on her phone as the man approached Ricardo's sedan.

He casually pulled out a set of keys, took a look around and let himself in. Tate caught him by the sleeve and yanked him out before he could turn the key.

"Whatsa matter with you?" the man spluttered, his arm raised in a fist. "I got nothing worth stealing, man. You got the wrong sucker."

Stephanie held up a calming hand. "We're not going to rob you. This car doesn't belong to you. How did you get the keys?"

A sly smile appeared under the tangle of beard.

"Did you steal them?" Tate demanded.

"Nuh-uh. He gave 'em to me."

Tate pressed closer. "Who?"

"Guy in the diner. Traded me."

Stephanie's heart sank. "Traded you for what?"

The man laughed. "My old clunker. Told me I could have his wheels if I'd give him mine. Nice trade, huh?"

Stephanie groaned. "What type of car did you have?"

The grin appeared again. "My old VW Bug. Sweet, huh?"

Tate exchanged a look with Stephanie.

They'd been beaten. Again.

NINE

Tate exchanged an exasperated look with Stephanie. It could not be that Ricardo had evaded them again. There was another piece of information that he was reluctant to ask for, but had no choice. "Was the guy who traded cars with you alone?"

"Yep."

Tate let out a relieved sigh.

Scratching his head, the man continued. "Until some long-haired chick came in. Their talk was real serious like, and that's when he came over to my table, paid for my dinner and traded cars. Left right after. I finished my ice cream and came out to enjoy my new wheels." His eyes narrowed. "Got a problem with that?"

Stephanie shook her head. "No, no problem. Is it okay if I look in the car for a minute? Just to see if the man left anything in there? He's an...acquaintance of ours."

He shrugged. "Go ahead, but if he left any cash, it's mine fair and square. A trade's a trade."

Tate rolled around the facts in his mind while Stephanie searched the car. Maria left Devlin's shop and thumbed a ride with the semi driver. She scooted into the restaurant, right under their noses, and convinced Ricardo to ditch his car. His sister was smart, too smart for her own good—but not smart enough to keep herself from partnering with Ricardo. He felt like slamming a fist on the car hood.

Luca jogged out. "Hostess told me Ricardo and Maria left by the back exit."

"In a VW Bug they bartered for," Stephanie said miserably as she got out of Ricardo's car with a creased road map in her hand.

Tate's self-control snapped. "So I guess your tracking device isn't worth two cents now. Treasure Seekers isn't worth much, either." Frustration rose in him like the clouds of dust kicked up by the VW as it drove away. "Computers, fancy cars, the people you're paying. It turns out to be nothing but show." He'd expected outrage, anger—hoped for it really, a way to release the emotions building inside, a wall for him to slam into.

Luca looked more surprised than angry. "So that's what your problem is? Money? You resent the fact that we've got resources?"

"No," he said, looking away.

Luca must have read some truth in his voice. "I think that's it. You got a chip on your shoulder because of our net worth. It's always goaded you, hasn't it, Tate?"

Tate's teeth clenched. "You're no better than me."

Luca raised an eyebrow. "I know that and you never heard me say it, did you? Or imply anything of the kind? Ask Stephanie, and she'll tell you the same thing. The problems we have with you, Tate, have nothing to do with your finances. Whatever inferiority complex you've got going is of your own making, so don't lay it at my doorstep."

Tate walked away a few paces, sucking in air, rage giving over to some other emotion. Much as he wanted to, he could not fault Luca, true enough. The decision four years ago, the last-minute switch of vehicles with his father, could not be foisted off on Luca as much as he desperately wanted it to be. The naked truth was, Tate had convinced his father to let him use the car because he was embarrassed to take Stephanie to a Gage family picnic in his own battered Ford pickup.

It was a decision driven by the same shame that made him avoid their other family invitations, excuse himself from certain Gage events. He was not of their strata. He'd thought he'd read it in their eyes, but maybe he was seeing only his own feelings reflected there. He rubbed his callused hands against his jeans, his father's words coming back to him.

The greatest man was a carpenter.

Tate remembered the way his father's hands looked, scarred and leathery, strong. *"You're worthy because He said so."*

Worthy. He tried on the idea as if it was a new jacket laid across his shoulders, and for a split second, he felt straighter, stronger. Worthy of respect? From Stephanie? From the Gage family? From the sister he'd failed? Flickers of the past shot through his mind, the pills he'd swallowed, the sight of Stephanie lying on the pavement, the accident that killed his father. Bottom line was, he'd convinced his father to drive the pickup, and that same pickup experienced brake failure on a steep section of sandy road. His father was dead. The hunger for comfort ate at him—a need which had previously sent him to the medicine cabinet.

You don't use pills anymore. You're going to fight through it, every day, every minute, like you have for the past year.

Looking over at Luca and Stephanie, he wished he could tell them.

I'm clean, and I'm going to stay that way.

Their heads were bent together, a team, a family.

"You had your chance, Tate," he whispered to himself.

Stephanie gestured for him to follow, and they headed into the diner.

"Going to ask some more questions?"

"No, going to get something to eat before I keel over," she said. "We know where they're headed anyway."

He nodded. "Bitter Song."

"Right. So I may as well not drop dead of starva-

tion on the way." She took the lead, and he smothered a smile. He'd learned way back in high school
that Stephanie, petite as she was, did not do well
skipping meals. His own stomach growled, and he
kept up the pace.

The waiter at the counter was a skinny teen
with hair to his shoulders. He took their order of
sandwiches for Luca and Stephanie and a burger
for Tate, to go. When he sauntered off, Stephanie
pulled out the Polaroid and squinted at it.

"Not a good quality photo." She flipped it over.
"No notes or dates on the back."

"Just looks like a violin to me," Tate said.

She held the photo closely. "I can see a gleam of
white here, a scrap lying next to the instrument."
She held it so they could see. Her eyes shone.
"Could be a label."

"Proving what?" Luca asked, taking a sip of tea.

"The Guarneri family labeled most of their instruments. Generally it was a piece of handmade
paper, and the text was in Latin. It would authenticate this treasure we've been killing ourselves
to find."

Tate raised an eyebrow. "If this thing is from the
1700s, would the label have survived?"

"It's possible." Stephanie considered it. "The
labels were attached inside the instruments. Do
you have a magnifying glass, Luca?"

He shook his head. "Didn't think to bring one.
Maybe we can get hold of one in Bitter Song."

She started pacing. "I wish they'd hurry up with that order. I need to get my hands on a magnifying glass."

"It's going on three in the morning. Where do you expect to find an open store in Bitter Song at this hour?"

She flashed him a smile that made his stomach tighten. "I'm a very resourceful gal. Ask anyone."

He didn't need to ask. She was resourceful and beautiful, and he was not surprised that her beauty had not waned one iota in the years they'd been apart. Now it seemed he would be shoulder to shoulder with Stephanie in the next leg of their adventure.

He had a feeling that finding an eighteen-million-dollar violin in the middle of the desert might just be the easy part of the trip.

Stephanie's phone buzzed and she clicked it on, unable to resist a smile as the gruff voice rumbled through the cell.

"I hate the desert. Too many bugs," Tuney said.

"You hate everything. It's good to talk to you."

He grunted, voice softening. "How you holding up, kiddo?"

"Okay, but we need this to be over. Do you have anything for us?"

She heard a crunching noise, and she knew the crotchety private eye was munching on his favorite snack, animal crackers.

"Matter of fact, I do."

Stephanie straightened, and both Luca and Tate caught her excitement.

"Had a talk with one Roger Goldberg, who is an incredibly annoying mechanic who happens to be a friend of a certain helicopter pilot who works for this Bittman character."

Her eyes widened. "What did he say?"

"Seems his buddy mentioned he had a flight to do in San Francisco for the boss on that Wednesday afternoon."

"Did Roger know the end destination?"

"No, Bittman scares his people enough that they know not to blab too many details."

Her stomach dropped. "Oh."

"But he does happen to know it was someplace local because he met the guy for an early dinner that same day."

She gripped the phone. "So Bittman didn't have my father taken out of the area. He's being held nearby. Maybe even in San Francisco."

"Looks that way, doesn't it?"

"Tuney, you're wonderful." She relayed the information to the others. "How did you ever get Roger to tell you all that?"

Tuney laughed. "Trade secrets, but tell your brother he's going to loan me that fancy fishing boat of his for a good long while."

"I'll tell him."

Tuney's voice sobered. "This isn't done. San

Francisco is forty-six square miles, and I'm going to cover every last one until I find your father."

Stephanie's throat thickened. "Thank you." Luca was gesturing for the phone, and she knew he would call in more people to help with the search. "Just remember, Bittman is…"

"I know—ruthless as a starving piranha. Well, guess what? I'm pretty ruthless myself, not to mention ornery, and no one scares me off a case."

She thanked him again and handed the phone to Luca, blinking back tears.

Tate took her hand and squeezed. "Staying strong?"

She felt the aching comfort of his touch ripple through her body before she withdrew her hand, nodding vigorously. "Absolutely," she said, ignoring the twisting in her stomach. She knew he was watching her, and she could not stand the feeling of those intense gray eyes on her for one more moment.

Leaving Luca to make arrangements with Tuney, Stephanie excused herself to visit the restroom. She saw her own reflection in the mirror, and for a moment did not recognize herself. Her hair was wild, eyes shadowed with fatigue, face drawn with worry. Every hour that passed brought them closer to the violin, but it meant another hour that her father was under the power of the crazy Joshua Bittman.

She splashed water on her face and tried to fix a

positive thought in her mind. He was probably fine; his stubborn, irascible personality had seen him through many a rocky time in his life, including the death of their mother when Stephanie was a baby.

A lady with ash blond hair entered and smiled as she washed her hands.

Stephanie smiled back, but did not encourage any conversation. She wanted to get on the road without any further delay.

"Visiting?"

Stephanie started. "What?"

"You're not from around here." The woman's eyes played over Stephanie's jeans and jacket. "On vacation?"

"Business trip."

The woman smiled, and there was something sly in the expression. Stephanie's skin prickled.

"Most people don't come to the desert for business," the lady said, painting a coat of pink onto her lips.

Stephanie quickly dried her hands.

The woman stepped between Stephanie and the door. "But then, you don't look like most people. Where are you headed?"

Pulse thudding, Stephanie took in her size—she wasn't big, but she looked strong. Her hand was in the pocket of her jacket. "Not sure."

The woman moved closer—close enough that Stephanie could smell her perfume, a heavy floral. "I thought you were a business woman, but you don't know where you're going?" She inched one more step, crowding Stephanie back toward the stalls.

Stephanie forced a smile. "Sorry, in a hurry."

"That's not very friendly." Keeping one hand in her pocket, she brought the other to her face, long nails tapping thoughtfully on her front teeth. "What kind of business are you in anyway?"

"The kind that's not your business," Stephanie said.

The woman put her hand in her purse and pulled out a knife. "Suppose I make it my business."

Stephanie eased back as much as she could and got into a ready position. She'd practiced the scenario many times in her mixed martial arts class.

The woman's eyes flickered as she caught the movement. "You some kind of Bruce Lee?"

"No," Stephanie said. "But I'm good enough to get that knife out of your hand and take you down in the process."

The would-be assailant hesitated before she slipped the knife back in her purse. "I'm not getting paid enough for that."

Stephanie kept her ready stance. "Who paid you and why?"

"Dunno his name," she said with a shrug. "Just told me to slow you up. I wasn't really going to hurt you."

"Silver crew cut?"

"Yeah. Gal's gotta make a living somehow. No hard feelings?"

Stephanie didn't bother to answer. With a quick movement, she elbowed the woman aside and escaped into the hallway. She made her way quickly back and found her brother and Tate waiting. The lady did not emerge from the restroom.

"Let's go, right now," she said, nearly sprinting for the door.

"What's going on?" Tate asked, falling in behind her.

"Some lady in the bathroom was paid by Ricardo to give me a hard time."

Luca took her shoulder and turned her around. "Did she hurt you?"

"No, but she thought about it for a while." Stephanie felt another rush of prickles along her arms. "Bittman has people everywhere, keeping tabs on us, and now Ricardo is getting in on that game."

Though Luca and Tate both wanted to look for the woman, Stephanie convinced them not to. "We've got to get to Bitter Song. Maria and Ricardo are already there, and I want to get a feel for things before we decide on a plan for tomorrow—actually today."

She glanced over her shoulder, but there was still no sign of the woman. "Besides, the longer we stay here, the more information is reported back to Bittman or Ricardo."

Resisting the urge to run, Stephanie exited the

restaurant, back out into the cool air. The sky was a brilliant, star-spangled velvet over their heads, and she breathed deep. Tate was at her elbow. Though he didn't touch her, she felt his presence strongly, like the cool breeze on her face.

When Luca steered her toward the rental car, she did not resist.

Keep as much distance between you and Tate as you can.

It was a relief to slide into the darkened car interior. Luca started the engine, and she leaned back her head, suddenly overwhelmed by fatigue. Then an email popped up on her phone. Just a photo, no message.

Cold fear squeezed the breath from her. It was a picture of a handkerchief. She held the phone up to Luca with trembling fingers. "It's Daddy's," she whispered. "I gave it to him on his last birthday."

The dark corner of the photo showed black, illuminated by the dome light Luca flipped on.

They looked at each other in horror, transfixed by the spot that looked very much like blood, an ugly blot against the sheen of the silk.

TEN

Bitter Song lived up to its name, as far as Tate could see when he awoke just before dawn the next morning, stiff from sleeping in the tiny area in the back of the truck covered by a camper shell. The temperature was chilly in spite of their desert location. He hadn't wanted to admit that he didn't have the money to rent one of the small rooms at the Desert Spur Inn, where they'd arrived only a couple hours before. He knew if he'd said something, Luca and Stephanie would have paid for his room without any comment. Probably stupid to refuse, but he had to hang on to his remaining self-respect with every ounce of strength he possessed.

He turned his back on these thoughts and sucked in a deep lungful of clean desert air. All he really needed anyway was a bed and access to the small shower in the pool area. A dark-haired and sun-weathered guy had been cleaning the pool deck with slow, deliberate strokes when Tate had helped himself to the shower earlier. He hadn't said anything.

The stinging hot water hadn't washed away the image. He'd gotten the gist of the final shock, the delivery of the handkerchief photo. Bittman was playing a sick game, and it made his blood boil. The thought that Maria was involved in the mess added salt to the wound. There was still no further word from Gilly, and Tate had tried again several times to leave messages for Maria, just in case she was checking. He'd wanted to say something along the lines of, "What's the matter with you? Don't you know who you're tangled up with? Ricardo's no better than Bittman."

His own words surprised him.

Sis, I know I've been harsh on you. I'm sorry. Let me help you. Call me, please.

He gazed out into the stark landscape of sand flats, distant canyons and the abrupt range of mountains that punched into the rapidly lightening sky. The inn seemed to be perched on the edge of a vast nowhere, bisected by a ribbon of road that led to the half-dozen buildings that comprised downtown. It was almost as if the great Mojave Desert was in the process of swallowing up the town like a snake ingesting a helpless rodent—like Bittman would do to his sister if he didn't find a way to put a stop to it.

He shook his head and did a few stretches to try to work out the stiffness in his leg, wondering why he didn't see any sign of life from the two rooms occupied by Luca and Stephanie. They were exhausted, pushed to the limit by fear and fatigue, but he did not think it was enough to keep Stephanie in bed.

He was proven right when he finally noticed them sitting under the shade offered by a sun-bleached umbrella stuck in a ragged patch of grass, a makeshift picnic area for weary travelers, perched on the far edge of the parking lot. She saw him and gestured him over.

Luca's attention was fixed on his laptop screen, but Stephanie had a curved piece of glass in her hands, and she peered through it to the picture below—the picture Devlin had left in the shop.

"You found yourself a magnifying glass?"

She shook her head, nose wrinkled as she squinted. "I took the makeup mirror apart in the bathroom and borrowed the glass."

"I always said if life didn't give you a door, you'd make a window." He laughed. "Why didn't I think of that?"

"Probably because you don't have any use for makeup mirrors. Can you read this?" She took his hand and pulled him down on the bench next to her, where he tried hard not to feel the softness of her body pressed next to his as he stared through the glass.

"Just looks like squiggles to me." She pressed her face to his, and the sensation made his stomach tumble.

"There," she breathed. "Doesn't that look like letters?"

The satin of her skin next to his made him want to hold her face with his hands and press her lips to his. "Too small to read," he muttered as he stood, pacing up and down the small area.

Stephanie continued to stare at the scrap of paper.

Tate circled until he could stand it no longer. "Time's a wasting. We're going after the crazy desert guy today, right? Shouldn't we get started?"

Luca looked up from his screen. "That's what I'm doing. Checking law enforcement records and newspaper references for anything having to do with a Guarneri."

Tate shook his head. "How about we just go look for some crazy guy with a violin? How many could there be in the desert?"

Luca sighed. "Treasure hunting is mostly research—weeding through historical documents, diaries, talking to someone's great grandfather. You've got to be methodical."

"We're looking for a fiddle, not the lost treasure of the Aztecs."

"An eighteen-million-dollar fiddle, and this is not something we're going to find with 3-D deep-seeking metal detectors and radar units. We have to do some groundwork, otherwise we're just wasting time. We've got to think smart here." He turned back to the laptop.

Tate burned with restlessness. He wasn't about to sit still staring at pieces of paper and computer screens when his sister was running around the desert, working with a possible murderer.

He let himself into the pool area. "Hey," he said, giving a friendly nod to the worker.

The man nodded and offered a polite smile.

"We're looking for someone who lives around here. A guy with a beard. Know anyone like that?"

The man shook his head. "No."

"You sure?"

He nodded again and moved to the trash can, pulling out the filled bag and inserting a new one. Tate moved closer.

"Look, I'm going to level with you. My sister's in a lot of trouble, and this guy can help me figure out where she is. I don't want to make trouble for him—all I want to do is help my sister."

The man looked up, a web of wrinkles appearing around his narrowed eyes as he took in Tate's full measure, from his worn boots to his faded baseball cap. "You got a limp, I seen you. What happened?"

"Tried to get my dad out of a car wreck. The explosion shattered my femur. My sister is all I've got left."

He considered. "She got hurt in the accident, too?"

Tate sighed. "Not on the outside."

"Sometimes the inside is worse." He picked up his broom and leaned against it. "I got a sister."

The man chewed his lip for a moment and crooked his finger in Tate's direction.

A squad car pulled up, and Stephanie had to blink several times to clear her vision from staring into the glass. "Luca…" she breathed. There was no time to do anything but close the laptop and try to paste amiable looks on their faces before the cop got out, strolling by their cars before joining them at the table, her khaki uniform perfectly matching the shade of the gravel under her booted feet. An alert German shepherd looked out the open car window, eyes trained on his master, flared nostrils catching the airborne scents.

The officer stood, fingers tucked into her belt as sunlight found the crow's feet circling her eyes. She chewed a piece of white gum with quick movements of her jaw. "Good morning, I'm Officer Sartori. Welcome to Bitter Song."

Stephanie forced out the words. "Thank you. How nice to receive an official welcome."

"We aim to please. Enjoying your stay? Strange place for city folks to come and vacation."

"We like the desert," Luca said.

"Uh-huh." The officer shot them a smile that was completely devoid of humor. "I've got a substantial to-do list, so let's get down to it," she said, gesturing to the dog. "Bear doesn't like to be in the car very long."

Bear stiffened at the mention of his name.

Luca raised an eyebrow. "Is he liable to jump out of there when he gets bored?"

"Not from boredom, but if I start to sound stressed he's going to think about it, so why don't you give me the truth right off the proverbial bat? Why are you in Bitter Song, really?"

Luca waved his hand and offered a dazzling smile that would have caused many other women to melt. "Who wouldn't want to come here?"

Sartori's expression didn't change. She remained silent except for the cracking of her gum.

Stephanie exchanged a look with him. They could not lie to the police, but they might be able to avoid certain details. "We own a Treasure Seekers business, and we followed an evidence trail to Bitter Song."

She pursed her lips. "Let me guess—you're looking for a violin, right?"

"How did you know that?" Stephanie said.

"Got a call from the sheriff at Lone Ridge this morning. He mentioned there had been a few visitors in town. We don't get many visitors." She continued chewing her gum, eyes scanning the table. "Love your bag. Coach?"

Stephanie swallowed hard. "Yes."

"Pretty. You visited the music store in Lone Ridge."

"We talked to Mr. Devlin and asked him if he had seen the violin."

"Had he?"

Sweat rolled down Stephanie's face. What if Bittman's contacts were watching right now? Reporting her conversation with the police?

"No," Luca cut in. "He'd spoken to someone who brought in a picture of a violin, but the man didn't leave an address and there was no way to verify the authenticity by a picture. We came to Bitter Song to ask around, see if we could dig up the name of the man Devlin talked to."

"Why did you go back to the music store last night? A resident saw your car there some time after midnight."

How much did Sartori know? Ice cold shivers went up Stephanie's back. "We got a phone message from him, and we went to meet him but he wasn't there."

Tate joined them and introduced himself. "Nice dog."

"Not nice. Effective," Sartori said. "I've seen him bring down a two-hundred-twenty-pound biker. Scared the guy so bad he wet his pants. You're Tate Fuego, the same Tate Fuego arrested for driving while under the influence of drugs four years ago?"

Stephanie watched the color suffuse Tate's face, and she felt herself aching for him as their prior conversation replayed itself in her mind.

Supposed to be forgiven, right? That Christian thing?

If God forgave, why did his past sins keep getting dredged up for the all the world to see?

Not past, Steph, she told herself, remembering the pill bottle in his backpack.

"Yes, Officer," Tate was saying, chin high. "But I'm clean now. Have been for a year."

"Good. Hate to see a guy with plenty of miles ahead of him wipe out in the first leg of the race. Why are you with these two?"

Tate shrugged. "My sister is involved in looking for the violin, too. I want to be sure she stays out of trouble."

"It might just turn out that trouble's already here," Sartori said, the gum flashing between her teeth.

Stephanie felt a ripple of dread course through her. "What do you mean?"

"Early this morning the local cops recovered a body, victim of a hit-and-run. Two problems with that. First off, not too many hit-and-runs here. We're not exactly a speedway, you see."

"And the second problem?" Luca asked.

"Dead guy looked as though he'd been beaten before he was run down, like somebody was trying to get some information from him. Maybe he made a break from his attacker and met the front end of a vehicle."

Stephanie's stomach churned with dread as Sartori continued.

"Oh, and one other strange thing. Dead guy had your business card in his pocket." She pulled out a notebook and consulted it. "Treasure Seekers, proprietors Stephanie, Luca and Victor Gage." She stopped and quirked an eyebrow. "Where is Victor, anyway? You didn't bring along the other brother on this treasure hunt?"

Luca shook his head, eyes intense. "He's in the hospital recovering from an accident."

"And you're here in the Mojave? Chasing a violin? Strange priorities, if you don't mind me saying it."

Stephanie finally found her voice. "The dead man…who is he?"

Sartori cocked her head and gave her gum another good crack. "You know him. Bruno Devlin, owner of the music store you visited just last night."

Stephanie's cry hung for a moment in the thin desert air.

Sartori's expression remained relaxed, but Tate could see that her eyes didn't miss one single iota of their reactions.

"The poor man," Stephanie whispered.

"Yeah. Lived in Lone Ridge for years. Never caused a lick of trouble. Never even got so much as a parking ticket." Sartori stared at Stephanie.

"Did anyone see the car that hit him?" Luca asked.

"No, but you can believe I checked both your vehicles before I stopped to talk to you. So you have no idea why Mr. Devlin wanted to meet with you a second time?"

The moments ticked by. Tate waited to see if Stephanie would tell the rest about finding his sister in the shop and about finding the Polaroid, which she had hastily placed under a loose sheet of paper. She opened her mouth, and the agony unfolded on her face. The crackle of a radio on Sartori's belt broke the silence. She took a step away and listened before returning with a look of disgust on her face.

"Seems I've got to go. Somebody much higher on the food chain is rearranging my day." She leveled a deadly serious look at them. "Stay in touch. I'll be wanting to finish this conversation real soon." She got back into her cruiser and peeled out of the parking lot, bits of gravel zinging against the bottom of the car.

Luca waited until she was gone. "Who do you think is responsible for Devlin's death?"

"My money is on Ricardo," Tate said, eyes on Stephanie.

"But why kill him?" she mumbled. "He was just a man who sold instruments. He didn't have the violin."

"Maybe he knew where it was, and he was going to tell us."

Tate waited for the two of them to say it aloud, that Maria could have been the driver that struck and killed Devlin. The unspoken accusation hovered there until Luca got up from the bench and gave his sister a hug.

"I'm going to have Tuney make an anonymous call to the police and describe Ricardo and the VW. Maybe it will give them enough to work with. We've got to move faster, find the violin before someone else gets hurt or we're thrown in jail for obstruction."

"So let's go then," Tate said, pulling the keys from his pocket.

"Where?" Stephanie asked. "We have no leads."

"Speak for yourself. While you were sitting around, I did some research of my own."

Luca's eyes narrowed. "Really."

"Yes, really. Rocky, the janitor at this place, has worked here for fifteen years, and he knows everybody."

Stephanie's lips parted. "Everybody?"

"Yeah, including a man who goes by the name Eugene. Big guy, wiry beard, loves to hike up to the ruins and paint pictures. Even has a little place way outside of town."

Luca shook his head, but Tate thought he caught the slightest hint of admiration. "Good work, Fuego."

Tate couldn't resist. "Real good. I guess you'll have to put me on the Treasure Seekers' payroll pretty soon."

"Don't bet on it," Luca said, as he packed up his gear.

ELEVEN

Stephanie had no luck finding the location Tate had been given for Eugene's home on her GPS. As near as they could glean from the elderly gas station attendant, there was a small stone structure about fifteen miles out of town that had been vacant for periods of time, but for the past few years was inhabited by a man matching Eugene's description.

"Have you spoken to him before?" Stephanie asked, pushing her wind-whipped bangs out of her face.

The attendant shrugged, arching a grizzled eyebrow. "Not much of a talker, except to himself. Carries around a sketch pad and scribbles all the time. Don't like people much. That's about all I know."

Stephanie thanked him and turned to go.

"Plays real nice, though," the attendant added.

Luca's eyebrows shot up. "Plays?"

The man nodded. "Yeah. I heard him one time

when I was taking my grandkids out for a dune buggy ride around the stone house. We were resting in the shade near his place. Heard some sort of fiddle or something. Sounded real nice, but he stopped quick like when he heard us, I guess. As I said, he don't like people much."

"Thank you," she said. "You've been very helpful."

"One more word," he said, stabbing a callused thumb at the sky. "Better not go out there today."

"Why not?" Tate asked.

"Windy. Real windy. Not a good time to be out there near the dunes."

Stephanie nodded, and they returned to their cars. "Well, we're not calling off the search on account of a little wind."

Tate frowned, looking at the trees, their needles undulating like bristly fingers. "Sandstorms can kill you."

Luca shifted. "I don't know anything about them. I'm not a desert guy."

"Maria and I used to go with Dad and do some four-wheeling."

Stephanie saw the flash of pain ripple across his face and felt the urge to reach out to him, but she knew the gesture wouldn't be welcome.

He cleared his throat. "Anyway, we don't have a choice, do we? Clock's ticking down for your father and my sister."

Stephanie's stomach clenched. "And it's a matter

of time before Sartori comes back with another set of questions we don't want to answer."

Silently they loaded up, she and Luca in the rental and Tate following in the truck. Luca headed in the direction the attendant had given them, down a dirt road that rose steadily in elevation against a brilliant sky, dotted with gossamer clouds. It was an arid, hostile environment, like an alien planet resistant to human life.

She closed her eyes for a moment, exhausted in body and spirit. *Daddy, where are you?* She prayed for the hundredth time that he was safe, that Victor would recover. That she could snatch her life back from Bittman's grasp. With her big brother beside her and Tate following behind, had she sucked them all into a goose chase that might come to a disastrous end?

When the panic began to threaten, she said another quick prayer and tried again to examine the photo Devlin had given her, but the bouncing of the car made it hard to focus.

"Who could have killed Devlin?" she mused aloud. "He was just a music store owner, not a threat to anyone."

"Ricardo might have killed him to keep him quiet, I suppose." Luca paused, then shot her a look. "There's another possibility, too."

Stephanie shook her head. "Maria is not a killer. She's impulsive and hot tempered, but she wouldn't do that."

Luca didn't look convinced. "When I politely declined a date, she told Tate that I came onto her. That doesn't say much for her character."

"She's desperate to have someone love her, Luca, and rejection freaks her out. I think that's why she fell in with Bittman. He was probably charming, gave her presents, a job, anything she wanted to string her along until he grew bored of her."

"So if she was in love with the guy, why go after his violin? What changed?"

Stephanie shaded her eyes against the sun-washed rock that rose on either side of the path. "That's what we'd better find out fast."

They drove for miles, climbing to the top of breathtaking vistas and back down to the endless acres of sand dunes, pushed along by the wind. Stephanie was beginning to worry that they'd made a wrong turn when they spotted a flat-topped stone structure, tucked into a dusty hollow below the road. Stephanie's heart sped up as she got out and they joined Tate, who was peering through a pair of binoculars.

"Doesn't look like anyone is home," he said, handing them to her.

She took a close look at the house, perched in the shade of a scraggly mesquite. There were only a few scrubby junipers growing close by, nothing to provide good cover. Wind tossed grit into her face, and she lowered the binoculars. "Any ideas?"

"Only one way to find out who's home," Tate

said, starting down a gravel trail that led from the road to the house.

Stephanie didn't waste any time in following him. When they reached the house, they stopped to listen. Luca slipped around the back, returning after a few moments with a report. "All closed up tight. Shutters are drawn, but someone's been here recently."

Stephanie gasped. "How do you know?"

"There's a half-burned newspaper out back. Looks like someone had a campfire going. Date on the newspaper is three days ago."

Tate held up a hand. "Did you hear that?"

Luca and Stephanie froze.

"I didn't hear anything," Luca said. "What?"

Tate listened for another long moment before shaking his head. "Nothing I guess. Just my imagination."

Stephanie approached the door. "Enough wasting time."

Both men protested, but she shrugged them off. "A woman at the door is less intimidating," she said.

"Depends on the woman," Tate murmured, his mouth quirked in a half grin. Luca and Tate took up positions on either side of the door as Stephanie knocked.

"Eugene? My name is Stephanie. I wanted to talk to you."

No sound came from inside the stone house.

"I'm not here to bother you. I just have a quick question."

No response.

She put her hand on the door and turned the handle. It gave slightly. "It's unlocked," she mouthed.

Luca shook his head and put out an arm to stop her from entering.

"We've got to," she whispered.

This time both Tate and Luca moved to stop her as she pushed open the door. They stood frozen as it swung wide with a low groan. The interior was dark and cool. Stephanie could make out a tiny living room with a rocking chair and a rickety shelf overflowing with books of every shape and size.

"Eugene?" she called again. "My name is Stephanie. I need your help. My father's in trouble. I'm going to come in so we can talk, okay?"

This time both Tate and Luca pushed in front of her and entered first. Biting back both fear and irritation, she followed them in. The house was perfectly quiet. A shadowed hallway led to the kitchen, and she followed Tate into the cramped space.

Tate tried his best to keep Stephanie behind him. At least he was able to ascertain that no one was in the kitchen before she pushed in. The yellowed tile counter was immaculate, in complete juxtaposition to the round table, which was covered with feathers, each fixed to an index card with a pencil sketch of a bird.

He picked up one and looked close. "Guy's a good artist," he whispered.

Stephanie tried a light switch with no result before she opened the refrigerator. "It's empty. No electricity."

Tate pointed to a cooler under the table. "Low-tech fridge."

She pulled open the lid of the cooler and perused the supplies floating in half-melted ice. "Water, and jars of peanut butter and jelly. Eugene lives simply."

Luca called them back out to the living room. "No one here. Bedroom's got nothing in it but a sleeping bag tossed over the box spring. No sign of a car, so I wonder how he's getting around."

"Even my trailer looks cushy compared to this," Tate said. "Hard to believe this guy's been in possession of a priceless violin all these years. Why hasn't he sold it? Maybe we got the wrong info."

"I don't think so," Stephanie said, picking up what looked like a small bar of soap. It was scored and scratched across the surface. "Violin rosin."

Tate held up a hand. "Quiet. Hear that?"

They froze, and a faint creaking sounded faintly.

"He's here somewhere," Tate mouthed.

"There's a closet in the bedroom, but I checked," Luca said, voice low. "It was empty."

"Eugene is probably better at hide-and-seek than you are," Stephanie whispered to her brother.

Tate headed for the bedroom, which was, as

Luca described, bare of personal effects, save for the worn sleeping bag. Luca caught his arm.

"I didn't shut the door."

Now the door was firmly closed. Tate wrapped his fingers around the handle and counted to three before he wrenched it open. Eugene was not there, only a set of three empty hangers and a knitted cap tossed onto a wooden peg. One of the hangers moved ever so slightly. A waft of cool air hit Tate's face. Looking in the back, he saw the source—a small door hidden in the back wall, which had not been fully closed. It opened with a creak of old wood, exposing a tunnel.

Tate took a penlight from his pocket and immediately plunged into the gloom, followed by Luca and Stephanie. The old tunnel had a cement floor and walls covered in broken brick. Thick wooden beams were lined up every four feet along the ceiling, hanging with cobwebs that trailed into the gloom. Tate had to stand bent over to avoid bashing his head on the low beams.

Their eyes adjusting to the darkness, they moved forward, Stephanie stumbling and falling to her knees. Tate helped her up, momentarily pulling her body against his, feeling her warm breath on his neck, the silken caress of her hair. Her hands squeezed his biceps for a dizzying second while she regained her balance.

"Thanks," she said.

My pleasure, he thought, remembering how he'd

used to hold her in his arms every day, then how he'd thrown her away along with his own happiness. Shaking the feel of her out of his head, he moved along, wishing they'd thought to bring a flashlight. The space grew narrower as the tunnel pinched in, the air stuffy and dank. He jerked in surprise as a drop of cold water landed on his neck from one of the rafters overhead.

"Must be an underground spring close," Luca said, swatting at a cobweb that clung to his face.

"This is old. The original home owner must have wanted his own private exit."

"Or he was storing something down here that he didn't want the world to see," Luca added.

Tate wondered if the walls were still sound, with the deteriorating powers of water and age working away at them. He inhaled the aroma of dead air. It was the same smell he'd experienced hundreds of times, working shoulder to shoulder with his father. It never ceased to amaze him how solid brick and steel could be reduced to rubble in a matter of moments. A wrecking ball or a series of precisely placed holes filled with TNT or C-4, and a perfectly constructed building could be obliterated. There one minute, gone the next.

A moan echoed through the tunnel, making the hair on the back of his neck stand up.

"Why won't you leave me alone?" the thin voice wailed.

A swaying light blinded Tate until his vision

recovered and he could make out the shivering form of the man he guessed to be Eugene, thrown into strange illumination by a lantern he held in one hand. He was slight but tall, his hair long and unkempt, the beard bristling from his chin. His eyes shifted uneasily from Luca to Tate and on to Stephanie.

"Hey there," Tate said, voice low. "I'm sorry if we scared you."

Eugene shook his head so violently that the lantern light bounced crazily around the tunnel. "You're not sorry. You're here to take it."

Stephanie moved closer. "Eugene, we're not going to hurt you."

"Those are lies," Eugene whispered, his voice pained. "You all tell lies, every one of you."

"No, it's not a lie," Stephanie said. "We're here to try to help my father. I'm sure you can understand that."

"Father?" he cried. "Poor father."

"Yes. I'll bet you love your father, too."

Anguish seeped into Eugene's words. "They're gone, everyone's gone and I'm alone. I want to be alone. Go away and don't come back here."

"Why don't you tell us who is bothering you?" Luca said. "Maybe we can help you."

"Get away!" Eugene shouted, the cry bouncing off the walls and ringing through the space.

"Please..." Stephanie started, but Eugene was edging back into the darkness. He must have hung the lantern on a nail because the light was suddenly pinned in place, bringing Eugene into dim focus.

"Is that…?" Stephanie started.

Tate's stomach dropped as he saw what Eugene clutched in his other hand. He knew the power of dynamite. Fuego Demolitions had used a range of explosives over the years, but the kind Eugene gripped was an altogether different beast. It was old, the type of dynamite made with a mixture of nitroglycerin and sawdust. Relatively harmless— if the blasting cap was absent.

Heart thumping, he looked closer. The cap was still affixed to the eight-inch stick, clutched in the man's trembling fingers.

"Does he know what he's doing with that?" Luca whispered.

"If it's unstable, it may not matter," Tate murmured back. Old dynamite stored improperly would sweat out the nitro, forming crystals on the outside of the sticks, causing them to become highly sensitive to the slightest shock or friction. Dynamite of any kind was dangerous. Old dynamite was deadly and unpredictable. "Eugene, put that down. It's not safe."

"You're not safe. You're here to take it. I have to do it." Tears streamed down his hairy cheeks. In spite of the potentially lethal situation, Tate felt a stab of pity for the man who he realized was mentally challenged and obviously terrified. He had the feeling Eugene had been through his own kind of nightmare. A match flared.

"No, Eugene," Tate said, stepping forward. "Put down the dynamite before you hurt yourself. You can go. We won't stop you. I give you my word." Tate figured they had maybe ten seconds before the match died out.

Eugene shifted, eyes rolling in thought. "I don't know."

Seven seconds left. "You don't want to hurt anyone," Tate said. "I can tell."

Time stood still as the match burned a hole in the gloom.

Five seconds. "I don't want to hurt anyone," Eugene repeated. "But I've got to get away."

The last seconds ticked away.

Eugene touched the match to the fuse.

"Eugene, no!" Tate yelled, leaping forward. Eugene scrambled backward as the fuse caught, tossing the dynamite behind him as he ran. Tate reversed course.

"Run!" he shouted, urging Stephanie and Luca in front of him, toward the entrance, knowing in his heart it was too late.

A deafening boom shook the tunnel, and chunks of debris began to rain down upon them.

TWELVE

Stephanie lost her footing, sprawling stomach first as bricks smashed into the floor around her. A solid weight pressed down on her, and she realized Tate had covered her back with his torso in an effort to shield her. The world spun around her in a dark maelstrom of noise and choking dust. She felt the secondary impact as heavy rock fell on top of Tate. Sharp bits cut into her cheeks as he pressed her to the cold floor.

The rumbling grew in intensity, and Stephanie feared the tunnel was collapsing around them. They would be buried under tons of concrete, beneath an empty stone house. No one would find them until it was too late. She fought to breathe against the dust and panic.

"Hold on," Tate said into her ear, as if he could read the terrifying thoughts racing through her mind. His hands wrapped around her arms, squeezing some courage back into her.

There was one last groan of protesting wood

before the vibrations tapered off, the sound softening and dying away. Debris still poured from
above, but it had lessened to a trickle. Tate eased
off her. An unsteady light emanated from a burning hunk of wood above them, glowing strangely
through the thick curtain of drifting dust. "Tell me
you're okay," he said, mouth pressed to her ear.
There was such longing in his voice, such tenderness, that her eyes filled with tears. He helped her
roll over, and she looked into his dust-streaked face
in the flickering light.

"I think so," she whispered, putting her hand to
his cheek. He clasped it there for a moment and
closed his eyes, breathing hard. It was the same
sweet connection they used to share, and it cut to
her very core.

"That's my girl," he said.

She could only manage a smile before fear clawed
her gut.

"Luca," she cried, trying to scramble to her feet.
Tate gripped her arm.

"Move slow. This place is unstable now."

She got to her feet and picked her way through
the clots of broken rock. The light was not suffi-
cient to illuminate the dark crevices. She could see
no sign of her brother. "Luca?" she called again,
her voice shrill. Victor lay broken in a hospital bed,
her father was lost and now Luca. It was too much.
She would not allow it.

Give me the strength, God.

Filled with energy born of fear and faith, she began pushing rocks out of the way, calling her brother's name every few moments. Her back and legs ached with myriad bruises and cuts. With every second that passed, her anxiety edged up a notch until she found herself holding her breath, fingers clenched into rigid fists. "Say something, Luca!" she screamed.

"Here," Tate called from a few feet away. "He's under here."

She waded through the rubble as fast as she could manage. Luca was lying face up under a fallen beam. Tate grunted as he struggled to lift the wood. "Too heavy. Need some leverage."

They looked around for something to use, and Stephanie came up with a long piece of wood, probably knocked loose in the explosion. She shoved it at Tate. He wedged one end under the wood and balanced it over a chunk of cement. "When I lift, slide him out, feet first."

Stephanie nodded, heart pounding.

With an effort that made sweat pour down his face, Tate threw all his weight on the end of the wood.

"It's not moving," Stephanie cried.

Tate did not answer, instead redoubling his efforts, pushing so hard the veins bulged in his neck. Shifting rubble proved that the beam was moving, inch by precious inch, until there was enough clearance for her to haul out Luca from under the beam by gripping him around the ankles.

When he slid clear, she knelt next to him, her cheek to his mouth, checking, praying for a puff of air on her face.

Luca grunted, and Stephanie nearly squealed with joy. "He's alive." He mumbled something else, and she put her head closer to his lips.

"Your hair is in my mouth," Luca said.

She laughed and brushed the debris off his face as best she could. "Are you hurt?"

He shifted as if he was going to sit up, but she held him down. "Not until you answer me."

He exhaled, eyes closed for a moment. "As far as I can tell, I'm okay. I can feel all my limbs and move all my fingers and toes. I might have a concussion...."

"Sounds like a clean bill of health to me," Tate offered.

"Right," Luca said. "Can I sit up now?"

She held his shoulder and helped him ease into a sitting position. Dirt fell from his hair and shoulders. He blinked several times.

"Yeah, everything seems to be working, but my ankle hurts." His eyes scanned the ruined tunnel before they came to rest on Tate. "Thanks for digging me out."

Tate nodded but didn't answer.

Stephanie ran her fingers along his ankle. "Nothing feels out of place, but you might have a fracture."

He eased the ankle back and forth, grimacing. "Just a sprain."

"Uh-huh," she said. "Let's get you out of here, and we can take a look when the light's better."

Luca cast a chagrined glance down the tunnel. "Eugene's long gone, I suppose."

"Yeah," Tate agreed. "But we'll catch up with him." He offered a hand to Luca, and he and Stephanie helped him to his feet.

Luca tried to walk and nearly fell. "I guess I really did mess up my ankle," he grumbled. "Need some ice and it will be fine."

They didn't reply, making their way out. Stephanie exited first, Luca following, awkwardly hopping, using Tate's shoulder for support as he hefted himself along.

When they arrived back in the kitchen, Tate steered Luca to a chair while Stephanie retrieved some ice from the cooler and wrapped it in a towel, applying it to Luca's ankle after they removed his boot.

"It's very swollen," she said. "We'd better get you to a clinic."

"It's only a sprain. It will be fine in the morning."

"Did anyone ever tell you you're stubborn?" Stephanie asked.

"Family trait," Tate murmured, earning a glare from Stephanie.

Luca shook his head. "I didn't think Eugene would resort to dynamite to get rid of us. He seemed harmless enough, but I guess I was wrong about that."

Stephanie wet another towel and used it to dab at a cut on Luca's face before she turned to examine Tate.

He waved her off. "I think Eugene is scared. Maybe he had a run-in with Ricardo. For whatever reason, he's decided that violin belongs to him."

Stephanie pulled the Polaroid photo from her back pocket and held it to the light from the kitchen window. She shook her head. "I've been focusing on the wrong thing."

"What?" Luca said, wiping grit from his shoulders.

"I've been trying to read the label to authenticate the Guarneri, but there's another way." She held the photo up for them both, pointing to the scroll. "The Quinto has a scar on the scroll from the building collapse, remember?" She peered closely. "It's not definite, but see that mark there? It could be the same scar."

Tate looked at her. "So Bittman is right. The Guarneri really did escape the fire all those years ago."

Stephanie bit her lip. "And it seems that Eugene might be the one who stole it."

"And set the fire to cover his tracks?"

"Bittman said it was another man who set the fire."

Tate sighed. "Ricardo. He's the only other person involved in this besides Maria."

Stephanie nodded, feeling the prickle of fear along her spine. "Ricardo won't stop until he murders Eugene and gets the violin that he tried to steal all those years ago. He killed Devlin because he didn't want Devlin to lead us to Eugene."

Tate sighed. "That leaves us caught between crazy Eugene and a murderer with nothing to lose."

"And don't forget Joshua Bittman," Luca said, voice grim, "a certifiable psychopath."

Tate and Stephanie herded Luca to the car in spite of his efforts to shoo them away, and Stephanie got behind the wheel. It was late afternoon; the sun, low on the horizon, cast long shadows across the road. No one said it aloud, but Tate found himself wondering how they would track Eugene now, with Luca barely able to walk.

You're not doing much better yourself. The pain in his leg was excruciating, aggravated by the extreme effort of hoisting the beam off Luca. He popped two aspirin, knowing it would do nothing more than dull the pain. He thought about the pills in his backpack and how easy it would be to fall back into the numbing narcotic haze. Then, as he had thousands of times in the past year, he made the decision to stay clean and sober. Something tugged at his mind. He thought of the moment the rumbling in the tunnel had stopped, and Stephanie lay still in his arms.

Something called out in his soul that moment, something deeper than his rational thought or his conscious mind. It was the same quiet sense of God stirring, urging him to stay sober every day— the same feeling he got when he sent up a plea for Stephanie's protection today. He was indeed the worst kind of sinner. An addict, a neglectful brother, a man who abandoned Stephanie Gage. Yet in that moment, he found himself again casting his deepest desire up to God for something other than his sobriety.

His every thought for the past year, his every anguished prayer had been dedicated to staying clean. Now his heart seemed to have expanded, allowing him to pray for something beyond himself. The prayer had been answered, and Stephanie was safe. He wasn't sure which was the greater blessing, that she'd been spared injury in a collapse that might have killed them all, or he'd once again surrendered his desires to God—desires that went beyond keeping the pills in the bottle.

He pushed these thoughts back down into the dark recesses of his heart, and bent his thoughts to the task ahead. Maria was still out there somewhere. In trouble up to her neck, no doubt. There had been no messages from her and no leads from

Gilly after he had pried into her computer files. What did she think she was accomplishing by trying to take Bittman's violin?

He guided the truck along for another half hour, looking for any signs indicating the direction Eugene had taken. A dirt path, so faint he might have missed it altogether, caught his attention. He tapped the horn to signal a stop and got out, willing his leg not to buckle.

Stephanie joined him, and Luca hobbled up.

Tate pointed to the path. "Could lead to the tunnel exit," he mused.

Luca frowned. "Then again, it could be a hunting trail. Doesn't look like anyone's used it in a while."

Tate shook his head. "I'll check it out. Be right back."

"I'll go, too," Stephanie said. "Luca, why don't you call home and check on Victor?"

She didn't wait for his answer before plunging down the path, which sloped sharply away from the road. The day was hot and the cloud cover pressed warmth down upon them as they pushed past a screen of mesquite shrubs. The wind, which continued to blow, brought no hint of cooling to the sultry air.

Stephanie stopped, listening.

He gave her a questioning look.

"Just wanted to make sure my brother isn't trying to follow. He hates being left out of the action."

Tate hid his smile and pressed on, the uneven ground agony on his leg. Teeth gritted, he continued along, the journey passing in a haze of pain. After another thirty minutes he stopped, under the pretense of checking for broken twigs or marks on the ground. He felt her fingers on his wrist.

"It's your leg, isn't it?"

He shrugged. "I'm okay."

"No, you're not. You're in serious pain. I can tell."

He soaked in her eyes, luminous and gentle. "You get used to it. Doc says this is probably as good as it gets. I can handle it."

She stared, his own face mirrored in her gaze. "How do you handle it? By…" She looked away.

Shame and anger boiled up inside him. "By abusing drugs?"

She shook her head. "That's not what I was going to say."

He put a hand on her cheek and forced her to look at him. "Steph, you never lied to me. Don't start now. You think I'm still using, don't you?"

She gripped his hand and then pulled it away. "I don't want to think so."

"I'm not."

He saw the doubt in her eyes, and his heart broke all over again. The worst thing, even worse than losing her love, was losing her respect. He did not trust himself to speak so he moved ahead, deeper into the tangle of undergrowth. The path was overgrown, and he was beginning to think it was nothing more than an abandoned hunting trail. Then it dumped into a small clearing, crowded by bristlecone pine trees.

A rocky outcropping rose some twenty feet, with boulders piled along the bottom. They moved closer, and Tate was able to discern an opening between the boulders.

Bingo. The exit to Eugene's tunnel.

"At least we know where he came out," Stephanie said. "But how is that going to help us?"

Tate examined the ground carefully, noting a faint set of imprints pressed into the dust. "He's got a motorbike." The tracks led through the grove of trees. They followed on foot to a well-packed path that paralleled the road—wide enough for a vehicle, as least as far as they could see before it twisted away through the trees.

Stephanie wiped her forehead. "We'd better go back and get the cars. We'll never catch up on foot."

"We're going to have to wait until morning."

"No," she said firmly. "There's another few hours of sunlight. We can make headway, sleep in the cars if it gets too dark."

He stood as straight as he could manage. "It's another half hour back to the car, and we're all tired and banged up."

"Then I'll go by myself," Stephanie snapped, eyes flaring, "if you're not in a big hurry to find them."

He tamped down his own surge of anger. "I'm

in just as much a hurry to find my sister as you are to get your father back, but one thing I've had hammered into my own thick head these past four years is patience."

She studied his face, and he could see the anger simmer down in hers. A slight smile quirked her lips. "I never would have thought of you as the patient type."

"People can change." *I've changed.* He wanted desperately to say the words aloud, but they refused to cross his lips. Her gaze held his for a long moment before she turned and headed back up the path with no further comment.

Tate did his best to keep up, but it was still three quarters of an hour before they made it back to the car to find an irate Luca. As much as he appeared to chafe at this delay confronting them, he agreed with Tate that a night search after Eugene was foolhardy. They returned to the hotel at sundown, dirty, famished and exhausted.

They picked up some sandwiches from the deli and piled into Stephanie and Luca's room to eat them, debriefing the day's insanity.

"Good news is, we found Eugene, and we can be pretty sure he's got the violin," Luca said.

"Bad news is, we lost him again, and Maria and Ricardo are still at large." Stephanie sighed.

A knock at the door startled them. Tate looked

through the peephole. "More bad news," he whispered. "Officer Sartori has come back for another visit."

THIRTEEN

Stephanie felt her stomach lurch as Tate opened the door. Officer Sartori stood, hands on her hips, looking every inch the cop, even though she wore jeans and a T-shirt.

"Please come in," Stephanie said. "Sit down."

Sartori gave her a thorough once-over. "No need. This will be a short visit. Where have you three been?"

Luca gestured to his ankle, propped on a chair under another bag of ice. "We went looking for the violin, and I had an accident."

Her eyes narrowed. "Uh-huh. I'm not a patient person, as you've probably gathered. Now I'm impatient, and I'm also angry."

Stephanie swallowed. "Why?"

"Because someone high up on the political food chain is pressuring the sheriff into taking me off this investigation."

"What do you mean?" Luca asked.

"The sheriff's getting heat from the county supervisor to direct his resources elsewhere—in other words, he's pulled me from the Devlin case."

"And the supervisor is leaning on the sheriff because…?" Tate said.

"The official line is that we're pulling back to focus on an identity theft ring, so we're leaving the Devlin case up to the Lone Ridge law enforcement, which basically consists of a really hard-working full-time officer and two volunteers who don't have the time or resources for this investigation."

Stephanie willed her feet not to pace. "What's the unofficial line?"

"Are you asking me what I think?" Sartori said. She nodded.

"I think I'm being pulled off because someone with power and money wants to cover up something. I think that someone has a lot to do with you three and this violin or whatever it is. And you know what else I think?"

The three remained silent.

"I think I'm going to work this case on my own time until I figure out just what Treasure Seekers is really doing in Bitter Song." She pulled a photo out of her pocket. "Do you know this person?"

Stephanie felt her entire body grow cold as she gripped the photo, forcing out the words. "He's a man I used to work for years ago. His name is Joshua Bittman."

"That part I know. I did some digging, and I found out that twenty years ago he claimed his father lost a Guarneri violin. Interesting coincidence that you just happened to be looking for a Guarneri at the moment."

"Interesting," Luca agreed solemnly.

Sartori put the picture away. "Is Bittman the guy you're working for now?"

Stephanie's heart pounded so hard, she thought it would break out of her chest. "We're working on our own behalf."

"Is that right? And when you find this violin, who are you going to give it to?"

Luca cleared his throat. "We'll establish legal ownership and hand it over to the correct individual. For us it's about the find, not the money."

"Well, isn't that big of you? I think I'll have to give Mr. Bittman a call and see if his story jibes with yours."

"No," Stephanie cried out before she could stop herself.

"No?" Sartori repeated, folding her arms across her chest. "And why wouldn't you want me to call him?"

She looked directly into Sartori's eyes. "Joshua Bittman is a dangerous man."

Her eyes narrowed. "I've looked up the esteemed Gage family. Well connected, plenty of money, no legal scrapes pending, no illegal activities under the respectable exterior. So what's this Bittman got on you?"

Stephanie pressed her lips together. Her legs felt

as if they were boneless, barely able to support her weight. What could she say that would not result in her father's death? Tate joined her and put an arm around her shaking shoulders. "Officer, we're not the bad guys here, I can promise you that."

Her gaze traveled from Luca to Stephanie and finally rested on Tate. "Okay. I'll leave it for now because I can see you're not going to make it easy on me. That's no problem. I don't like things easy." She opened the door. "But I promise you I'm going to dig up the truth, and I'd better not find out that you're on the wrong side of the law, or I'll make it my mission in life to lock you up. Am I making myself clear?"

"As crystal," Luca said.

"You can expect to be seeing me in your rear-view mirror. I'll be your personal shadow while you enjoy the finer things in Bitter Song." She smiled. "Have a great day."

Sartori left, and Stephanie's legs would not hold her up anymore. She sank down on the bed, sucking in a shaky breath. "If she calls Bittman, he'll kill Dad."

Luca hopped over and sat next to her. "He wants the violin. If we can convince him we're close, he won't hurt Dad."

Stephanie knew that deep down, Luca was just as scared as she was. "Call Tuney. Maybe he's found out something." She focused on breathing, keeping herself calm while Luca dialed, putting Tuney on speakerphone.

There was a clatter of noise on Tuney's end.

"Where are you?" Luca asked.

"Clinic. Got a lead on your dad. Followed it to an apartment, only someone was waiting and I took a bullet to the shoulder."

Stephanie gasped. "Oh, no. Tuney, are you okay? You could have been killed."

"I'm fine. Your father was being kept there, I think, but they moved him."

She felt like screaming. "We've got a cop here who is onto the truth. She's going to contact Bittman."

Tuney grunted. "Then I'd better pick up the pace over here."

"We can't ask you to risk your life," Stephanie said, choking back a sob.

"You're not asking. Talk to you soon." Then he was gone.

Stephanie closed her eyes, head spinning. "This is all going wrong."

Tate took her hand. "I think we need to call Bittman. Tell him we're close. Buy ourselves some time to find Eugene."

Stephanie gripped his fingers, trying to stem the panic flowing through her veins. "I don't think I can talk to him without losing it."

"I'll talk," Luca barked, picking up her phone.

"Luca…" Stephanie started as he punched in the numbers.

"I know what the stakes are, sis." He listened for a few moments, frowning. "He's not answering." Luca spoke to the answering machine. "We've located the man with the violin. We'll pick him up tomorrow, and you'll have your prize. We'll turn it over when you return our father." He clicked off.

"So what do we do now?" Stephanie asked.

"We try to get some sleep," Tate answered.

And count the minutes until morning, Stephanie thought.

Tate stretched out in the camper of Gilly's truck and fell into a restless sleep, interrupted by the pain in his leg. Stephanie had argued with him to let them pay for a room until she'd run out of breath. He awoke hours later, disoriented, to find it was still dark, his watch showing a few minutes after four in the morning. Lying there, willing his body to come awake, he listened, trying to figure out what had awakened him.

A soft crunch made him bolt upright. The sound came from the rock pathway that skirted the small hotel. He pulled a corner of the curtain aside and peered out. A sliver of moon did little to illuminate the area. Holding his breath, he stared intently into the darkness.

A flicker of movement from the bushes alongside the building caught his eye. Pulling a T-shirt on over his jeans, he didn't bother with shoes. Slinking into the front seat, he tried to ease open the driver's side door without making any noise. His plan fell apart when the creak of the metal hinge sounded loud in the predawn. Throwing caution aside, he leaped from the vehicle and barreled into the bushes.

There was a muffled exclamation and a cry of surprise as he wrapped his arms around the figure, holding tight.

"Stop it, Tate."

He was so surprised by the voice that he let go, and his sister climbed to her feet.

"You big dummy. You could have killed me."

"Maria?" He didn't know which emotion to act upon. He settled for a hug of profound relief. He squeezed her to his chest and rocked her back and forth. "I'm so glad you're here." He pulled her to arm's length and looked her over thoroughly. "Are you okay? Are you hurt?"

"No, I'm not hurt," she whispered, brushing the leaves from her hair. "No thanks to you." She looked around. "Let's sit in the truck. More private."

Mystified, he followed her to the truck. She sat in the passenger seat, darting nervous glances out the window.

She took a deep breath. "I can't believe this is all happening."

He frowned. "Did you come here to find Bittman's violin?"

She twisted her long hair between her fingers. "Yes, that's how it started."

His frustration boiled over. "Why would you do something like that? You know what kind of man Bittman is."

"I didn't," she fired back, eyes gleaming. "I thought he loved me. At first he was really nice, and I thought we were…" She broke off and wiped a tear from her face. "Never mind. I can't undo any of that. Please don't rub it in my face."

She was right. It was not the time for blame. "Okay. I'm sorry. I was just crazy with worry about you."

She pressed her fingers to her temples. "So why did you and the Gages come here anyway? Just to find me?"

He took a deep breath. "Not just for that. Bittman kidnapped Wyatt Gage. If Stephanie doesn't find the violin for him, he'll kill Wyatt."

Maria's dark eyes rounded in shock. "He's a monster."

He squeezed her hand. "You aren't to blame for that."

She shook her head, eyes wet. "I didn't listen. Stephanie tried to tell me, and you did, too, but I didn't listen."

He took a deep breath. Maybe they could salvage things before they got any worse. "Let's focus on getting you out of this situation. Tell me why you decided to go after his violin in the first place."

"That's not important. The point is I did, and when I got here I found out I wasn't the only one looking for it. This guy named Ricardo was spying on me when I was with Bittman, and I think he followed me to Devlin's shop."

"Bittman's pool guy."

She nodded. "He met me as I was leaving the shop and convinced me we could find the violin faster if we worked together, and we could sell it and split the money. He said the Guarneri belonged to his great uncle or something, and Hans Bittman stole it from him. He's been working undercover at Bittman's to turn up any leads. I believed him." She shot Tate a look. "Was that another dumb mistake?"

"Finish the story. What did you and Ricardo do next?"

"We contacted Devlin. He said he could get a picture of the violin, but when I went back, he wasn't there. Devlin had told me about the guy who came into the shop with it, so I started asking around. Somebody pointed me to Bitter Song, and I came here and found the man. His name is Eugene."

Tate tried to keep down his growing excitement. "So do you know where the violin is right now?"

"I think it's with Eugene. I've been visiting him, gaining his trust." She flushed. "So we could get him to tell us where it is."

"But he hasn't so far?"

"Not yet. Ricardo said Eugene was a thief, the

vagrant who took the violin from the music store years before, but…" Her forehead wrinkled. "The more I talked with Eugene, tried to gain his trust, I found out he's really sweet. Confused and scared, but not the cutthroat guy Ricardo made him out to be. I'm supposed to meet him up at the ruins in two days."

"What ruins?"

"A ghost town called Lunkville, north of Eugene's stone house. When I get the violin, I'm to contact Ricardo to meet me there." She shook her head. "I thought it was a good plan, but now I'm not sure anymore. That's why I came here, to talk it out with you. It doesn't seem right to take it away from Eugene. He doesn't care about the money, and I'm sure he didn't know it was wrong when he stole it from Bittman." Her voice hardened. "Bittman doesn't deserve the violin anyway, if his father took it from Ricardo."

Tate took Maria's hand. "Listen to me carefully, Maria. Ricardo is not who you think he is. His family never owned the violin. We think he set fire to Bittman's shop all those years ago and killed Bittman's brother, Peter. As soon as he gets his hands on that Guarneri, he's going to kill Eugene and probably you."

Her eyes widened in fear. "No. That can't be true."

He squeezed her fingers. "I'm not lying to you. You know that."

She sucked in a breath, and her eyes filled with tears as she yanked away her hand. "Oh, no. What have I done? How could I have made such a mess of everything?" A trail of tears flowed down her face.

His heart constricted at the misery in her eyes. "You made mistakes. We can fix it if you let me help."

"No, Tate. This time it can't be fixed." She was sobbing in earnest now. "What would Dad say if he could see me now?"

Tate's breath caught. It was a thought he'd entertained a thousand times through his own struggles. What would his father say to see his son addicted to pills? His relationship with Stephanie ruined? Fuego Demolitions facing bankruptcy?

"He would say you made a mistake, and he would forgive you." Tate felt a swirl of comfort speaking the words aloud, and at that moment he knew he needed to believe it as much as his sister. "Listen, Maria. You got off track when Dad died. You started looking for love, and you thought Bittman could give that to you, but he isn't capable of it. Lesson learned. It's my fault, too. I should have been there for you, and I wasn't. I'm sorry."

She shook her head, wiping her face with a tissue. "I can't wish it away that easily." She turned a tear-streaked face to him, vulnerable as a child's. "Oh, Tate. I'm scared."

"I'm not going to let anyone hurt you."

"What about Eugene? Ricardo will find him and kill him."

He raised his voice over her rising hysteria. "Not if we get there first."

"We? I can't involve you and Stephanie any more than you already are." She looked at her lap. "Or Luca, especially after I accused him. Tate, I lied about him. I wanted him to like me, and when he didn't, I lashed out. He was never anything but kind to me." Tears started again. "My life is a wreck. I'm so ashamed."

"Honey, we all have things we're ashamed of, but God forgives all of it, just like Dad said." He was startled at his own words. He recalled that it had been the first step on his road to recovery, asking God to forgive him and make him whole again. It felt good to put that into words for Maria, at long last.

She stared into his eyes. "Do you believe that?"

He smiled and caught her tear on his finger. "You know, I think I really do."

Maybe people couldn't forgive. He thought of the distrust in Stephanie's eyes, the anger in Luca's.

But God could.

She sniffed. "I came earlier to talk to you, but I saw a woman here so I left. Who is she?"

"Cop."

Maria started. "What did she want?"

He hoped his words wouldn't drive Maria further into despair. "She's investigating the murder of Bruno Devlin. He was run down the same night we found you in the shop."

Even in the weak light, he could see all the color drain out of her face. "Oh, no. Ricardo told me that he had some business to take care of." She bit her lip. "I think he went back and killed Devlin so he wouldn't tell Bittman we were getting close to his violin. He's a murderer." Her voice fell to a whisper. "I've been helping a murderer."

"You didn't know. You couldn't have." He checked his watch. "It's almost five. I'm going to wake up Stephanie and Luca. We'll make a plan to get to Eugene before Ricardo does." He got out of the truck and went around to the passenger side.

Maria rolled down the window, anguish written plainly on her face. "Tate, I'm sorry I got you into this mess."

He stroked her cheek. "Hey, there. Don't beat yourself up. Fuegos are famous for making messes, but we always clean them up, right?"

She didn't answer, so he leaned in to kiss her on the cheek. "Stay right there. I'll be back in a minute."

Maria nodded, and he trotted to Stephanie's door. A knock at five in the morning was never good, and he knew they were both dog tired, but he had the sense that every moment wasted left a greater window for Eugene to disappear—or worse, for Ricardo to get hold of him before they did.

Stephanie opened the door in seconds, hair

mussed, eyes smudged with fatigue, and still the most beautiful woman he'd ever seen. He swallowed the sudden onslaught of emotion at the terror he'd caused her with his early morning intrusion. "Sorry to wake you."

"I wasn't sleeping."

"Maria's in the truck."

Her mouth opened. "Is she okay?"

"Yeah. She's set up a meet with Eugene day after tomorrow. We can intercept them."

Stephanie gasped and immediately turned to wake Luca. "Bring her in. Let's go over the details."

He trotted back to the truck, something like hope beating in his heart. They'd turned a corner, finally. His sister was safe for the moment, and maybe, just maybe, they could get Bittman's violin back before Ricardo tried to kill Eugene.

As he neared the car, the hope was replaced by a growing dread. Maria was not in the front seat—only a scrap of paper and a note scrawled in pen.

I'm sorry. I'll fix it. I love you. M

"Maria!" he yelled, heedless of whom he might bother. He ran in the direction he thought she must have taken. There was no sign of her. He kept searching anyway even though he knew it was hopeless.

Eventually he returned to the truck and banged his fist against the side.

He looked up and saw Stephanie standing there,

understanding in her eyes. She knew it, too. Maria was going to walk right into Ricardo's hands, and it would destroy any chance of saving her father.

FOURTEEN

Stephanie felt like screaming. One step forward and three steps back. She plopped down onto the battered chair and pulled up on her laptop some satellite maps of the area while Tate related Maria's confession. She could not fault the girl entirely—after all, she'd been unable to discern Bittman's true nature as well, but now the morass was deepening, and if things didn't change, none of them would get out of it alive.

"In order to get to this ghost town," she said, "I'm thinking we should follow the trail from Eugene's house that we found yesterday."

Luca considered. "Makes sense. We may even find Eugene along the way if he stopped to camp."

"Agreed." Tate's mouth was still tight with frustration, though. He looked like he was about ready to explode.

Luca was unable to suppress a groan as he tried to put weight on his damaged foot. "I'll be okay."

Tate and Stephanie exchanged a skeptical look.

"Come on," he growled, limping to the car.

Stephanie pointed to a section of the map, and Tate peered over her shoulder. "Looks like Lunkville is down on the sand flats, maybe about three hours from here. It's an old railroad town, or what's left of it." She looked at Tate. "How is Maria planning to get there?"

He shrugged. "I don't want to think about it. She's resourceful, and she thinks she's going to fix everything. I just hope she doesn't hitch a ride and get into even more trouble. She's stubborn."

Stephanie shot him a look. "Family trait?"

He didn't reply, instead turning to Luca and shoving his hands into his pockets, his brow furrowed.

"Luca, Maria told me that she accused you of... pressuring her when it wasn't true. It was wrong of her to do it." He took a deep breath. "She's sorry, and so am I."

Luca didn't speak for a moment. "I guess if it came down to it, I'd take my sister's side, too."

Tate rubbed a hand over his eyes. "She's not a bad kid, just insecure. After Dad died, things only got worse. Too much happened all at once, and she can't get past it."

A hint of a smile lit Luca's face. "That can keep a person stuck in one spot, all right."

Stephanie saw the wistful expression in Luca's gaze, and she knew he was thinking of another woman, a woman he'd loved and lost. It brought

Brooke to mind, the woman deeply in love with Victor, and her heart ached. The Gage family had had their share of trials, too.

"Anyway, I'm sorry," Tate said.

It had never before occurred to Stephanie how difficult it was to say those two words, or how hard it was to accept them. He'd tried to apologize after the accident, but she had turned away, sickened by his addiction and deeply hurt by his abandonment. If Bittman hadn't taken her father, she might never have seen Tate again. It would be the easy way, but for some reason she knew it would not have been right. They needed to clear the air between them so they could both start their lives fresh. She would not allow herself to love him again—but maybe it could be a tenuous bridge between them, unsteady though it might be.

If they could somehow climb out of the present mess.

Luca clapped Tate on the shoulder. "Forgotten. Let's move on and get to Eugene."

They hurriedly packed up bottles of water and the leftover sandwiches from the night before. They had another surprise waiting when Tate tried to start the truck. Several turns of the ignition using the key yielded no results. It took him another minute to find the reason. He groaned. Maria had ripped away the ignition wires.

Tate got into the back of the rental car, his face a mixture of anger and amusement. "Good thing you didn't leave yours unlocked, or she would have disabled it, too."

Stephanie allowed herself a smile. "At least she didn't steal it."

"She probably would have if I didn't have the keys in my pocket," Tate grumbled.

As they rolled to the edge of the parking lot, Stephanie driving and Luca in the passenger seat, Rocky the janitor jogged up, broom and cell phone in hand. "Call for you," he said, thrusting the phone through the window.

Stephanie thanked Rocky and took the cell, her stomach clenching into a knot. "Hello?"

"I'm okay, little lady. Don't let him…"

She sat forward, electrified. "Daddy! Has he hurt you? Tell me where you are."

"He is unharmed for the moment," Bittman said, coming on the line. "But I am losing my patience. This investigator, Tuney, he is causing some inconvenience to me."

Stephanie was unable to answer, her father's voice still ringing in her ears.

Luca took the cell and jabbed the speakerphone button. "If you hurt him, it will be the last thing you ever do."

"Such bravado, but we've no time for this. I have had to intervene with the local authorities already. Another annoyance. I thought I spelled out very clearly that you were to stay away from the police."

"Sorry, but there's been a murder here," Luca snapped. "Cops don't turn a blind eye to that."

"The music store owner." Bittman's voice was thoughtful. "It proves me right."

"About what?"

"Whoever burned down my father's store is after my violin, and he's eliminating any potential witnesses. Perhaps he'll eliminate Maria, too. I surmise they are working together."

"Enough," Tate shouted.

"Aah, the oaf is there with you. Stephanie, you are worthy of so much more. You were better off without him."

"Stop it," Stephanie hissed. "I want to talk to my father again."

"I've no more time to waste, and neither, it seems, do you. Call off Tuney, or I will be forced to kill him. Keep the cop away, or she will also meet with an accident. And find my violin. Quickly. I'll tell your father goodbye for you." He hung up.

Luca snapped the phone shut, and Stephanie held it out the window to the waiting Rocky.

"How does he know where we are?" Stephanie managed. "I haven't seen anyone following us." Her voice shook.

"Doesn't matter." Tate shifted impatiently on the seat. "We've got to get moving."

Luca took out his own phone and reluctantly

dialed Tuney's number, then left a message. "I doubt he'll give it up. You know Tuney."

Stephanie shivered. She could not bear it if something happened to Tuney.

She eased down the driveway and headed out of town, keeping an eye on the rearview mirror. She wasn't sure who she was looking for. Ricardo? Sartori? Maria? Alternating waves of panic and rage swept through her. Tate's face in the rearview was grave, Luca's tired, haggard and tinged with pain. It all came back to her decision long ago to work for Bittman, to let him into her world.

He'd permeated her life like a toxic gas, enveloping the people she loved the most: her father, her brothers and Tate.

The thought startled her. Not Tate. Not anymore. She shot a look at him again.

"...past is passed, just like you said. Supposed to be forgiven, right? That Christian thing?"

Could she forgive Tate for the hurt he'd heaped upon her? For the stupid choices he'd made when he'd fallen into addiction? For shutting her out?

Something shifted inside her, like a sheet of ice breaking to reveal a pool of water underneath. Maybe she could forgive him, and reconcile herself to his continuing addiction, if indeed he was still using.

But she could not love him.

Not again.

Pressing harder on the gas pedal, she aimed the car away from town, toward the yawning desert.

Tate clamped down on his rage toward Bittman and tried to decipher the map Stephanie had printed as they retraced their route to Eugene's. The highway shimmered before them, basically flat except for gentle swells and dips. The road on either side stretched out in endless miles of sandy ground, covered by a scalp of low bushes. Mountains rimmed the horizon in the distance, scraping their peaks against a sky so blue it hurt to look at. Under other circumstances, it might have been beautiful.

Wind buffeted the car as they drove, easing only slightly as they took the turn to the stone house. He was relieved to see no sign that any recent vehicles had disturbed the dust around the structure. At least Ricardo hadn't made it there—not by car anyway.

Tate let himself into the house to do a quick check, in case Eugene had returned. He hadn't, but Tate made an interesting discovery that he shared with the others.

"Peanut butter is gone from the cooler. I think Maria made a stop here before she took off."

"Could have been Eugene," Luca said. "Maybe he came back, changed his mind and headed off in another direction."

"Nope, it was Maria."

Luca raised an eyebrow. "Why so certain?"

"Because she hates jelly, and that was left in the cooler." Tate climbed back into the rear, and they drove once again to the trailhead they'd found the day before. His leg was not as painful as it had been, but the memory of his conversation with Stephanie was every bit as uncomfortable.

How do you handle it? By abusing drugs?

She thought he was an addict.

She thought right—he was and always would shoulder the risk of using again.

But he would never touch another narcotic as long as there was any life left in him.

That's the part she didn't know.

He would die before he allowed himself back into that abyss.

Stephanie eased the car down the slope, the sides scraping against the bushes that crowded in from either side. The jostling tossed them around, and Tate could tell it wasn't doing Luca's ankle any favors. Just when the trail pinched in to the point where he thought they would have to stop, they emerged at the exit to Eugene's tunnel.

On the other side of the clearing, the narrow road climbed sharply as it wound through the trees, and he wondered how far they would be able to go in the car. With Luca's ankle injured, they would not cover much ground on foot.

Wind scattered leaves across the windshield, and Stephanie clutched the steering wheel in concentration. The makeshift road sloped downward through a canyon speckled by crystal-flecked outcroppings of rocks. Minerals colored the cliffs in stripes of gold and red as they reached the bottom and began a gradual ascent that took them to the top of the canyon and out onto an inhospitable landscape of rock and sand.

Stephanie slowed as they took in the barren panorama. "What's that?"

Tate looked in the direction she pointed. A small ridge in the distance marked the edge of a ravine.

She was already unbuckling. "We can get a look at what's below." She had to heave the door against the wind.

"Steph…" he started, but she was already marching resolutely, hand shielding her eyes against the flying grit.

Luca unbuckled his belt and made to follow her.

"I'll go," Tate said. "Rest your ankle."

"It's fine." Luca grimaced. "Just a sprain."

Tate was about to reply when a movement on the horizon stopped him. Behind Stephanie, starting from the far edge of the plateau, a massive cloud of sand began to form, a gigantic chimera rising from the desert floor.

"Sandstorm," Luca breathed, pushing at the door. "Stephanie!" he yelled as he struggled out of the car.

"Stay here. I'll get her."

Luca shook him off. "No, she's my sister."

Tate grabbed him by the shoulders, his face

inches from Luca's, yelling over the wind, which had begun to howl. "You can't help with your ankle like that. Get back in the car." He didn't wait to see if Luca would follow his commands. Instead he took off, sprinting after Stephanie.

He saw her stop and turn, her face tilted toward the monster bearing down on her.

He tried to call her name, but the huge tower of sand sent out a wild shriek that swallowed up his voice. The wind was screaming now, bearing down on them both with speeds that must have topped fifty miles an hour. They could not outrun it.

His brain understood, but his legs did not.

Get to Stephanie was all he could fathom over the roar of the storm.

Forcing his body to move through the blasting wall of sand, he kept on.

The most serious risks from sandstorms, he knew, were suffocation and blindness from the airborne avalanche of sand. He tried to put it out of his mind as he pushed ahead, nearly falling as the ferocious blast forced his weight on to his bad leg. Grains of sand cut into his face, pricking at his eyes, causing them to tear up.

He fell, struggled back to his feet and fell again.

"Stephanie!" he yelled. She was no more than twenty feet away now. "Get down!"

She might have shouted something back, but he could not hear it as a wall of moving desert closed in around them, and he lost sight of her.

FIFTEEN

One moment Stephanie was surrounded by clear blue sky, and the next, she was enveloped by a massive cloud of stinging sand. Tate appeared just before the storm swallowed her up, and then he was gone, overtaken by the undulating cloud. She began to cough, gasping for air as stinging particles flew into her mouth and eyes. She wanted to run, but she no longer knew which was the way back to the car and which led to the edge of the ravine.

She covered her nose and mouth with her elbow and ran blindly anyway, panic fueling her flight. Anything to escape the painful suffocation. Sand and grit cut her cheeks, and the wind hammered against her. Suddenly a pair of arms wrapped around her legs, bringing her to her knees. Tate.

Tate wrapped her in a bear hug, and they pressed their faces together as the storm howled around them. Somewhere in the back of her mind, she realized he was wearing short sleeves, leaving nothing to shield him from the onslaught, so she pressed closer, lifting her arms and trying to cover them both with her jacket. A sudden shock sent them tumbling as a branch careened by them, powered by the wind. They clung together as the storm crashed over them and a cocoon of sand piled up around their bodies, sifting into their hair, looking for entry into their noses and eyes.

Pounded by the wind, Stephanie lost track of time. *Just hold on,* she told herself, tightening her grip as much as she could around Tate. She felt a second sharp impact as an object, perhaps another branch or rock, ripped from the ground and hit home, knocking the breath out of her. The rage she felt against the storm, against Bittman and even Tate, gave her the strength to fight, but even that strong emotion ebbed against the power of the wind-frenzied sand.

I won't let go.

Her clawed fingers began to lose their hold, and she felt herself tearing away from Tate.

"No!" she yelled, and tried with every bit of strength she had left to hang tightly to him. He was strangely passive in her arms. "Tate!" she yelled.

He did not answer, nor did he stir in her arms. A cold chill of fear crept into her body.

"Hold on!" she screamed again. Was it her imagination, or was the gritty cloud beginning to lighten?

The wind hammered with such violence that in

spite of her most heroic effort, he began to slip from the circle of her arms.

She tried to grasp him under the shoulders, but he was pulled away.

"No!" she yelled again, mouth filling with grit as she threw herself on top of him.

Just as her hold began to fail, the storm passed, whirling away into the ravine.

The silence was shocking. The only sound coming from her was labored breathing and the hammering of her heart. She spit out a mouthful of sand before sucking in as much fresh air as she could hold.

She let go of Tate and sat up, blinking the sand out of her eyes, shaking it from her ears and unloosing piles of it from her jacket.

"I can't believe we made it," she said, coughing and shaking more sand.

Tate lay on his stomach, unmoving.

For a moment, she could only stare in horror.

"Tate?" He was so still. She could not see the rise and fall of his chest. Crawling over to him, she gently turned him over. His face was covered in blood, seeping from a wound on his forehead where something had struck him. She tried to brush it off with her sleeve, but there was so much—a crimson tide that ran down his neck and soaked into his shirt.

She ripped off a piece of her shirt and balled it up, pressing it onto the wound.

He still did not move.

She looked frantically for Luca, who was nowhere in sight. Her phone was back in the car where she'd left it.

Terror rose inside until she could not form a coherent thought. She pressed her mouth to his neck.

"Please do not leave me," she whispered, fingers trying to find a pulse.

Her trembling fingers would not obey.

"Tate," she whispered, her tears dropping onto his face, etching trails onto his dusty skin. "Tate, Tate, Tate" was all she could manage, tracing her fingers over his head, his cheeks, the curve of his chin, the hollow of his throat.

She could no longer feel the ground under her or the wind, suddenly gentle, that toyed with her hair. She pressed her lips to his, desperate to feel an answer there. He remained motionless. The last of her strength left her and she put her face to his chest, tears soaking into his ruined shirt.

She felt movement as he inhaled deeply. Jerking to her knees, she stared into his face as his eyes slowly came open, confused and disoriented.

"Tate?" she whispered.

"You okay?" he mumbled.

She could only fight to control her cascading emotions as the gray eyes cleared and he struggled to sit up. He tried to get to his feet, but he toppled over. She tried her best to keep his head from hitting the ground. She rolled him onto his side and pressed her face to his cheek.

"Stay still, just for a minute," she whispered into his ear. Holding him around the shoulders, crouched next to him, her cheek touching his, an overwhelming current of some deep emotion flowed between them. She was transported back in time, past the anguish of addiction, the pain of being shut out. She thanked God again that Tate was alive. It was truly the only thing that mattered.

Tate clutched her hand in his, and for that brief second she wondered if the past was erased for him, too. It was Tate and Stephanie again, facing the journey ahead together, their back turned on the ugly road they'd already traveled. Did he feel it as strongly as she did?

A shout from the direction of the car broke the spell, and Stephanie got on her knees to find Luca hobbling up, using a stick for support. "Stephanie!" he yelled again.

She waved both arms to show him that she was unhurt and turned her attention again to Tate, who had now raised himself to a sitting position.

"I think I took a rock to the head," he said.

Stephanie reined in her emotion and forced a grin. "Won't do it any harm. You always said Fuego craniums were made out of cement."

"Plywood," he corrected.

She gave him her arm to help him get up, and he leaned against her briefly as dizziness overtook him. "You probably have a concussion. We'll take you to the hospital."

"Not likely," Tate said. "Let's go. We've already lost too much time. Besides, Maria might have been caught in the storm, too."

He straightened and headed tentatively back to the car, Luca and Stephanie staring after him. Luca examined Stephanie closely. "I tried to call for help, but there's no signal up here. Not sure who I would have called anyway."

She rolled her shoulders. "He should go to the doctor."

"But he won't," Luca said. "He's as stubborn as I am."

She shot him a look. "Yes, but I guess we're all guilty of that character trait. We'll bandage him up as best we can, and I'll watch closely in case he really does have a concussion." She could just make out his tall frame, limping slightly on his way to the car.

Had it all been imagined, the warmth between them—a by-product of trauma? How could he still have such control over her emotions, this addict, this ruined man who had meant everything to her? She felt angry at herself for imagining feelings that didn't exist.

Luca put a hand on her shoulder. "You sure you're okay?" he asked.

She nodded. "Scraped up is all."

"You look strange, like you just discovered something."

"What would I discover in the middle of a sandstorm?" she snapped. She felt Luca's eyes on her as she walked to the ridge to take a look, now that the storm had passed.

Tate allowed Stephanie to fuss over him with the first-aid kit because he knew she wouldn't agree to leave otherwise, and it gave him time to get himself together. He still felt confused. One moment he was plunging through a wall of sand, and the next, lying with Stephanie at his side, stroking his cheek, murmuring something unintelligible in his ear. He was sure he'd imagined the longing he heard in her voice, the tenderness that made his breath grow short, even now, as she wiped the blood from his face and affixed a bandage to his forehead. He didn't want to experience the strange warmth that coursed through him and sent him off balance. The strange disequilibrium eased a bit, though the pain in his leg flared anew, and now his head throbbed, too.

She avoided looking into his eyes, muttering something about hospitals and stitches. Then she got behind the wheel, though he tried to edge her out.

"I'm the only able-bodied one around here," she said. The engine coughed to life, and they continued on. "It looks as if once we get across these dunes, there's another road—a trail, more like. It heads in the direction of Lunkville, according to the maps I downloaded."

Tate let her talk while he kept his eyes trained for any sign of Maria. He prayed she'd not been caught by the same sandstorm. More and more, he felt the urgency to extract them both from the mess that brought Stephanie back into his life. The violin was the key—find it, and maybe everyone really would get what they needed. He hoped it was quick. He did not understand the intense feelings that he'd experienced over the past few days. It felt like he was standing on dangerous ground, the sand shifting under his feet.

Luca tossed down his phone in frustration. "Useless until we get another satellite link."

Stephanie approached the end of the plateau, which fed them through a narrow gap between two massive rock cliffs. "What were you researching?"

"Emailing back and forth with the retired cop who handled the music store fire." Luca rubbed at a spot on the window. "He told me Ricardo's last name is Williams. He worked at Bittman's store, doing odd jobs and janitorial stuff. That must be how he saw the Guarneri and decided to take it for himself."

Tate tried to forget the dull ache in his head. "Why set the fire, though? Why not just run with the violin?"

"He probably figured it would slow down the investigation and give him time to vanish."

"Which he did," Stephanie added. "For twenty

plus years. Last laugh was on Ricardo when he burned down the shop but didn't get the Guarneri."

Last laugh's going to be on us, if he gets his hands on it now, Tate thought.

"But Ricardo never stopped looking for it. He must have been keeping tabs on the music world, too. When he heard Bittman was on the trail, he tried to get close, worked as the pool guy even." Luca laughed. "Bittman's gonna have a conniption when he figures that one out."

It gave them all a small sense of satisfaction, Tate knew, to think of one way Bittman had been fooled.

The rock cliffs pinched together until there was only a passage barely wide enough for one car. As they crawled toward the gap, trees poked through the earth with limbs twisted and shorn off by the untamed wind.

Stephanie rolled down the window, checking the clearance on the driver's side. Tate did the same out the passenger window.

"Going to be a tight squeeze." She pushed the hair out of her face.

"Not as tight as the Manhole." He wished immediately that he hadn't said it. A flush colored her cheeks petal pink, and his own face warmed. He remembered the situation in perfect detail, recalling it from time to time in his happier moments. It was their first foray into spelunking at a cavern in Gold Country back before the accident, before everything had gone bad. She'd pushed ahead into the darkness broken only by their headlamps, teasing him about being too slow, and shimmied into a hole dubbed the Manhole by cavers over the years. Stephanie had promptly found herself wedged in. While others might have panicked, Stephanie laughed until her face was wet with tears while Tate crawled around to the other side of the hole and yanked her out by the ankles. He'd called her Pooh Bear, after Winnie the Pooh's famous "stuck" scene, for months afterward. They'd enjoyed reliving the memory perhaps more than the actual trip.

Stick the memories back in the past where they belong, Tate. There was only pain in recounting his time with Stephanie. She'd moved on, and he could not blame her.

Stephanie poked her head out the window again and eyed the sides of the car. Tate did the same. No more than a few inches clearance, but it would be enough if the path didn't narrow any further. He reached out and snapped off a twig of a spiky shrub to examine it closer. Freshly broken, as were many others.

"Someone's been this way recently," he said.

Stephanie flicked a glance at him. "Eugene?"

Tate shook his head. "He was on a motorbike. I don't think he'd have caused this much damage."

"Maria?" Luca suggested.

"Hope so." Tate didn't want to think about the other possibility—that Ricardo had already passed by, killed Eugene and taken the violin. A sudden movement along the rocks made them all straighten until Tate caught site of the source. "An animal, ground squirrel I think. Wait a minute—do you hear that?"

Luca stiffened in the backseat. "There's a car following."

"I'll check it out." Ignoring Stephanie's protest, he climbed out the window since there was not enough space to push open the door. Scrambling onto the rocks, he climbed upward to the nearest flat one, where he could get a look at the path they'd just traversed.

The vehicle was leaving the sand flats. He caught a glimpse of a dark-colored truck before it began to climb the slope. It moved slowly but steadily, vanishing into the tree-covered incline that would lead right to them.

He returned to the car and crawled back inside. "Truck. Don't recognize it."

"So we have a decision to make then," Luca said. "Move forward and get to Eugene, or stop and find out who's behind us."

Tate rubbed at his throbbing head. "We've tried the waiting thing already. I say we go. The window of opportunity to save Eugene and this violin is small."

In silent assent, Stephanie started the car forward, the sides scraping against overhanging branches. They climbed another hundred yards before they reached the pinnacle. Out the back window the truck was visible, winding its way through the same sunbaked route.

"Closing the gap," Luca said. "Can you push faster?"

Stephanie tightened her grip on the wheel and stepped harder on the gas. Gravel pinged against the undercarriage as they traversed a hill that looked down onto another seemingly endless plateau of corrugated ground, cut through by cracks filled with dry grass and creosote bushes. There was no sign of any human habitation as they took the last turn before entering the flatlands. Stephanie rounded the corner and slammed on the brakes, but not quickly enough to avoid the improvised spike stick, a narrow strip of wood bristling with nails. One front tire rolled over the stick with a loud pop that sounded like gunfire.

The car lurched slightly, the rear wheels skidding to one side.

Tate was out immediately. "Front tire is blown. Do we have a spare?"

"One," she said with a groan.

He looked around. A rock-strewn slope behind them, and in front, miles of sunbaked nothing. Behind, he heard the relentless approach of the oncoming truck. They had only a few minutes, not enough time to change the flat.

He felt the wild surge of reckless energy from days gone by.

"Okay," he said. "Here's what we're going to do."

SIXTEEN

Stephanie's heart thundered in her chest as she crouched behind a rock, looking down on the road below them. Luca sat behind the wheel in their car. She didn't like it. He was vulnerable, and though he was one of the toughest people she knew, he was injured. If the person in the truck was Ricardo, he could walk up and fire a gun into the driver's side.

Her mouth went dry, and she tightened her grip on the soccer-ball-size rock she'd eased to the edge of the slope, praying Tate's desperate plan would work. Her eyes watered as she peered across the bleached landscape, trying to spot where he'd gone. In spite of his leg and the head injury, he had quickly disappeared into the rock maze after he'd helped her shimmy the rock into place and tuck herself out of sight.

The truck was close now. She could see the glint of sun on metal as it approached the final curve. She leaned forward slightly, hands pressing the rock. The truck pulled to a stop.

Her fingers were slick with sweat. She blinked against the dazzle of the sun. Was it a man behind the wheel? A woman? She could not tell. Leaning forward, she braced to shove the rock down the slope if the driver turned out to be Ricardo. It would provide a momentary distraction only. She prayed a moment would be enough for Tate to gain control of the situation.

The door of the truck opened and a figure got out, hair covered by a baseball cap, untucked plaid shirt over worn jeans. Then she saw Tate edging out of hiding, just behind the driver.

Pulse pounding, she leaned forward. The sandy soil underneath the rock gave way, and the weight of stone carried it to the road below. Both Tate and the stranger looked up at exactly the same moment.

Stephanie's breath caught. "Look out!" she shouted.

Tate grabbed the arm of the driver and yanked. The rock sailed by, across the path and down into the ravine below.

Stephanie scrambled down from her hiding place as Luca shot from the car.

"It's Officer Sartori," she called, too late.

Tate helped up Sartori from the ground. "Sorry," he said. "We thought you were somebody else."

Sartori glared at the three of them, brushing the dirt from her clothes. "You were expecting Ricardo Williams, maybe?"

Stephanie sighed. True to her word, Sartori had

been researching the case in spite of the sheriff's order. "We weren't sure."

"Uh-huh." Sartori looked over their rental car. "Somebody left a little booby trap for you? Could be miners. There are still a few old-timers around, looking for that big gold strike."

Stephanie shrugged. "Are you following us?"

"Maybe. It's my day off. Would have intercepted you sooner, but I caught the tail end of a sandstorm." She eyed Tate's bandaged head. "You, too?"

"Yes." Stephanie pushed the thought of the storm firmly away. "But we're okay."

"Why are you headed out here? Lunkville's this way, but it's nothing but a ghost town."

Stephanie knew there was no use trying to hide information from Sartori any longer. She sucked in a deep, shuddering breath. "We got a lead that a man named Eugene is in possession of the violin and he's come this way."

"Eugene? Guy with a wild beard?"

"Yeah." Luca leaned on his good ankle. "Know him?"

"Not well. Moved here about five years ago, I think. Took up at the stone house, squatting really, since it belongs to some city guy who hasn't lived here in twenty years. Eugene's got mental problems, but he's pretty harmless. We don't hassle him because he doesn't make trouble. Just wants to be left alone." She raised an eyebrow. "So he's got Bittman's violin?"

"We're not sure." Tate pointed to the flat tire. "Could be he left us this present. I've got to change it."

Sartori shrugged. "I'll give you a hand, but you're going to have to follow me back to town, I'm afraid."

Stephanie shook her head. "No, we can't do that. We've got to check out Lunkville and see if Eugene is there."

"Nope," Sartori said. "I don't think so."

Stephanie felt a prickle of annoyance, but she kept a level tone. "We've been through a lot already, and we're not giving up now. We haven't broken any laws, and you're not technically supposed to be following us anyway."

Sartori held up a hand. "Different issue. The reason I drove up here was to give you a message. Rocky called me from the hotel and said he couldn't get you on the phone, but he'd heard you talk about where you were headed."

Tate cocked his head. "What message?"

"From the hospital," Sartori said.

Stephanie felt as if the ground shifted under her feet. The word *hospital* unlocked the terror inside her that seemed to whiz around her head and heart, creating a buzz so loud she could hardly hear herself ask the question. "What is the message?"

Luca stepped up behind her and put a firm hand on her shoulder. Tate looked at Stephanie with a mixture of worry and fear written on his own face.

Frozen in a terrified tableau, they waited for the words to come.

Sartori's face softened. "I'm sorry to be the bearer of bad news, but your brother Victor has developed a blood infection."

"How bad?" Stephanie whispered.

Sartori shifted uncomfortably. "Seems as though he's spiked a fever they haven't been able to control." She cleared her throat. "They suggested the next of kin should be present."

Next of kin. Her head spun, and her legs began to shake until Luca guided her to the car so she could lean on the back bumper. The rest of the conversation seemed to come from a distance.

"There was a follow-up message from a Brooke Ramsey." Sartori cleared her throat. "She said she contacted the pastor of your family church."

Luca peppered her with a list of questions ranging from what time the call had come in to airport information. Sartori fielded the questions patiently. "I'll help change that tire and give you all a moment." She busied herself working with Tate to hold the lug nuts when he loosened them.

Luca embraced Stephanie, but she felt no comfort from it. Victor was not going to make it. They could not save him. Just like they were unlikely to save her father. She felt sickened and numb.

"...the next flight," Luca was saying.

"I'll go with you to the airport," Tate answered. "Then I'll come back and continue the search."

Tate and Sartori labored together to replace the ruined front tire with the spare. They worked in silence, the only sound coming from the clank of the lug wrench and the murmur of Luca on Sartori's satellite phone as he inquired about flight information.

She sat on a rock, the heat seeping into her, yet not warming the cold place deep inside.

He's won. He's killed Victor, and he'll kill Dad, too.

From the moment she'd walked away from Joshua Bittman, she'd feared something like this would happen. He was interested only in acquiring everything he desired, and the means to that end were unimportant. He would get his violin, without their help if it came to that. With Victor and her father gone, she knew he would not stop pursuing her, stalking her, watching her. She flicked a glance at Luca and Tate. If anyone else got in his way, he would take care of them, as well.

She felt the bitter taste of defeat. Nothing she'd done since the moment she'd learned of Victor's accident had made the slightest difference. After a while she felt Luca's hand on her shoulder again. "There's a flight out in three hours. We can just make it."

She stood up, looking over the vast sprawling vista below. No matter where she went, how deeply she buried herself, the past was still there. Bittman was still there, as sure as the sunset.

"Let's go, Steph."

She squeezed her eyes closed. *Lord, I got myself into a mess, and only You can help me get out of it. Heal my brother and give me the strength I need.* Something rose inside her, not courage exactly, but a feeling she'd forgotten in the recent crush of events—the feeling that she wasn't alone, and God would walk with her through the desert like He'd always done. "No," Stephanie heard herself say.

Both men stared at her.

She stood up. "Luca, you go back. Be there for Victor and Brooke. I'm staying here, and I'm going to get that violin. It's the only chance left for Dad."

Luca grabbed her fingers and squeezed until she looked at him. "We'll keep looking for Dad. Tuney and me. You need to come with us, for Victor." He shot a glance at Tate. "We'll help you as much as we can from back there. I can ask some buddies of mine to come and search for Maria."

Tate didn't answer.

"I'm going to help Victor my way, Luca. It's my fault he's in that hospital. It's my fault Dad's with Bittman. I can't help either of them in San Francisco. The only thing I can do is stay here."

"No," Luca said.

She looked him full in the face. "I'm staying."

He opened his mouth, anger and resignation warring there. "You need to be with Victor, in case…" His voice broke, and at that moment her heart did also.

"I'll be praying every moment," she whispered to him, clutching his hands.

Luca cleared his throat. "It's not safe to leave you here alone."

"I'm not alone. Tate will stay here with me."

Tate remained silent, but gave a slight nod.

Luca looked at her again and gave her a fierce hug.

Fighting tears, she hugged him back, the pain in her heart almost too much to bear.

Tate could not think of a single thing to say to help the situation. He watched Luca kiss his sister once more as she got into the car, head bowed, lips moving. It was probably the hardest decision she'd ever had to make, to stay behind when her brother was likely to die. If there was something he could do, anything to ease the anguish on her face, he would do it in a heartbeat. The only thing left was to find the violin, find his sister and save her father's life.

Luca drew him aside as Sartori got into her truck and started the engine. His eyes were shadowed with fatigue and pain. "So it's on you now," he said, eyes glittering. "I'm sorry to leave things like this. It's dangerous and…"

"And you don't trust me," Tate said flatly.

Luca exhaled. "I guess I don't have a choice." He looked away for a moment. "You've shown me someone different through this whole treasure hunt, though, a Tate I didn't know before."

Tate felt a sudden thickening in his throat. He was different; at least he desperately wanted to think so. He settled on a nod.

"But you're not good for Stephanie. You tossed her aside and messed her up so badly that she went to work for this psycho."

The truth cut into him. Nothing had really changed at all because in Luca's mind and Stephanie's, he would always be locked in the past, bound so tightly to his sin that he could never be free.

"We'll get the violin," he said.

Luca gave Tate an appraising look. "I know you care about her enough to keep her safe, so I'm going to have to rely on you to do so, but that's it." Luca stared at him. "She's better off without you, and she knows it. I don't want to be cruel, but I've got to watch out for her, like you would for Maria."

He nodded. She was better off without him, probably always had been. "I'll take care of her."

Luca offered a hand. His grip was crushing. "I will hold you to that." They locked eyes until Luca let go, hobbling to the truck without a backward glance. Tate got into the car. Stephanie did not protest when he took the wheel. Sartori walked up and handed them a handheld radio and a folded paper through the driver's side window.

"It's a satellite radio. It will work even if your

phone doesn't. I think the paper is a bill or something from the hotel. Rocky was afraid you were going to skip out, I think. Probably figured you for criminals, due to my frequent visits." She checked her watch. "I'll be back up here after I drop off your brother and take care of a few things."

"To arrest us for something? Trespassing in Lunkville, maybe?" Tate asked.

Sartori grinned unexpectedly. "Maybe. Or maybe I'll just tag along for the treasure hunt. You all are sort of growing on me."

Stephanie gave her a wan smile. "It's dangerous. People who hang around me—" she swallowed hard "—have a tendency to get hurt."

"Then I'll bring Bear," she said. "Bad guys have a tendency to get hurt around him, too." Sartori returned to the truck and backed down the trail. Stephanie waved, fingers trembling, face pale, until they were out of sight.

Tate could not stand her stricken look. He took her hand, pressing some warmth back into the cold fingers. "We'll find the violin. I promise."

She bit her lip and forced a deep breath. "What did Luca say to you back there?"

Tate shook his head. "Nothing I didn't already know," he answered, gunning the engine to life.

They followed the road down, scouting ahead for any more spike sticks, but there were none. Arriving at the bottom, they continued on for what seemed like an eternity. The late afternoon was warm, the air that rushed in through the open windows sultry and pine scented. Stephanie spotted the turnoff toward Lunkville.

"There. It's overgrown, but that's got to be it."

There was no way to tell on the rocky entrance to the trail if any other vehicles had passed there recently. He took it slow, easing over the uneven ground. The last thing they needed was another flat, especially with no spares left. Under the sparse canopy of a Joshua tree were the ruins of a log cabin, roof slanted crookedly and windows long gone.

He pulled the car to a stop and got out, intending to check it out before Stephanie joined him. But true to form, she made it to his side before he did so. The interior was dark and smelled of rotted wood as they peered through the window gap.

"Empty?" she breathed in his ear, tingling the skin along his neck.

"Looks that way." They entered, picking their way carefully to avoid the places where floor planks had caved in, revealing dark recesses underneath. He inhaled, catching the tang of something unexpected.

"Cigarette smoke," he said.

Stephanie nodded. "Maria doesn't smoke, and there was no sign that Eugene did, either."

Tate had a sudden flash of memory. When he'd tangled with Ricardo in the alley, he'd filed away an important detail in his memory. Ricardo had had a distinct odor about him—the acrid smell of cigarettes.

SEVENTEEN

In the next several miles there were four more structures in various states of decay. One was a mere shell with walls, a few ruined fireplace stones and a small windowless jail. The others had been homes and the remnants of a building, which Tate decided must have been some sort of garage. Over time the airborne grit had scoured the paint off the sides and worn away the edges of shutters and railings, as the desert inexorably reclaimed the town. None of the buildings revealed any clues or hiding places where Eugene or Maria might be holed up, but most held the faint scent of cigarettes. Hours passed before they had completed their search and stopped to rest, sweaty and tired.

Leg and head throbbing, Tate climbed to the top of an old steel tower and surveyed the surroundings.

"Looks like the rest of the town is clustered in the hollow about a mile from here," he called down to her. "There's a railroad track just beyond the hill." He eyed the sky as he climbed down. It was dusk, and the sky was darkening, rapidly cooling the air around him.

Stephanie looked at him. "I know what you're thinking. We should wait until morning."

"No, I was thinking we should rest, eat something and wait until dark."

Her eyebrows lifted in surprise. "Really?"

He almost smiled. "Really. Ricardo is here so we've got no time to waste, but if we go marching into town while it's daylight, we're sitting ducks." And truth be told, he desperately needed to regroup if there was to be any kind of physical encounter in the next few hours.

He let her lead the way to the car, so she wouldn't see how badly he was limping. She retrieved a bag and handed him a sandwich and some water. They sat in the car and ate greedily, gulping down the water in spite of its warmth.

"It's another two hours until sundown, and we'll tack on one more to be sure it's dark." He got out of the car.

"Where are you going?" Stephanie asked.

"To rest in the cabin over there. Didn't look like any critters call it home."

She cocked her head. "You can lie down in the backseat."

"Nope."

"Why not?"

"Because you need to lie down in the backseat."

He finished off his water bottle. "See you in a few hours. Lock the doors and keep the radio close, just in case."

She grabbed his sleeve. "Wait. Here." She pressed something into his hand.

He looked down and found a bottle of aspirin in his palm. "Am I limping that badly?"

"Yes. And I know you don't have…"

"Have what?" The realization dawned on him. "Painkillers."

She flushed.

He pulled his arm away. "Listen to me, Steph. I don't use anymore. I told you I didn't, and I was telling the truth."

"But I saw them in your backpack."

He closed his eyes and bit back a groan. "Yeah. I keep them there. You know why?"

She shook her head.

"Because every day I ask God to help me keep that bottle closed, and every night when the lid is still on, I know I beat it. Every single day, I beat it with His help." The anger throbbed in his throat, the injustice that he would never be clean in her eyes. And he wouldn't allow himself to become any more vulnerable around her.

You're not forgiven, not by Luca and not by Stephanie. And you never will be.

She might have called out to him, or it could have been the mournful sound of an owl winging its way over the darkening landscape. He did not turn. He could not. She would look at him through eyes filled with bitter memories, and he could not stand to see it on her face. Instead he settled into a corner of the old shack and tried to sleep.

Stephanie stretched out on the backseat, eager for sleep that did not come. She wondered if Tate was able to get any shut-eye. The angry scene replayed in her mind.

Because every day I ask God to help me keep that bottle closed...

Every single day, I beat it, with His help.

She felt conflicted by his outburst. Day by day, he was beating back the addiction that nearly ruined him. The strength it took to do that, she could not imagine. But addicts often lied, didn't they?

They did, but something in Tate's gray eyes told her that he was not lying. Besides, of all the things he'd done to her—shoved her away, blown up when she'd tried to stop him from using, forbidden her to work for Bittman—he'd never lied to her.

Never.

She let herself entertain the incredible thought. What if he was clean? Would there be a chance at reconciliation between them?

For a moment, her heart felt light, dancing on an ethereal hope until the dark feelings took over again. Memories trickled across her mind, stinging like crawling insects.

Tate bleary from the drugs. *Let go of me, Steph.*

Her grasping desperately at his arm. *You can't drive. I won't let you.*

I don't want your help. I don't need it. I don't need you.

Those words had hurt more than any of the rest. *I don't need you.*

She'd made up her mind right then not to need him, either. Ever. In spite of what her aching heart told her, the emptiness of her arms was a feeling to be pushed aside and buried deep.

I don't need you, either, Tate Fuego, and I never will again.

She prayed for Victor then, hands clutched so tightly her fingers ached. With no chance of sleep, she powered up her laptop, scanning emails to find one from Tuney. There wasn't one, and none from Luca, but she chalked that up to the inconsistent wireless connection. She checked her watch. Luca was probably just landing in San Francisco. Her heart throbbed again thinking about Victor.

She shut down the computer and shoved her hands in her pockets to ward off the chill that was settling in as the temperature dropped steadily. Her fingers found the paper from Rocky. He'd been helpful and kind. She was not sure what gave him the idea they'd skip out on paying the bill.

She unfolded the note. It was a printed copy of an email sent to the hotel.

Please forward this message to Stephanie Gage, without delay.

Stephanie, as it is September 20th, the anniversary of the date I first met you, it was my pleasure to send flowers to the hotel, the deepest azure, the color you wore upon our meeting that day. You were not there to receive them, I have been informed. Please call me with all haste and report on your progress. When you have found my violin, we will celebrate. Devotedly, Joshua.

She bit her lip to keep from screaming. Flowers. She used to love them, but now every blossom reminded her of Joshua—the parade of bouquets sent to her for the anniversary of their introduction, her birthday, Valentine's Day. She felt sick. It had started out so innocently. She'd been referred by a client of her father's to do a computer consulting job for Joshua. There should have been some sign in his pale countenance, some hint of madness in his eyes, but she had seen nothing to give her pause until much later, until it was far too late.

She tapped out a message on her phone, anything to keep him off her back for a few hours longer so he would not take action against her father or Tuney. *Getting close, S.* Without much hope that she could communicate a message from such a remote location, she hit the send button.

The hours passed in agonizing slow motion. Finally, when the stars showed against a brilliant black velvet sky, she let herself out of the car, pocketing the keys and putting Sartori's radio in her back pocket. Tate met her in front of the cabin.

"Get any rest?" she whispered.

"No. You?"

"No. That bill from Rocky was actually a message from Bittman." She relayed the contents. Though she could not see his face, she felt him stiffen next to her. Something made her take his arm for a moment. She felt a flood of guilt that she'd kept such a hard heart, that she hadn't believed he was finally clean. "Tate, you were right about Bittman. I should have listened to you."

He sighed, a small sound filled with the same wistfulness she felt twining through her own emotions. "Lots of people fall for his charm. I just hope we can keep him out of this before anyone gets hurt."

"He seems to know my every move," she said as they started up the winding trail.

"This time we're going to get there first." Tate pushed ahead of her. "We'll stick to the rocks as much as we can. Radio?"

"Got it."

He pressed something into her hand, encased in a hard leather sheath. "Your knife?"

"Yeah, just in case."

She pushed it into her other back pocket, and

they crept along past the ruined buildings that cast otherworldly shadows in the moonlight. They found the broken railroad tracks and used them to guide them into what had once been Lunkville, a thriving town supported by the productive borax mines.

Tate stopped to let her catch up. "There," he said, pointing suddenly to a lopsided building in the distance. "I saw something, a flicker of light."

She held her breath, staring until her eyes burned. "I don't..." A gleam of light shone for an instant before it vanished again. Tate was already crouched low and moving fast, keeping to the shadows as much as he could. She jogged behind him, pulse pounding.

They pulled up even with the building. There were a half-dozen windows that Stephanie could see, but all of them were too high to peek through. Tate edged his way around the ramshackle structure and she followed, avoiding some of the beams that protruded like splintery claws. They found themselves at a back door, pulled crookedly closed, the handles rusted through. Tate flicked on a flashlight and cupped his hand around it to dull the light.

"It's been opened recently," he whispered, peering at the marks in the earth. "I can't make out any footprints. Contact Sartori on the radio and tell her what we're up to."

"No time," Stephanie said. She grasped the corrugated handle and heaved, the whine of distressed metal thundering through the air before she darted inside, Tate at her heels. Her eyes struggled to adjust to the near darkness. Moonlight shone dimly through the gap where a window had been. The interior of the cavernous space was filled with oxidized mining equipment, all coated by a dull layer of grit. She turned on her own flashlight and pointed it to the floor. Footprints shone distinctly in the grime.

Stephanie saw her own surprise mirrored in Tate's expression. He held up two fingers.

She nodded. There were definitely two sets of prints leading to the rear of the space. Walking carefully to avoid tripping over the odd collection of antique equipment, they moved farther into the darkness.

Stephanie felt the aching mixture of fear and hope. The footsteps were mismatched, one large and one smaller. It had to be Eugene and Maria. Anticipation rose inside her. Ricardo might have given up, left Lunkville without his precious violin. She held her breath as they approached an enormous rusted cart, which she surmised had transported loads of borax ore to the waiting trains decades before. Now it crouched like some prehistoric animal waiting to devour them. The smell of mold tickled her nose, and she caught a musky scent of animal, as well.

Tate pulled her to his side, forcing her to come to a stop. She stood in the shelter of his arm, motionless except for the blood that raced through her body. A soft swooshing echoed through the building. Above them? From behind the cart? She could not tell as the sound bounced wildly.

She turned sharply as the noise intensified; skin prickling, as she tried to pick up the origin. Tate aimed the beam of his flashlight at the rafters far above. The light caught dozens of beady eyes staring, a column of skittering mice traversing the beams above them. Ears twitching, they surveyed the trespassers down below.

Stephanie gritted her teeth, trying not to think of the living freeway of rodents right over her head. If one dropped down onto her, she was not sure she could prevent herself from screaming.

Tate kept hold of her hand, and she clutched the strong fingers. Her tension mounted as they edged by the cart, giving them an unobstructed view of the rear. Piles of rotting boxes stood along the wall in what had once been a tidy arrangement. Now they had spilled through the ruined cardboard, disgorging their reddish contents onto the floor.

Stephanie's breath hitched as she viewed the outline of a door. It probably led to a smaller storage area. They both saw the gleam of light at the same time, a slight glimmer under the threshold.

Tate let go of her hand and moved stealthily to the door until his foot caught on a discarded length of chain. He kept his footing, but the chain scraped against the floor. There was a scuffling beyond the closed door. Tate turned to look at her just as the door crashed open. Eugene, eyes wild in his tangle of hair, tore out of the storage room, clutching the straps of his backpack.

"Wait," Tate called, but Eugene pushed by him, knocking him into the pile of boxes.

Tate righted himself and took off after Eugene. Stephanie overcame her shock to join in the pursuit when she heard something inside the storage space. Fearing it was Ricardo, she drew back into the shadows.

"Tate?" a voice whispered, soft and tremulous. "Is that you?"

With a surge of relief, Stephanie hurried inside. "It's Steph, Maria. Tate is here, too. He went after Eugene."

Maria was huddled in the corner, her face luminous in the dark. She clicked on a small lantern that blinded Stephanie for a moment.

Maria's long, dark hair was pulled into a loose braid. She wore a torn pair of jeans with an oversize shirt. There was a rolled-up sleeping bag in the corner, along with the remains of a box of crackers and a half-empty bottle of water. "You found me."

"It wasn't too hard. We knew where you were headed. How did you get here?"

Maria shrugged. "Thumbed a ride from a guy who mines for turquoise. I gave him my watch in exchange. I guess I'll never be on time again," she said with the ghost of a grin.

Stephanie's tension boiled over, and she could not restrain her impatience. "We've been chasing you for days. Why did you decide to go after Bittman's violin?"

Maria's face went sullen. "I loved him, at least I thought I did. He led me to think we were going to be married, but then he changed his mind. I realize now he never really loved me at all."

Stephanie didn't voice the truth. *He didn't. He isn't capable of it.* "He's got my father and…" Her voice failed as she thought of Victor.

Maria moved closer, and Stephanie could see honest regret in the lines around her mouth. "I'm sorry. I'm truly sorry. I had no idea he would force you into helping him." She paused. "Or maybe I did know, deep down. Our last fight was about you. I sneaked into his office and found a whole display of pictures of you. It was almost like a shrine or something." Her eyes flashed. "I told him that things had to change now—he had to let go of his sick fascination with you."

Stephanie closed her eyes. "He'll never let me go," she whispered.

"That's what he told me. Then he threw me out."

Stephanie's anger ebbed away, leaving a numb horror in its wake. "Maria, I'm so sorry. I didn't see the truth about him at first, either. I wish I'd never introduced the two of you."

She shook her head. "Doesn't matter now. I knew that his precious violin had surfaced. It seemed like the perfect way to get back at him and start a new life."

"But Eugene didn't want to part with the violin, did he?"

"No. That doesn't matter anymore, anyway. Tate told me that Ricardo is a murderer, so I came to warn Eugene." Her eyes glimmered in the lantern light. "He's a bad guy. Eugene said Ricardo was here in Lunkville, sniffing around. We decided to wait it out here until he left."

Stephanie noticed a window, one pane of glass broken and the rest glazed with dirt. She walked over, stood on a crate and peered out, looking for any sign of Eugene or Tate. "Did Eugene have the violin with him? Was it in his backpack?"

Maria laughed. "You know, Eugene is a little slow in some ways, but he's as crafty as they come."

"How's that?"

Maria walked over to the corner and pushed the backpack aside. She loosened a floorboard and pulled something out of the space below. Grinning, she held the violin case in her hand. "Tate is chasing after a guy with a backpack full of peanut butter and jelly."

Stephanie felt a surge of relief so strong that it almost brought her to her knees. Sucking in a breath and fighting back tears, she managed a smile. They'd found it, the one chance to save her father's life. She took a step toward Maria, when suddenly a gunshot exploded through the air.

Stephanie watched in horror as Maria crumpled to the filthy floor.

EIGHTEEN

Tate sprinted after Eugene until the man came to an abrupt stop at the mouth of what must have been a mine shaft. It was covered over with weathered boards, except for a V-shaped gap. Eugene stood with his face to the wood, one trembling hand pressed there. Tate reached out and tugged the ragged hem of Eugene's shirt, causing him to whirl around. His eyes were round, mouth open to suck in gasping breaths.

"He's here, he's here," Eugene wheezed.

A gunshot rang out.

Only one, and the night slipped back into silence.

Ricardo? Had he found Stephanie? Tate's mind wheeled between the echoing sound and the man before him. "I need the violin, Eugene. Please."

"No. It's mine. I have to keep it safe." He stabbed a dirty finger at the warehouse. "From him."

Tate moved forward as Eugene eased back.

"Where did you hide it, Eugene? Is it in your backpack?"

Eugene shook his head violently. "It's in a safe hiding place, with a friend."

Tate felt his gut tighten. "Your friend is a girl, right? With dark hair? Her name is Maria, and she's my sister. If you gave her the violin, then someone is after her, too. Is that what you want?"

Eugene's eyes clouded, shifting from Tate's face to the warehouse and back to Tate.

"Go back," he whispered. "She's in there."

Tate looked toward the building where he'd left Stephanie, where his sister might very well be holed up. Eugene used the moment of hesitation to disappear into a gap between the boards covering the entrance to a defunct mine shaft.

Stomach twisted in terror, Tate left off his pursuit of Eugene and ran as fast as he could over the uneven ground, back to the warehouse. All the while he tortured himself with thoughts of what had happened. He'd left Stephanie behind, with Ricardo somewhere close by. If she was hit... Her perfect face rose in his memory, laughing eyes, glinting with life, heart filled with lion-size courage. She could not be dead. He would not allow himself to think it. Nor would he imagine similar things happening to Maria.

He pushed faster until he pulled up at the back door, panting and shirt damp with sweat. It had been opened, the mark of booted feet showing clearly in the loose dirt. Moving as quickly as he dared, he retraced the route they had followed moments before, stopping every few feet to listen.

He thought he caught the echo of a shoe on the hard floor.

Stephanie. His heart pounded a frantic rhythm, and he prayed with every step.

Please keep her safe.

Even though her heart would never belong to him again, he knew at that moment he would lay down his life for hers.

Just hang on, Steph.

From outside the building, he got the crazy notion he'd heard a helicopter somewhere close by. Maybe Sartori had returned like she'd promised, with reinforcements. Hope burned hot in his gut.

There was a blur of movement from behind a pile of rusted metal. A bullet cut through the air by his head. He threw himself to the ground, belly first. Another shot followed, ricocheting off the metal cart and pinging upward, sending the mice swarming in all directions along the rafters. His breath disturbed swirls of dust on the ground, and he tried not to inhale.

"Hey, boy," Ricardo called out. "Didn't think you'd make it."

Tate looked around, knowing that the longer he stayed in one spot, the easier he would be for Ricardo to shoot.

"You are not going to take what's mine," Ricardo growled.

Tate scooted under the cover of a tower of dilapidated wooden crates, his mind racing. He had to get to Stephanie, and the only way was to keep Ricardo talking until he could figure out how to take him down. "The violin isn't yours. You tried to steal it from Hans Bittman. It never belonged to you."

Ricardo snorted. "I did the work, I planned the theft. I even burned down the building to cover it up, and then what do I find?" Ricardo snapped out the words as Tate kept moving, now ducking behind a deteriorating steel barrel. "Some homeless guy runs off into the woods with the Guarneri, and I'm left with an empty case and arson on my plate."

"And murder," Tate yelled. "Don't forget the fire killed Peter Bittman, and it was you who killed Devlin, wasn't it?"

"Yes. I wanted him to tell me about Eugene, but he refused. Things got out of hand." Ricardo laughed. "I'll give you points for persistence, boy. I thought the spike stick would slow you down until I finished up here."

"You let Eugene slip away with the Guarneri. Bad mistake."

"The violin is mine!" Ricardo roared. "I will have it back."

"And then what?" Tate asked, trying to get a fix on Ricardo's location. "You'll kill Eugene because he witnessed you set the fire all those years ago?" There was no answer, and Tate stared into the darkness, his nerves screaming. "Well, now there are more people who know the truth. You can't kill us all."

The chilling silence lingered, and then Ricardo's reply came from somewhere above Tate. "Oh, yes I can, boy. And I will," he heard, just before the tower of crates crashed down on top of him.

Keeping low, Stephanie tried to tend to Maria, whom she had dragged behind a stack of palettes. She'd done her best to secure the door, wedging a piece of wood under the jamb. If Ricardo climbed through the window, there was not much she would be able to do about it, but the window was small and it would be an awkward entry.

Breath coming in pants, she held the flashlight close to the whimpering Maria. Tears streaked the girl's face.

"It's okay. Let me see where you're hurt."

"My side," Maria moaned. "Oh, Steph. Is it deep?" Abject terror shone in Maria's eyes, and Stephanie raised her shirt as gently as she could. The wound was just below the ribs, and though Stephanie was no nurse, she did not think it was deep, but rather a shallow laceration caused by the bullet grazing her. A hole in the back of the garment told her it had passed through. She breathed out in relief.

"It's not bad," she said, taking off her jacket to tie around Maria's waist in an effort to stop the bleeding. As she did so, her fingers grazed the soft swell of Maria's belly. The truth dawned on her in one blinding flash. Maria was indeed trying to start a brand-new life, but not just for herself.

"Maria, are you…?"

Maria's eyes locked on Stephanie's and she nodded, a fresh flow of tears painting trails on her dirty face. "I thought he would be happy, but he didn't want the baby. He kicked me out and called me a tramp. I was going to get us a fresh start."

Stephanie held Maria's hand, swallowing her sadness at Maria's clumsy attempts to take responsibility for her unborn child. This poor misguided girl was going to be a mother, if they made it out alive. The stakes had just risen even higher—if that was possible. "It's okay. It's going to be okay." There was the thump of a booted foot on the door.

Maria let out a little yelp.

"Open up," Ricardo barked. Maria and Stephanie froze in terror.

"I'm coming to get my violin."

Stephanie looked around frantically for an exit. There was no back door, and the window would be impossible for Maria to climb through since she'd been shot.

A fist slammed into the door. "I've got plenty of bullets and lots of time. Open the door, and I'll make it quick for both of you."

Stephanie raced around the small room, thinking there had to be something she'd overlooked, something they could use to defend themselves, when

Ricardo pushed through the door. Tate's small knife would be useless against a gun. Searching desperately for some sort of hiding place, her eyes were drawn to a square cut into the floor. It was the faint outline of a trapdoor.

Her eager fingers found an indentation that must have served as a handle. She yanked on it with all her strength. At first, it did not budge. Then with a groan, it came loose and Stephanie hauled it upward. The space below was ink dark and cold—some sort of basement, she guessed.

She hurried back to Maria. "I'm not sure it will help. We could find ourselves trapped down there with no way out."

"It will buy us some time," Maria whispered. "Until Tate comes back."

For a moment she thought she heard the sound of a helicopter, but she could not be sure over the pounding of her heart. She felt a thrill of fear picturing Tate walking into the warehouse with Ricardo lying in wait, but she could think of no other option. Returning to the edge of the opening with the flashlight, she saw a sloping set of stairs. "Can you manage it, Maria?"

Maria was already crawling toward the opening, one hand clutching the violin case. After a moment to steady themselves, Stephanie started down first, her flashlight making only a minuscule dent in the oppressive darkness. Cobwebs brushed her face, and she thought about the hundreds of mice she'd seen earlier. Putting them firmly out of her mind, she tried to support Maria, who clung to her arm as they made their unsteady way down fifteen steps, testing each one gingerly first. Mercifully the wood held, and when they got to the bottom, Stephanie raced back up the steps and pulled the trapdoor closed from the inside. There was no way to lock it. Ricardo would find them, but perhaps not right away.

What would happen to Tate? As she rejoined Maria, she suddenly remembered Sartori's radio. Pulling it out of her back pocket, she was dismayed to find that it appeared to be dead. "The basement," she groaned. "It won't work down here."

Maria gave a half sob and Stephanie put an arm around her, trying to lend some warmth back into her shivering body. She checked the makeshift bandage as best she could by flashlight, pleased to see that the blood had not begun to seep through the cloth.

She felt Maria's terrified gaze on her. "Bandage is holding," she said with forced optimism. "Now let's find a way out of here."

Leaving Maria leaning against the wall to catch her breath, Stephanie explored the basement.

It was a small rectangular space, with cement walls. A series of pipes ran along the ceiling, and the floor was damp. Water dripped from cracks in the rock ceiling, indicating there was some source of groundwater nearby. Stephanie realized that she was becoming more chilled with every moment. Pushing aside her growing fear, she held the light as high as she could, searching for an exit.

Maria screamed, and she scrambled to her. "Something crawled over my feet."

"Mice, I think." Stephanie wished she had another jacket to give Maria. She worried the girl would go into shock or start bleeding profusely if the bullet wound was deeper than Stephanie had realized. Certainly the cold and fear was not good for Maria or her baby. "We'll get out of here soon. Let me check around some more."

Maria gave a shaky nod, cradling the violin, and Stephanie resumed her search. Her heart leaped when she saw a metal door, tucked behind a stack of bricks. The handle didn't budge when she turned it. She did not know if it was rusted shut or locked, but no matter how hard she tried, she succeeded only in loosening flakes of paint from the surface of the steel.

"Stephanie," Maria whispered. "I heard something."

Stephanie's stomach lurched. "Mice?"

"I don't think so."

The muffled sound of a gunshot filtered down to them. Stephanie's eyes locked in terror on Maria's.

Maria's hand went to her mouth. "Tate?"

Stephanie fought down the panic. "No. No, I'm sure it's not Tate. Maybe Ricardo is shooting through the door."

"Then he'll be down here in a few minutes. What are we going to do?"

Well, we're not going to give up, she thought, gritting her teeth. She prowled the space again, once more throwing her weight against the door until her shoulder ached. It still refused to give even the tiniest bit.

"Look for something we can use as a weapon." She had Tate's knife in her pocket, but she did not want to have to get close enough to use it unless it was a last resort. Stephanie poked around the piles of debris until she came up with a section of a metal pole. It was not sharp, but it would do as a club since nothing better was at hand.

Stephanie pulled Maria behind the pile of bricks. It was a scant four feet high, but it was the only shelter available. Maria's lips were trembling as Stephanie tucked her behind the brick screen.

"Stay there. I'm going to stand at the bottom of the stairs, in the shadows. I'll trip him up or knock him out if I'm able to. Be ready to get up the stairs as fast as you can, okay?"

Maria shook her head. "I can't. I'm scared. I'm too scared."

Stephanie put her hands on Maria's shoulders to quell the mounting hysteria she heard in the girl's voice. "You can do it. You're tough, like your brother."

She didn't answer, so Stephanie bent her head to

look Maria right in the eye. "Just get up the ladder and run. Find a place to hide."

Maria half sobbed. "Stephanie, what will happen to you?"

Stephanie forced a smile. "I'm tough, too, like *my* brothers. I'll meet you when I can."

"But what should I do with the violin?"

"Get it to Luca if you can. What's most important is that you make it out alive."

Maria caught Stephanie's hand before she moved away. "I'm really sorry. I'm so stupid. Forgive me."

"Forget it, Maria. You're forgiven as far as I'm concerned." Stephanie was comforted to know that she really meant it. It was a sweet feeling to truly forgive. She thought about Tate.

Because every day I ask God to help me keep that bottle closed...

And she realized in that moment that she had never asked God to help her forgive Tate, because she'd never wanted to. Being angry at him, resurrecting the past every time she thought of him, allowed her to keep from being hurt again.

Allowed her to hide from the pain, like he had hidden, buried deep in drugs.

A crash from above made them both jerk. Grasping her makeshift weapon, she gave Maria one final squeeze before she scurried to the stairwell. She paused to tuck the flashlight on top of a box and turned it on, the beam illuminating only the last few steps before she hid herself in the shadows at the foot of the staircase.

The creak of the trapdoor swinging open was followed by the thump of the cover being tossed aside. Stephanie fought to keep her breathing quiet.

Maybe the person coming down the stairs was Tate.

She hung on to the thought. He'd caught up with Eugene, and he was back looking for them.

But he would have called out, wouldn't he?

Maybe not, if he'd heard the shots.

Her palm grew sweaty where she gripped the iron bar. A squeal from the stairs indicated someone was on their way down.

One step, then another. Then a pause. Then a few more steps.

Stephanie kept count in her mind. Fifteen steps, and the person coming down had made it through seven. Five more steps, and they'd know if it was Tate…she swallowed hard.

Or Ricardo.

Her courage faltered for a moment, and she wondered if she would have the strength to overcome the man who'd shot Maria. If she didn't, Maria would have no chance, and neither would her baby.

Gripping the bar tighter, she waited for the footsteps to come closer.

A shadow crept into the glow of the flashlight. Stephanie's heart pounded so hard she thought the person approaching must be able to hear it. Willing her knees to stop shaking, she watched as the shadow descended.

Her heart thudded to a stop. The shoes coming down the ladder were not Tate's.

She raised the bar.

It was wrenched from her hand so abruptly, she staggered back.

The figure stepped down into the light and tossed the bar into a far corner with a deafening clang.

"I've missed you, Stephanie," Joshua Bittman said.

NINETEEN

Tate opened his eyes. When the blurriness subsided, he remembered why he was lying underneath a pile of broken crates. Ricardo.

Jerking fully to his senses, he kicked as hard as he could, knocking enough wood aside for him to scramble free. He was not sure how much time had passed as he ran to the room where he'd left Stephanie. The door was pocked with bullet holes and smashed open with such violence that the jamb had splintered.

Fear twisting his gut, he pushed inside, not sure what he might find.

The room was empty. A flicker of movement from outside the broken window caught his attention. He made it to the broken glass in time to watch Ricardo vanish into the tree line in the direction he thought he'd heard a helicopter earlier.

He's checking it out.

If Tate was right and Sartori had returned via

helicopter, she'd have a chance to arrest him. Sartori was tough and savvy, a good match for Ricardo.

He returned his attention to the empty room. Droplets of something dark stained the corner floor. Blood. He swallowed the panic and searched farther, finding his way to the open trapdoor in moments. Some sort of basement.

His mind screamed at him. *Stephanie, get to Stephanie.* Throwing caution aside, he plunged down the ladder into the darkness, emerging at the bottom.

Stephanie stood there, seemingly unharmed, staring at him as deep gratitude filled every fiber of his body. He started forward, stopping abruptly as Joshua Bittman drew into the circle of light.

"What…?" The pieces fell into place. The chopper had not been Sartori's.

Bittman waved a small handgun in Tate's direction. "Ah, the oaf." He handed Stephanie a pair of plastic restraints. "Put them on him, please."

Stephanie's lips were pressed tightly together as she walked forward, circling his wrists with her fingers. Fear and anger shone in her eyes. She was trying to tell him something, but Bittman shifted so he could see her face. "Now."

He nodded to reassure her. *Buy time,* he wanted to say. *We'll get out of this somehow.*

Her touch was ice cold as she slipped the restraints around his wrists.

"Tightly," Bittman advised.

Stephanie complied. "You don't need to do this," she said. "We will get your violin."

"I know, but things were dreary back in San Francisco. Your father is a crotchety old man, trying to escape at every opportunity. He's quite wearing out my staff. I knew you were here in Lunkville."

"Did your spies fill you in?" Stephanie spat.

"When you worked for me, I had a device placed in your phone that activates the GPS and pings your location back to me." He laughed. "It also triggers the camera in your phone. I've gotten plenty of interesting snapshots of your life—everything from picnics to pie." His eyes swept over Stephanie.

Rage boiled up inside Tate. Bittman was more than a crook; he was a deranged stalker, obsessed with Stephanie. "You're sick," he barked.

Bittman trained the gun on him. "And you are nothing. Poor, uneducated, powerless. You should have died in that crash instead of your father."

Tate jerked. "So you've been keeping tabs on me, too?"

"Only to make sure you were removed from Stephanie's life."

Tate opened his mouth to press further, but Bittman cut him off. "Where is she? Maria?"

Stephanie shrugged. "I don't know."

He smiled, teeth glinting in the lantern light. "Such a bad liar. There was blood in the outer room, and you're not injured. Either you managed to wound the person who shot up the door and window, or she's in here." He flicked on a small but powerful light and beamed it around the space.

"Maria, why don't you come out from behind those bricks? It's filthy back there."

Tate's mouth fell open as Maria emerged, violin in hand. His eyes were drawn immediately to the makeshift bandage around her waist.

"Are you hurt?"

She gave him a small smile. "Only a little. Ricardo shot through the window."

Bittman's eyebrows raised. "Ricardo? The man who worked at my father's shop?"

Tate watched Bittman as he mentally filled in the rest.

And the man who set the fire that killed my brother.

"He's out there right now, checking out your helicopter," Tate said. "He was on his way to find Stephanie when he heard your approach. He might have shot you if you'd arrived a few minutes sooner. Pretty lethal for a pool guy."

"What are you blabbering about?"

Tate gave him a slow smile. "Oh, you didn't know that Ricardo was working at your estate trying to ferret out information about the Guarneri? You have state-of-the-art security systems, and you didn't even know the enemy was right there on your property?"

Bittman's face was incredulous for a split second before the mask settled back into place. "Immaterial."

"You probably never even bothered to meet the pool guy. It must have been beneath you to rub elbows with the common folk. Feel stupid now, don't you, Bittman?"

Bittman's lip twitched. "He knew the Guarneri had resurfaced. He presumed the fastest way to find it was to let me do the work."

"Probably beats cleaning pools."

Bittman took a step toward him, and Tate figured he was in for a fist to the face. Stephanie tensed by him, but instead Bittman handed Stephanie another pair of restraints. "You may bind her, too."

Stephanie complied, leaving the bands loose around Maria's wrists until Bittman forced her to tighten them. While she did so, Bittman prowled the space, keeping the three in his peripheral vision.

With a catlike movement, he snatched up the violin. His eyes glittered, mouth curved into a smile. When he spoke, it was almost a whisper. "The Guarneri. Finally."

He gestured for them all to sit on the steps while he balanced the case on top of an overturned pallet. With trembling hands he opened it, his gaze roving over the interior like a hungry lion sizing up its prey.

He removed the violin and brought it closer to

the lantern, which picked up the gleam of the rose-colored wood. Suddenly he jerked the violin from its case.

The three prisoners watched in astonishment as he brought the violin down full force on the pile of bricks, smashing it to bits.

Stephanie cried out as pieces of the ruined instrument scattered over the space. "What are you doing?"

Bittman regarded the debris strewn across the floor. Then he turned to Maria. "It's a fake." He moved closer, and Tate stood in front of the two women.

"She didn't know that," Tate said.

Bittman raised the gun. "I don't care about you or your sister. I would be happy to kill both of you." He stared at Maria. "Where is my violin? Tell me, unless you would like me to shoot your brother, one limb at a time."

"No!" Maria cried.

"Don't tell him anything," Tate hissed.

Stephanie desperately tried to think of a way to help. Her hands were free, but she did not dare make any moves with Bittman's gun leveled at Tate.

Bittman's tone was flat. "You know I mean it, Maria, don't you? I am not a sentimental man. I will start with his crippled leg, and then the other. Then one arm…"

"Eugene has it," Maria yelped. "He must have given me the fake. He ran out with his backpack. He's here somewhere, close by, but he's not a troublemaker. Please don't hurt him."

Bittman shook off her comment. "That's better. We're going to find my violin and this tramp who took it. Back up the stairs. Now."

Stephanie went up the ladder after Maria, who moved slowly. She wondered how much blood Maria had lost from Ricardo's shot.

As they made their way out of the warehouse, she scanned the tree line. Ricardo would have discovered by now that the helicopter was Bittman's. In another few minutes, he would return to finish what he'd started. Stephanie saw Tate chafing against the restraints, which did nothing but cause them to cut into his wrists.

They left the building. Bittman surveyed the area. "Where would he hide?"

Maria shrugged. "Probably in one of the abandoned buildings along the road. We'll have to search."

Bittman stared at Tate. "Or maybe there's a faster way. Eugene!" he shouted. "You're here somewhere. I know you have my father's violin. I want it back. Come give it to me, and we'll let the whole matter drop."

The silence was broken only by the sound of an animal scavenging through the bushes.

"He's not here," Stephanie said.

"Eugene," Bittman said louder. "I'm sure you're a reasonable man. You don't want to be responsible for a murder, do you?"

Stephanie's blood went cold. Murder?

Bittman shoved Maria forward.

Tate charged, headfirst like a bull, but Bittman cuffed him on the head with the gun. He crashed to the ground, and Stephanie ran to him. By the time she'd helped him to his feet again, Bittman had the gun pressed to Maria's temple.

"This girl, she says she's a friend of yours, Eugene. Why don't you come out so we can talk? If you don't, I'll have to shoot her. She's pregnant, you know, so it would be two birds with one shot, so to speak."

Tate jerked, his eyes shifting from Maria to Stephanie.

She could see the question there. Pregnant? Stephanie nodded slowly, and Tate's face crumpled as he realized the truth.

It was as though she could see all the regret and shame unroll across his face like the subtitles in a movie. She'd told Bittman about the pregnancy, and he'd rejected her. Tate had failed his sister, removed himself from her life while he fought his own addiction. Now she was pregnant, with a gun to her head.

Bittman's attention was fixed on the entrance to the tunnel.

Stephanie remembered the knife in her pocket

and the radio clipped to her belt. She sidled up a few inches closer, and Tate understood her intent. He quickly pulled the knife from her back pocket and hid it between his hands. She was trying to figure out how to access the radio without attracting attention when a voice floated out of the mine tunnel.

"She's my friend. Don't hurt her," a thin voice wailed.

Bittman smiled. "Of course I won't. Come out, Eugene. We have plenty to talk about."

"No."

Bittman shifted slightly, his tone soothing as if he spoke to a child. "Then I'll have to shoot her. That would be sad, wouldn't it, Eugene? She's so pretty. It would be your fault, too."

Stephanie wanted to call out to the terrified man, to tell him about the monster named Bittman, but she was too scared of the gun pressing into the side of Maria's head.

The board across the cave entrance trembled. "Don't hurt her. You can come in."

Bittman's eyebrow raised. "How do I know you have the violin?"

There was a long pause, and then the sound of music, light and delicate as windblown petals, danced through the air.

Stephanie had never heard any sound more beautiful.

The reaction in Bittman was shocking. He

tensed, mouth slightly open, the veins on his neck standing out.

"You learned that song from my father. He played it all the time." Bittman's hand tightened around the gun.

She saw Tate edging closer, and she did the same.

The music kept on, Bittman's voice rising over the sweet melody. "You learned that from my father, and then you stole his instrument. How dare you? He let you live in our shop, eat from our table, and you stole from him." A drop of spittle flew from Bittman's mouth. "Stop playing, stop immediately."

The song died away.

Bittman took a deep breath, and his tone was calmer when he spoke. "I will kill her if you don't come out."

"You'll kill me if I do," Eugene said, voice hoarse.

Bittman wiped a hand over his mouth. "We're running out of time. There's another man here, the one who set the fire. It is a matter of time before he arrives to kill you. I merely want the violin. Give it to me, and I will let you go."

"And Maria?"

Bittman looked at Maria as if he'd forgotten about her. "Yes."

A soft thud indicated Eugene was kicking at the

boards from the inside. One finally fell away, revealing a dark hole.

"You can come in," Eugene said. "If you promise not to kill her."

Bittman smiled, and the chill in his expression took Stephanie's breath away.

No, Eugene. He'll kill you. He'll kill us all.

But no words would come.

Bittman shoved Maria ahead of him, then gestured with the gun for Stephanie and Tate to follow her. In his panicked state, if Eugene had a weapon, he would use it on one of them first, she thought grimly.

With hands thrust before her, she stepped into the perfect darkness.

TWENTY

Tate kept the knife pressed between his palms, waiting for the chance to cut off his restraints. For all his intellectual prowess, Bittman had made a mistake by having Stephanie cuff his hands in front instead of behind. All he had to do was work the knife blade back and forth. The mine was dark enough to allow him cover. The blade was positioned point up, toward his wrists. As he wriggled it into place, the blade cut into his palms. Gritting his teeth, he began to saw away at the plastic.

The interior of the shaft was a small space, no more than eight feet across, and he had to duck his head to keep from hitting it on the ceiling.

"No games, Eugene," Bittman said. "Turn on a light."

Instead the sound of the violin filled the tiny cavern, echoing along the low beams that supported the ceiling. It was the same haunting melody.

"Stop it," Bittman's voice thundered. "Stop playing my father's song."

"He meant for me to play it," Eugene said over the music. "He meant for me to have the Guarneri."

Tate could hear Bittman's teeth snap together.

"He meant it for his son, for my brother, Peter, you cretin."

The music stopped abruptly. "Peter."

There was an odd questioning tone in Eugene's word. "Peter," he repeated. "Peter Bittman. Have you seen him?"

Bittman grunted. "He's dead. Ricardo burned down the shop and killed him."

"That's sad," Eugene said, beginning to play again.

"Stop!" Bittman roared.

The music kept going, faster now.

Tate's fingers kept time as he sliced away at the restraints.

Bittman yelled and Eugene continued to play, the song growing wilder with each measure.

Bittman fired off a shot that drilled itself into the ceiling, hurting Tate's ears. The impact of the bullet made a tiny puff of sparks.

Eugene broke off playing.

"Now," Bittman said quietly as a lighter flared to life in his hand, illuminating the gun still pointed at Maria. "There is a lantern there, hanging on the wall. Light it."

Tate felt the plastic beginning to give.

Eugene lifted a trembling hand to the lantern

and lit it. He stood there with the violin cradled in his arm, his beard covered by dust.

Bittman moved forward into the lantern light. "Give me the violin."

"*Vater* meant me to have it. He would not have wanted it to burn. I ran. I ran to keep it safe." His voice dropped to a whisper, hands stroking the violin. "Safe."

Bittman stared at Eugene. *"Vater?"* He moved closer to Eugene, who cowered against the wall, then staggered a step back as if he'd been struck. Tate was dismayed to see he did not lower the weapon. "Peter."

"Peter," Eugene repeated thoughtfully.

"You are my brother, Peter," Bittman whispered. "But you died in the fire."

Stephanie spoke quickly as the truth sizzled through her. "The body was badly burned. It was twenty years ago. It was probably the homeless man your father took in. Peter was the one who took the violin. Peter was the one you saw that night running away."

Bittman's glance flicked from Stephanie back to Eugene.

Tate's wrists finally came clear of the restraints. He lunged at Bittman, knocking the gun from his hand, which skittered away into the darkness. Eugene let out a cry and shrank back.

Tate tumbled to the floor, fighting for a grip on Bittman, who was trying to dig his fingers into

Tate's throat. They crashed into the stone walls, thrashing as Tate grappled to loosen Bittman's choke hold.

Tate was fueled by a strength he didn't know he had. This time he would not fail his sister, and Stephanie would be free of Joshua Bittman forever. Inch by inch, he managed to force Bittman's hands away from his throat, maneuvering him onto his stomach. Tate's knee was across his shoulder blades.

He sat panting, hands bloody and leg twitching with pain.

"I will have my violin," Bittman said, his voice filled with hatred. "And my brother will come home."

Eugene looked confused. "Home?"

"Oh, I don't think so," came a voice from the mouth of the cavern. Tate's heart dropped like a stone as Ricardo stepped into the space, a gun gripped in his hand. "So I'm not responsible for killing your brother after all," he said.

"But you killed the homeless guy and Devlin," Tate panted. "You're still a murderer."

Ricardo shrugged. "It's like potato chips. Hard to have just one." He laughed. "I appreciate you doing the legwork for me, boy. Here is my violin, and all the people I need to kill in one spot."

Tate started to rise.

"Slowly," Ricardo warned. "I think maybe we'll take this party outside. Ladies first."

Tate got off Bittman, who climbed to his feet. They paraded out of the mine shaft into the predawn.

Ricardo took the violin from Eugene's hand. Bittman twitched as he watched Ricardo tuck the instrument under his arm.

"You know, I've got the perfect way to tidy up this mess." He led them down a dusty section of road to the old jail they'd searched earlier. "Everyone inside."

"My pilot will radio for help if I'm not back soon," Bittman said.

Ricardo shook his head. "He would if he was still conscious."

Tate's stomach lurched. "Let the women go. You don't need to hurt them."

He smiled. "Right. I'm sure they wouldn't tell anyone about me." He guided them inside. "No, I like the irony of this method. This way, Peter really will die in a fire, just like he supposedly did twenty years ago, only he'll have company. I just need to get the gas can from that ridiculous Volkswagen. It's hidden nearby. I won't keep you waiting long."

Tate tried desperately to find a way to fight back, but anything he might have tried would result in the death of one of their group. He followed the women into the jail, along with Eugene. Ricardo pushed Bittman inside last.

He whirled to face Ricardo, his body tense like a cat ready to spring. "I'll find you. No matter where you go, I'll find you."

"No," Ricardo said, leaning in as though he was divulging a secret. "You'll die."

Bittman's hands curved into claws. "I have people who will track you down, and you won't even realize they're onto you."

"Only if they take orders from a dead guy," Ricardo said with a laugh.

Bittman was trembling with rage. "A small puncture in your brake line, and you'll be gone."

Tate started. The brake line?

You should have died in that crash, instead of your father.

Tate's pulse thundered. "You tried to have me killed, didn't you? By tampering with the brakes of my truck."

Bittman's hatred was palpable. "And you managed to make a mess of that, too, and your father died instead."

Somewhere in the back of his mind, he heard Maria gasp.

"Why...?" Stephanie whispered.

Bittman turned to her. "He's a loser. A nobody, and he couldn't give you anything close to what you deserved."

Before Tate realized it, his hands were clutching Bittman's collar.

Ricardo laughed again. "I'm sorry to miss this, but I've got a plane to catch and a violin to sell. Adios."

The sound of the door swinging closed roused

Tate from his red-hot rage. He threw himself at it, fists making contact in time to feel the heavy bolt slide shut from the outside.

Stephanie could hardly absorb what she'd just heard. Bittman had tried to murder Tate and instead killed Mr. Fuego. She hadn't realized until that moment Bittman's level of depravity, his need to possess her. The list of tragedies that stemmed from Bittman's dark obsession was growing: Victor, her father, Mr. Fuego, Devlin and now more people awaited death in a space that would become an inferno if Ricardo had his way. For a moment she teetered on the edge of despair.

Lord, I'm still here. You made me strong for a reason. Help me now.

She and Tate immediately began to examine the walls as best they could in the darkness, the only light coming from cracks in the roof, testing for any weaknesses. Fifteen frantic minutes passed until there was a sound of crumpling paper and the acrid smell of gasoline.

Eugene's voice was a whisper. "Fire. He's going to burn it down." He began to cry.

Maria put her arm around Eugene. "It's going to be okay. I loved the song you played on the violin. Can you tell me about it?"

Stephanie shot her a grateful look. Maria was going to be a good mother, if they could get her out alive. She could just see Tate's staunch profile. He would not stop trying until they were free or dead. He was one of the few people who could match her determination.

All this time she'd refused to forgive him for his failures, deep down holding on to lingering resentment. Now it seemed that the situation had flipped. Her dealings with Bittman had cost him his father, ruined his sister. He would not be able to forgive that, and she did not blame him.

Remembering the radio in her pocket, she turned it on, only to receive buzzing static. She spoke into it anyway, explaining the situation in as few words as she could manage. Then she handed it to Maria. "Keep talking on it. Maybe someone will hear."

Bittman pulled out his cell phone. He got no signal, which was not a surprise. It wouldn't matter anyway. The flicker of flames showed under the gap in the door, and acrid smoke poured in.

Stephanie looked for something to stuff under the crack. Maria handed her the jacket that had been wrapped around her waist. "The bleeding has stopped. Use this."

Cramming the fabric in the gap slowed the smoke to a trickle, but it would not hold for long, Stephanie knew. She joined Tate, hands pressing over the rough bricks, looking for the smallest weakness in the old walls.

Bittman stood defiantly in the center of the space, occasionally looking at his brother, who was rocking back and forth next to Maria. The man who had wreaked havoc on so many lives was now powerless, like a snake with his fangs removed. Stephanie continued on, her fingers raw from the rough walls.

The crackle of flames grew louder as the fire traveled up the side of the old jail and started to gain a foothold on the roof.

"Fire, fire," Eugene moaned as Maria tried to comfort him.

The radio crackled, and a voice came through. "Repeat."

Stephanie felt a surge of hope. If Sartori was close...

There was another burst of static, and the voice died away. Maria began her message all over again, but there was no further acknowledgment. Stephanie turned away from Maria rather than see the hope die in her eyes.

Tate grunted, dropping to his knees in the far corner. She went to him, thinking he'd been injured.

"One loose," he said, pushing at a silvered brick with his palms. Slowly, the block began to move under the steady pressure. He got to his feet and began to kick at it. Stephanie could only imagine the pain it caused his damaged leg. When he paused to recover for a moment, Stephanie took his place, throwing kick after kick against the weakened spot.

Tate pulled her aside. "The smoke is thicker." He jerked a thumb at the others.

Stephanie needed no further instructions. She turned to Maria and Eugene. "Lay down on the floor where the air is cleaner." She spoke gently to Eugene. "May I have your shirt, Eugene? I promise I'll buy you another when we get out of here."

He nodded and gave her his outer flannel shirt, leaving him in a stained white T-shirt. She tore off the two sleeves and handed one to them. "Cover your nose and mouth. Breath through the cloth."

She turned with the body of the shirt in her hands and held it to Bittman. "You can use this," she forced herself to say.

"Stephanie, if only you had seen reason when we first met." He touched her hand, and she jerked it away.

"If I had been reasonable then, I never would have gone to work for you."

He laughed. "I have always admired your fire. That drive is what attracts me to you, and your refusal only increases that attraction."

"Why don't you try to comfort your brother?" She could not stand to hear one more word from Joshua Bittman. "Lie down if you want to live." She turned back to Tate just as he aimed a vicious kick at the loosened brick. It slid free, plopping into the dust outside the jail and letting in a stream of smoky light, the weak rays of early dawn.

He beamed a triumphant smile at her that made her breath catch.

"We just need to make an opening big enough

to crawl through." He began kicking at the bricks again, but she could see that his leg was weakening.

She edged in front. "We'll take turns. This round is mine."

Tate was panting too hard to answer, but he nodded and she went to work, blasting at the weakening spot as hard as she could, each impact jarring her to the bone.

A second brick gave a fraction of a centimeter, and it sent her energy into overdrive. She kicked like a wild horse until the second brick gave way, bringing a third with it.

Tate took over while she caught her breath. The air was now thick with smoke, curling upward to the rafters above. Pops and crackles filled the air. She realized that the outside roof had caught, and the fire was eating away at the beams.

In spite of his extreme effort, Tate only managed to loosen the next brick.

"Let me try now," she said.

He barred her with his arm. "No." His jaw gritted, and he struck out with renewed effort. The air had grown hotter with each passing moment, and sweat poured down both their faces. She shot a look at Maria and Eugene, who lay on their stomachs on the floor.

She was just about to insist that Tate give her another turn when an ominous crack sounded above them. Jerking her head, she was horrified to see a jagged piece of burning wood from the ceiling give way. It tumbled through the air, landing right next to Eugene.

He leaped up with a cry, waving his arms around. "Stop!" Stephanie yelled. "Please, Eugene, stop!"

Her words had no effect as he whirled madly, as the white fabric of his T-shirt caught fire.

Tate jerked toward the sharp cry of pain. Through the smoke he could make out Eugene flapping his burning sleeve, fanning the flames with his panic.

Bittman followed him helplessly. "Peter, listen to me, listen to me!" he shouted louder and louder until he was hollering, but his brother was so caught up in the fear he did not or could not hear him.

Tate moved as quickly as he could, his leg nearly folding underneath him. He pushed by Bittman and knocked Eugene to the floor, hearing the air forced from Eugene's lungs by the impact.

When they hit the floor, Tate began rolling Eugene back and forth. Mercifully the panic seemed to be knocked out of Eugene along with the impact, and he lay relatively passively while Tate smothered the flames. When he was satisfied the fabric was no longer burning, he got up and helped Eugene to a sitting position. Maria came closer, speaking soothingly.

Bittman pushed them both aside. "Get away. He's my brother. I will take care of him."

Bittman sat carefully on the floor, knees folded

underneath him, and put a tentative hand on Eugene's back. "When we get out of here, things will change, Peter. You will come back to live with me, where you belong. You will have anything you want."

Eugene's lips were tight with the pain from his burned arm. "I want my violin," he sobbed. "My violin."

Bittman's eyes glittered, hard and cold. "You will have it. I promise."

Tate did not have time to puzzle over Bittman's unfounded confidence. He'd managed to knock only four bricks loose, and he'd need to push out twice that many to make the hole large enough for them to crawl through. The jail was now alive with smoke and the ominous hiss and crack of the fire on the roof. He ducked down to avoid breathing in the black smoke and returned to the corner. Stephanie joined him, and they resumed their tag team effort. She was exhausted, he could tell by the droop of her head, but she worked as hard as humanly possible to shove out a brick, which took another one with it.

She grinned and gave him a double thumbs-up.

Suddenly the task seemed doable, fueled by the light in her eyes and the triumphant smile on her face. It had always been that way, he thought. With Stephanie in his life, he had the courage and optimism that eluded him in the dark days they'd been apart.

But not completely, he realized as he kicked out at the bricks. In the horrifying aftermath of his father's death, he'd summoned strength to beat back the addiction that clung to him like a shadow.

It was God-given strength; it could be nothing else. He'd been blessed with an extraordinary woman to love, and even in the darkest moments of despair he had the memory of that love to remind him he had been worth something—worth loving, worth grieving for, as he knew Stephanie had done.

His shame at his past began to fall away, like the flakes of mortar that drifted through the smoky air. It was true, he had been neither the man nor the brother he should have been, but he could push by that, kick away at the wall of sin and glimpse the brilliant future that lay on the other side.

He felt a surge of energy ripple through his body, and he hammered his boot against the wall, unaware that Eugene, Bittman and Maria had joined them until Maria cried out as brick number seven fell away.

Stephanie put her hand on Tate's shoulder, and he clasped it there for a moment, drawing new strength from her touch.

"I'll finish," Stephanie said. "You need to rest."

He looked at her, so tired, her face streaked with soot and more beautiful to him than raindrops on roses. This was a woman who taught him that he was worthy of loving. "No, Steph," he said quietly. "I'm going to finish this."

With his leg screaming in pain, he began anew until finally, with torturous slowness, another brick fell and two more besides. The hole would be big enough, barely.

Bittman made for it, pulling his brother behind, but Tate blocked them. "The women go first."

Bittman's lip curled as he considered. For a moment, Tate thought he would need to physically restrain Bittman and his brother, but suddenly he stepped back. "As you wish," he said, something in his tone causing alarm bells to jingle in the back of Tate's mind.

As Maria squeezed through, a burning beam fell through into the center of the space with a whoosh that catapulted burning embers in a whirlwind around them.

"Go now!" Tate shouted over the rising sound of burning wood. He grabbed Stephanie's shoulders and shoved her into the hole. He watched in relief as she wriggled through. It took coaxing from the women outside and the men inside to convince Eugene to shimmy through, scraping his burned shoulder as he did so.

Maria crooned to him the whole time, soft words of comfort, until he was gone.

Then Tate was alone with Bittman, flames licking the walls around them.

"Last men standing," Bittman said. "Ironic."

"Get going." A spurt of flame from above their heads distracted him just long enough. Bittman pulled a knife from his coat pocket and plunged it into Tate's side.

The shock was so intense that he stood there for a moment, just long enough to see the triumph on Bittman's face.

"Last man standing," he purred.

Tate pulled the knife out and fell forward, watching Bittman vanish through the broken wall of bricks.

TWENTY-ONE

Stephanie helped Maria try to soothe Eugene, but all the while she eyed the gap. Bittman emerged, as calm as if he'd just left a board meeting. The moments ticked by, and there was no sign of Tate. Flames were now dancing madly across the roof as she ran back to the hole, Maria right behind her.

"Tate," she yelled into the smoking jail. "Where are you?"

There was no answer, and she pushed her head and shoulders back in the gap. "Tate." Her heart convulsed as she saw him there, lying on the floor, blood staining his shirt.

"Get out," he said in a voice so soft, she almost didn't hear it above the flames.

She willed her voice to stay steady. "I'm coming in to get you."

"No," he said louder. "You need to get out. Keep Maria safe, and call the cops. The ceiling's going to go. Steph, I…"

Tate's words were drowned out by a massive

boom. She felt Maria yank on her shoulder, and she was drawn backward as the ceiling collapsed, forcing the brick wall to buckle.

"Tate!" she screamed. Even before the ground stopped rumbling, she was scrambling back toward him. Through a cloud of choking debris, she could just make out that the bricks had compacted, covering over the hard-won hole. Now the building was an impenetrable six-foot-wall of brick, crowned by a burning roof. She ran around it, desperately looking for a gap, a small opening that would allow her to get in, but she found nothing.

Maria pressed her hands to her mouth, her eyes round with horror. "Oh, Steph," she whispered.

Stephanie's body went cold even as her brain searched for options.

The fight wasn't over, it couldn't be. An idea shot through her brain.

She grabbed Maria's wrists. "Use the radio and call the police."

"What are you going to do?" she heard Maria call as she sprinted madly down the road.

What was she doing? The most insane thing she could think of, but it was the only way that might save Tate. She prayed as she tore along, stumbling and sliding on loose gravel, slapping branches out of her way. *Let him hold on, Lord.*

She'd found her share of priceless items, paintings and coins, pottery and gems, but never had she felt the excruciating urgency that coursed through her body. Inside that burning jail, buried under filth and ashes, was the greatest treasure she'd been blessed to possess, damaged though it was.

Nothing from the past mattered anymore. Not one moment of it.

Panting, sweat running down her face, she made it to the car, snatching the keys from her pocket with trembling hands.

In a moment, she'd gunned the engine and turned the vehicle back up the slope, bouncing over ruts, rocks pinging against the undercarriage.

Hold on, Tate. Hold on. Her mind screamed as she pushed the car faster, the tires spinning along the trail. Past the ruined houses and the tower. She could see the black smoke rising in a roiling mass just over the next hill.

The rear tire exploded, and the car skidded to one side. Stephanie fought to keep control. Now wobbling madly, the vehicle was a hundred yards from the jail. She shot past it and slammed on the brakes, the rear end skidding until the car was once again facing the jail.

It was almost concealed under a blanket of smoke, orange flames darting through gaps in the broken bricks. She aimed the car directly at the far side of the jail, farthest away from the spot she knew Tate had fallen.

With a last prayer, body prickled in goose bumps, she pressed the gas pedal to the floor. The car leaped forward, thunking on the ruined tire.

Faster and faster it accelerated, until the scenery flew by in a blur.

The gap closed quickly—fifteen feet, then twelve, six, four, three.

Stephanie closed her eyes just before the car crashed into the wall of bricks.

Tate watched the smoke billow in graceful arcs around him. It would kill him before the flames, he knew. At least the others had made it out. Stephanie would take care of Maria, and keep her safe from Bittman.

It was the one thing that pricked at his mind. Bittman had made it out unscathed. He would no doubt spend the rest of his life tracking down Ricardo, and Tate knew he would probably win in the end. He'd have his violin and his vengeance.

But he wouldn't have Stephanie. He would not possess the one thing he craved the most.

He pictured her smile again, giving him the double thumbs-up, eyes dancing with triumph.

A troubling fact intruded. Bittman still had Stephanie's father, and as long as he did, he'd have his hooks into her.

Pain rippled through his leg and the wound in his side. A fit of coughing escalated the agony, and he closed his eyes against it. Sparks rained down on him, and he became aware of an out-of-place sound—the sound of an approaching engine.

Maybe it was Sartori.

He felt a surge of satisfaction. She had probably missed the chance to capture Bittman, but knowing help was there for Stephanie and Maria eased his mind. The sound grew louder, but his coughing drowned it out.

A split second later, there was a grinding crash and the far wall of the jail exploded, sending bricks flying like cement missiles through the air. He covered his head, unable to fathom a reason for the implosion until he looked up again. There was the wrecked rental car, the front end jacked up on a pile of debris. The door opened, and Stephanie spilled out.

He was imagining it, the carbon monoxide confusing his mind.

She scrambled over the bricks, heedless of the smoke, and knelt next to him.

"Tate?" she whispered, face tight with fear.

"Steph, did you just drive the car through the wall?"

She nodded as she hooked her hands under his arms to help him rise. "You always said if there wasn't a door, I'd make a window."

In spite of the pain in his side, he laughed.

They emerged in the sunlight to see Sartori arrive with Luca in the front seat. Sartori took one look at them and grabbed the first-aid kit. Luca helped Stephanie ease Tate on a rock while Sartori pressed a section of gauze to the wound in his side as Stephanie told them the details.

"It's only a scratch," Tate said.

"More like a dent," Sartori countered, "but I think you'll live. Paramedics are on their way."

Luca wrapped Stephanie in his arms and kissed the top of her head as she told him about Bittman and Ricardo and Eugene's true identity.

Maria ran up and hugged her brother, tears streaming down her face.

"Tate, I was so scared," she sobbed. He rubbed a hand on her back.

"It's okay."

She drew back abruptly. "You're bleeding."

"Bittman decided to leave me with a final souvenir. He missed any vital organs, I think, because I'm still alive. He escaped with Eugene."

Sartori nodded, a look of satisfaction transforming her face. She jerked a thumb at the backseat of her police car. "Not exactly."

Stephanie jerked in amazement. Bittman sat in stony silence, staring out the window of Sartori's car. Bear stood outside the door, ears pricked and body on full alert.

"I told you Bear was effective," Sartori said. The dog twitched at his name but did not budge from his post near Bittman. "We saw him making his way back down to the main road, and Bear was obliging enough to catch him. We had plenty of grounds to arrest him because your father was quite happy to fill us in on his abduction by Mr. Bittman."

Stephanie gasped. "Dad? You found him?"

Luca beamed. "Tuney did, actually. He wasn't about to give up, just like he said. Dad's perfectly fine, except he's lost a few pounds and he's got a gash to the head. Tuney was trying to talk him out of storming here immediately to help."

Tears flowed down Stephanie's face, but she wiped them away and turned fearful eyes to Luca. "Victor?" she whispered.

"He's okay. He beat the infection, and he's fully conscious. As soon as I saw him, I turned right around to come back here."

Stephanie felt her knees crumple under her, and both Tate and Luca helped her to sit on the rock next to Tate. Her nerves were firing so many emotions at once, she was not sure which to feel first. Victor and her father were okay. The joy threatened to overwhelm her.

Luca looked solemnly at Tate. "You saved my sister, and you almost died in the process. Thank you."

Tate nodded.

Luca hesitated. "I've misjudged you."

"I gave you good reason." Tate lifted his chin, his face bruised and battered. "I'm clean. I want you to know that. I've been clean for a year, and I'm going to stay that way."

Luca cocked his head. "I believe you mean that." Slowly he extended a hand. "Let's make a fresh start then."

Tate and Luca shook hands. Stephanie saw the

look pass between them, a look of trust and respect. Her heart skipped a beat.

Luca chuckled. "You know, I can't believe we actually did it. We found the violin and Bittman's supposedly dead brother. Incredible."

Stephanie saw no sign of him. "Where is Eugene?"

"Sartori had another officer transport him to the hospital."

"What will happen to him?"

"We'll see that he gets the help he needs since big brother will be in jail," Sartori said. "Long list of complaints, abduction, your brother's accident, Devlin's death."

"And my father's murder," Tate cut in.

Sartori's eyebrows nearly vanished into her hairline. "I didn't know about that one. We'll have to get those details. I got word that they've stopped Ricardo Williams at the airport, so eventually Eugene, or Peter rather, may get his violin back."

An ambulance arrived, and the paramedics began to check over Maria and Tate. Luca used Sartori's satellite phone to call the hospital and fill in Victor and their father on the situation. Stephanie found herself drawn to the police car, to the rigid figure sitting in the back. She did not know why she wanted to see him—maybe to convince herself that he really was no longer a threat to herself and the people she loved.

Sartori saw her approach and called Bear away from the car.

Bittman turned to look at her, his gaze an odd mixture of regret and desire. "I could have given you anything you wanted."

Sometimes what you want isn't what you need. She needed a partner, a soul mate, a strong man who looked to God in the darkest of times. A man who drove a beat-up truck and matched her in both stubbornness and determination. Her throat thickened. A man who had nearly exchanged his life for hers. But too much had driven a wedge between them, including the man who sat there now, staring at her imperiously as though his hands were not in cuffs. Her eyes turned toward Tate.

"You made the wrong choice," Bittman said, following her gaze.

Yes, I did. Tate's eyes sought hers, and for a fleeting moment, she wondered if one more choice could change everything. Then he lowered his head and looked away.

She gave Bittman one final glance. "I don't belong to you. I never did, and I never will."

She returned to her brother, who was still talking on the phone. Maria sat nearby, a blood pressure cuff on her arm. She beamed a smile at Stephanie.

"The baby is okay. They heard the heartbeat."

Stephanie smiled. Maria's love would be enough for her unborn child. "I'm so glad, Maria."

Another paramedic worked on Tate and gave her a nod. "We'll transport him to the hospital."

"I don't need to go," Tate said, his chin set stubbornly. "It's just a scratch."

Stephanie folded her arms. "But you're going anyway because Baby Fuego is going to need his or her uncle around for a long time."

Tate grumbled and then cracked a smile. "Uncle Tate. Has a nice ring to it." He hesitated. "Are you okay? That was some crash."

She flushed at the way his eyes roved her face. "Perfectly fine."

Luca clicked off the phone with a grin. "When I told him how things worked out here, Victor let out such a whoop the nurse dropped her medicine tray. I believe his exact words were, 'we've got a wedding to plan.'"

Sartori called Luca over, and he clapped Tate on the back and gave Stephanie a kiss.

Stephanie couldn't help but smile. "A happy ending."

Tate was silent, staring off at the distant hills.

"Anyway, thank you, Tate." The words seemed woefully inadequate. "I didn't deserve your help." She felt the tears sting her eyes. "You put yourself on the line for my father, after Bittman took away yours."

He still kept his face turned away, and she knew

that he thought it, too: *if you had only listened to me...believed in me...*

"I didn't do any of this for your father," he said quietly.

She looked at Maria, resting in the shelter of a tree while the paramedics finished their work. He'd done it for Maria, to make up for his failure with her. Family ties really were the strongest. He loved his sister, she loved her brothers, and Bittman, perhaps as much as he was capable of it, loved Peter.

Luca's laughter caught her attention. Soon she would be home, back in San Francisco, working with her brothers again.

And Tate would be living his own life, as far away from her as two hearts could be.

She felt a stab of pain.

"I did it," Tate said, looking at her now, "for you."

Her stomach flipped as she looked into his clear gray eyes.

"I did it because I love you. In my mind, you are my perfect match."

She stared, not believing what was coming from his mouth. "What are you saying?"

"I've got an idea," he said, abruptly getting to his feet with a wince of pain.

"Sit down. You've been hurt."

"Nope. Gotta do this standing up."

Something in his face made her heart skip a beat. "Do what?"

"Your brother's finally going to have his happy ending with Brooke. Let's make it two."

"What do you mean?"

"A double wedding. Victor and Brooke…and you and me."

Stephanie's mouth fell open. "We can't."

"Why not?" Tate pulled her into the circle of his arms.

"We tried and things fell apart. I…I didn't want to forgive you."

"And I didn't want to forgive myself. But that's changed now." He traced his fingers over her face, keeping her gaze riveted to his.

"I brought Bittman into our lives, and your father…" Tears slipped down her cheeks.

He hugged her closer and traced the curve of her cheekbone with his lips. "We made mistakes. Both of us. I feel like I got a second chance to start over, and I want to spend the rest of my life celebrating that with you."

Her skin prickled as she leaned against him, his hand on the small of her back. "Tate, there's too much…"

"No," he whispered in her ear. "There's just enough. Just enough love to keep us together in this crazy life, to keep us strong for each other."

Just enough love? Did she have enough love and

strength left to turn her back on their dark past? "Tate, I…"

She broke off, lost in a rush of emotion that sounded over her like the sweetest note of a haunting song. All she had to do was give the past to God and take hold of the future with which God had blessed them both.

"I love you, Tate," she whispered, turning her face to his.

"I've sure waited a long time to hear that," he said, his voice hoarse.

She was almost sure, as his mouth found hers, that she could hear an exquisite melody that was theirs alone.

* * * * *

Look for Dana Mentink's next
TREASURE SEEKERS *novel,*
FINAL RESORT, available in February
from Love Inspired Suspense.

Dear Reader,

This week we watched a wonderful baby dedication at our church. The youth group led the little preschoolers in a song that brought down the house, so to speak. I know my eyes were certainly damp! We all cooed over the adorable children, God's precious treasures. It struck me that as we change and grow, like that innocent baby into adulthood, sometimes we lose our way and forget that we are treasures in God's eyes. Swept up in circumstances and world-weary, we drift far away from that understanding, don't we? The good news is, no matter how far we drift, no matter how broken we become, God will find us because we are His treasures, priceless in His eyes. *For the Son of Man came to seek and to save what was lost.* Luke 19:10.

Thank you for joining me in this second book in the Treasure Seekers series. The next book will focus on Luca Gage as he embarks on a wild hunt to find a "pearl of great price" inadvertently acquired by a missing man in the purchase of an abandoned storage unit. Dangerous times are ahead for the Gage family as this series wraps up.

I welcome comments from my readers. You can reach me via my webpage at www.danamentink.com, and my physical address is there also for those who prefer corresponding by mail.

Thank you sincerely for spending some precious time with me!

Fondly,

Dana Mentink

Questions for Discussion

1. Stephanie Gage is thrown into a deadly situation because of bad decisions made earlier in her life. How do past mistakes intrude upon our present lives? What are some biblical examples of how to handle such situations?

2. Joshua Bittman is a man obsessed with having his own way. Have you had experience with people who share this trait? How do they deal with defeat?

3. The Treasure Seekers pursue a priceless violin made by Guarneri del Gesu. What other prizes do modern-day treasure hunters seek? Can you recall any treasures that have recently made the news?

4. Tate shut Stephanie and Maria out of his life when he succumbed to addiction. Was it right to keep them away from the situation? Why or why not?

5. Stephanie and Tate are very different, but also share some strong similarities. What charac-

ter traits do they have in common? Are these helpful traits or hindrances?

6. How can we be mindful of our past failures, and still move forward to live the life God intends for us?

7. Do you think it's a good idea for Tate to continually carry around a reminder of his addiction? Why or why not?

8. Ex-cop Tuney makes an appearance in this story. What would be a happy ending for him? Do you suppose such an ending would be possible for a man of his character?

9. If you could embark on your own treasure hunt, what prize would you search for? Explain.

10. Tate will have to fight his addiction all his life, but he has chosen to look forward to his future. Is there an area of your life where you are making the same choice? What is the benefit to making that decision? The cost?

11. Stephanie's plan to free Tate from the burning jail is extreme. Would you have done the same? Why or why not?

12. Luca will take the lead in the final installment of the Treasure Seekers series. What treasure do you imagine he will be looking for? What roadblocks will he face on his way to finding a soul mate?

LARGER-PRINT BOOKS!

**GET 2 FREE
LARGER-PRINT NOVELS
PLUS 2 FREE
MYSTERY GIFTS**

Love Inspired®
SUSPENSE
RIVETING INSPIRATIONAL ROMANCE

Larger-print novels are now available...

LARGER-PRINT BOOKS!

**GET 2 FREE
LARGER-PRINT NOVELS
PLUS 2 FREE
MYSTERY GIFTS**

Larger-print novels are now available...

YES! Please send me 2 FREE LARGER-PRINT Love Inspired® novels and my 2 FREE mystery gifts (gifts are worth about $10). After receiving them, if I don't wish to receive any more books, I can return the shipping statement marked "cancel". If I don't cancel, I will receive 6 brand-new novels every month and be billed just $4.99 per book in the U.S. or $5.49 per book in Canada. That's a saving of at least 23% off the cover price. It's quite a bargain! Shipping and handling is just 50¢ per book in the U.S. and 75¢ per book in Canada.* I understand that accepting the 2 free books and gifts places me under no obligation to buy anything. I can always return a shipment and cancel at any time. Even if I never buy another book, the two free books and gifts are mine to keep forever.

122/322 IDN FEG3

Name	(PLEASE PRINT)	
Address		Apt. #
City	State/Prov.	Zip/Postal Code
Signature (if under 18, a parent or guardian must sign)		

Mail to the **Reader Service:**
IN U.S.A.: P.O. Box 1867, Buffalo, NY 14240-1867
IN CANADA: P.O. Box 609, Fort Erie, Ontario L2A 5X3

Not valid to current subscribers to Love Inspired Larger-Print books.

**Are you a current subscriber to Love Inspired books
and want to receive the larger-print edition?
Call 1-800-873-8635 or visit www.ReaderService.com.**

* Terms and prices subject to change without notice. Prices do not include applicable taxes. Sales tax applicable in N.Y. Canadian residents will be charged applicable taxes. Offer not valid in Quebec. This offer is limited to one order per household. All orders subject to credit approval. Credit or debit balances in a customer's account(s) may be offset by any other outstanding balance owed by or to the customer. Please allow 4 to 6 weeks for delivery. Offer available while quantities last.

Your Privacy—The Reader Service is committed to protecting your privacy. Our Privacy Policy is available online at www.ReaderService.com or upon request from the Reader Service.

We make a portion of our mailing list available to reputable third parties that offer products we believe may interest you. If you prefer that we not exchange your name with third parties, or if you wish to clarify or modify your communication preferences, please visit us at www.ReaderService.com/consumerchoice or write to us at Reader Service Preference Service, P.O. Box 9062, Buffalo, NY 14269. Include your complete name and address.

LILP11B

FAMOUS FAMILIES

YES! Please send me the *Famous Families* collection featuring the Fortunes, the Bravos, the McCabes and the Cavanaughs. This collection will begin with 3 FREE BOOKS and 2 FREE GIFTS in my very first shipment—and more valuable free gifts will follow! My books will arrive in 8 monthly shipments until I have the entire 51-book *Famous Families* collection. I will receive 2-3 free books in each shipment and I will pay just $4.49 U.S./$5.39 CDN for each of the other 4 books in each shipment, plus $2.99 for shipping and handling.* If I decide to keep the entire collection, I'll only have paid for 32 books because 19 books are free. I understand that accepting the 3 free books and gifts places me under no obligation to buy anything. I can always return a shipment and cancel at any time. My free books and gifts are mine to keep no matter what I decide.

268 HCN 0387   468 HCN 0387

Name   (PLEASE PRINT)

Address   Apt. #

City   State/Prov.   Zip/Postal Code

Signature (if under 18, a parent or guardian must sign)

Mail to the **Reader Service:**

IN U.S.A.: P.O. Box 1867, Buffalo, NY 14240-1867
IN CANADA: P.O. Box 609, Fort Erie, Ontario L2A 5X3